Expository Preaching
in Africa

Expository Preaching in Africa

Joel Kamsen Tihitshak Biwul, PhD

African Christian Textbooks
2019

Expository Preaching in Africa
Copyright © Joel Kamsen Tihitshak Biwul 2019

Published in Nigeria by:
Africa Christian Textbooks (ACTS),
ACTS International Headquarters,
Opposite TCNN Secondary School,
PMB 2020, Bukuru 930008,
Plateau State,
Nigeria.
Tel: +234 (0) 803-589-5328.
E-mail: publishing@actsnigeria.org
www.actsnigeria.org

ISBN
Print   978-978-905-435-0
e-pub   978-978-905-436-7
mobi   978-978-905-437-4

Interior production by Book Genesis, Inc. (https://bookgenesis.com)

This book is dedicated to the late Evangelist Paul Gofo Gunen Gindiri, an uncompromising Nigerian "firebrand" Evangelist, whose life of radical preaching of the Bible inspired mine; to late Evangelist Gyang Luke Dung, whose eschatological preaching motivated me; and to late Dr. Byang Henry Kato, whose insistence on biblical Christianity in Africa propelled my pursuance of Christian spirituality and encouraged my preaching biblically.

TABLE OF CONTENTS

FORWARD

The greatest need of the hour for the Church in Africa is the clear and unambiguous presentation of the Word of God. It follows therefore that the most important role of the pastor, the man/woman of God, the preacher and the minister is the clear presentation of the Word of God (2 Tim 4:2). The current trend where the emphasis on the pulpit is on healing, miracles, deliverance, story-telling, etc., is actually misplaced in terms of priority of the Word of God. The obsession with supernatural activities, and demonic activities is wrongheaded and dangerous. *Expository Preaching in Africa* by Rev. Dr. Joel Biwul is a bold and courageous corrective. The motivation for the book explicitly stated by the author, is "to assist pastors and teachers of the Scriptures to adequately let out the divine voice from the divine text to the contemporary African context."

The book, *Expository Preaching in Africa,* by Dr. Biwul examines the biblical and divine mandate of sounding out (explaining, making sense or expounding) the Word of God in the African Church. Most textbooks on homiletics (the art and science of preaching) used in theological schools are usually written from a non-African perspective. This book has Africa as its primary audience and therefore is very relevant for the African Church. The book is comprehensive and examines all the major aspects of preaching the Word of God. These include among others, African context of expository preaching, biblical foundations, elements of preaching, fundamentals and challenges of expository preaching and benefits of preaching for Africa.

The strength of this book lies in the fact that it is well-researched, well argued, well-articulated, Bible-based and relevant. Preachers, Bible teachers, Bible students and Pastors will find this book a ready tool for dealing with questions and solutions on biblical preaching in the African context. There are adequate examples in the book to illustrate the rudiments of good expository preaching.

Dr. Joel Biwul has done a great service for the Church in Africa by providing an excellent resource material which should find a place in each theological institution and a required textbook for all students in homiletics and especially on expository preaching. I am getting myself a copy and I enthusiastically recommend it to all who desire to preach the Word of God with integrity in the contemporary Church in Africa. Bravo, Rev. Dr. Biwul, for this great book!

Rev. Professor Samuel Waje Kunhiyop, PhD
Professor of Theology and Ethics
Former Provost of ECWA Theological Seminary, Jos, Nigeria, and
former General Secretary of the Evangelical Church Winning All
(ECWA),
March, 2018

PREFACE

Old Testament Professor John Bright rightly noted some years ago that the church lives in her preaching; always has and always will. "No church," said Bright, "can be any stronger than the gospel she proclaims." Dr. Joel KT Biwul in this insightful work on African preaching reconfirms what Bright declares to be the case about the strength of effective biblical preaching. Expository Preaching in Africa challenges us to return to the rightful exposition of scripture in our preaching. Biwul, in this marvelous work, is not calling us to become bibliophiles who merely love the book, rather he is calling on us to engage the whole counsel of God in our preaching of the Word of God.

Aberdeen Missiologist Andrew Walls and others have noted the decline of Christianity in the Western world and its explosive growth in the Global South, especially on the African continent. Consequently, Biwul is not merely writing for African preachers; rather this fresh word is an invitation for all who desire to know in a more creative and life-giving way the art and craft of preaching. This book beckons us to sit at the feet of a master homiletician in a part of the world where Christianity is thriving. Not only does Biwul lead us into a more in-depth understanding of biblical exposition in these opening years of the twenty-first century, but he also offers a corrective to African preachers who would misuse their God-given gift of rightly dividing the word of truth. In this work he calls to account those who seek to major in minor things merely to incur the favor of the believers. He challenges us to keep our focus on the inspired word of God in its depth and fulness. He has a stern warning for those who seek to minimize the expansive depth and richness of God's word; for those who would take the flashy and excitable aspects of scripture and present them as the whole of God's word to humankind in our day.

Biwul encourages us to lean into scripture so that we might hear the voice of God speaking anew to the contemporary listeners, primarily in the African context, but not only in that context. Biwul recognizes that the word of God has a way of breaking through contextual restraints and speaking to wider circles through the empowerment of the Holy Spirit. He leaves no stone unturned in his effort to identify and describe the basics of expository preaching. He writes in great depth about the nature of expository preaching along with its biblical and theological foundations. He demonstrates an intellectual and spiritual grasp of African contextual realities and then offers expository preaching as the answer to the pathos that results from our fallen existence in the modern world.

Biwul not only displays his broad knowledge of the plight and pitfalls of the African situation in the modern world in this volume, but he also outlines a very practical approach to the building of the expository sermon to meaningfully address those situations in life. This book contains step-by-step instructions on the most effective way to build a biblically-based, biblically-inspired expository sermon. A biblical sermon can be defined as one in which the scriptures take the lead in the shape and development of a sermon. In *Expository Preaching in Africa*, the Scriptures are front and center as Biwul walks us through the most effective ways of preaching the insight and understanding that comes through the proper exposition of the Word of God. Biwul shakes every door and rattles every window as he walks down the street of the human condition laying out a path that teaches us how best to bring out both the old and the new in these ancient yet living texts.

This is a must-read for all who desire to preach more faithfully Sunday in and Sunday out. Biwul not only inspires us with his knowledge and skill he also blesses us with the sapiential wisdom one derives from this work. This book holds the promise of making all preachers, those in Africa and beyond, better preachers. To God be the glory!

Cleophus J. LaRue
Princeton Theological Seminary
Francis Landey Patton Professor of Homiletics
Princeton, New Jersey
December 2018

ACKNOWLEDGEMENTS

Authors know that a good book is not entirely the product of the writer. The comments of preliminary readers to a book makes immense contributions to making such book a good one. This, then, calls for the recognition of such contributions.

First, I am highly indebted to Professor Samuel Waje Kunhiyop who graciously accepted to forward this book. His kindness and gracious words serve as an inspiration. Also, it is with gratitude that I acknowledge the useful comments of my reviewers: Thank you, Dr. Matthew Michael (Rabbi Mikhail), Post-Graduate Coordinator, Department of Philosophy and Religious Studies, Faculty of Arts at Nassarawa State University, Nigeria; Dr. Nathan Husseini Chiroma, Dean, School of Theology at Pan African Christian University, Kenya; Rev. Andy Birch Keith, a missionary to Spain; and Dr. Rick Creighton and Rev. David Colvin, both missionaries at ECWA Theological Seminary, Kagoro, Nigeria. Your objective observations and critiques have strengthened this work. I am also grateful to Prof. James Nkansah-Obrempong, of the Nairobi Evangelical Graduate School of Theology (NEGST), Africa International University, Nairobi, Kenya and to The Most Rev. Dr. Benjamin A. Kwashi, Anglican Bishop of Jos, Nigeria for their gracious recommendations.

Secondly, the friendship that Rev. Dr. Cleophus James LaRue of Princeton Theological Seminary, USA and I share is quite a fascinating one. At very short notice, he accepted to preface this book in your hand. Words are insufficient to express my immeasurable gratitude to this friend of mine.

Thirdly, I thank Africa Christian Textbooks (ACTS) Publishers who readily took up the publication of this book. I am particularly thankful to the Publishing Editor, Dr. William Paul Todd. As someone has said, "How can authors do without editors?" Dr. Todd has great confidence and unwavering belief in my writing ability. That apart, His editorial expertise spiced up this book and made it a great one. Thank you ACTS Publishers; thank you Dr. Todd.

Fourthly, Dr. George E. Janvier, a retired distinguished professor of education, is an exceptional source of inspiration and motivation to me. Since my doctoral studies days at ECWA Theological Seminary (JETS), Jos, Nigeria, where he served as its premier programme Director, he had great confidence in my maturity and writing ability. His continuous encouragement is indelible. Also, his book, *Biblical Preaching in Africa*, an ACTS publication, motivated this volume.

Fifthly, Rev. Dr. Samuel Olarewaju, the then Dean of Academics at JETS, asked me to teach preaching courses (homiletics and expository preaching). This was an exciting opportunity to sharpen my skills in preaching as one who has always loved to preach the Scriptures. My interaction with students in class about preaching further motivated my writing this book. Thank you Dr. Olarewaju; and thank you my students in JETS.

Sixthly, the preaching of late Evangelist Paul Gofo Gunen Gindiri and late Evangelist Gyang Luke Dung were a propelling force for mine. These departed heroes of the Christian faith fanned into flames my desire to be a preacher as a young Christian then. Additionally, I had always loved to listen to Dr. Stephen F. Olford expose the Scriptures over the Radio. His expository preaching and that of Rev. Dr. Amaechi Nwachuku deepened my thirst for preaching as well. Also, the feedback and endorsements to my book *Preaching the Scriptures* (HippoBooks 2018) were no less inspiring.

Seventhly, my wife and three children have been very understanding and supportive of my research and writing. A good family is a great gift from God. Thank you Riftie Kasaina, Johnny Bature, Andih Dorcas, Ahmetmu Seth, and Aputgurum Grayom.

Eighthly, Miango Rest Home (MRH) in Nigeria has become my second home. The Manager, Emmanuel Zamfara Benedict, and his management have graciously granted me permission to always use their facilities for research even when I do not check in as a guest. The benefit has been unquantifiable.

Lastly, let me thank my readers in advance, especially those of them who are expositors of the Scriptures. I hope this noble contribution of mine will spur you to develop a solid foundation of Christian preaching, and to expound the Scriptures honestly, faithfully, and reverentially.

INTRODUCTION

According to the Apostle Paul, "'The God who made the world and everything in it is the Lord of heaven and earth ... he himself gives all [people] life and breath and everything else. From one [person] he made every nation of [people], that they should inhabit the whole earth ...'" (Acts 17:24-26 NIV). All the people in the world, who came from this one person (Adam), no matter their geographical location,[1] their cultures, customs and traditions, their religious orientations, or even ethics, share certain characteristics basic to all humanity. Yet, the African peoples[2] are unique in their history, worldview, philosophy, traditions and customs, cultural expressions, norms and

---

1. Geographical location is termed, broadly, as continent. This broad sense is used in reference to the geographical grouping of land mass, that is, a continuous mass of land. The continents of the world, placed according to their order of size, are Asia, Africa, North America, South America, Antarctica, Europe, and Australia. What may appeal to the person in Europe – in Britain, Germany, Spain, France or Holland – may not necessarily appeal in the same way to the person from Asia – in Japan, China, Indonesia, Bangladesh, India or Korea. Equally, what is most cherished and monumental to the person from the Middle East – Jewish or Arab – does not necessarily convey the same mode of attraction to the person in Africa – in Egypt, South Africa, Nigeria, Kenya or Democratic Republic of Congo.

2. The use of the plural form *peoples* for the homogeneous Africans is significant here. Idowu, one of the indigenous founding fathers of the formative study of African anthropology and religions, offers an explanation in defence of the term *African peoples*. He says, "... there is the bewildering situation of myriads of languages and dialects. ... we have in Africa a continent of multitudes of nations, myriads of peoples, countless languages or dialects, and peoples of various levels of cultures. Africa is confluence – which often turns to a whirlpool – of intermingled races and cultures, the origins of most of which are obscure." See E. Bọlaji Idowu, *African Traditional Religion: A Definition* (London: SCM Press Ltd., 1973; repr., Nigeria: Fountain Publications, 1991), 82.

value systems, religious beliefs, and sociology and lifestyle within their different contexts.

Traditional Africans lay claim to the Fatherhood of God as Supreme Being and Creator. As J. N. K. Mugambi explains, they discern his Fatherhood in his providence as he discloses it in the world he has created and sustained. As a Father, then, all that there is in the universe ultimately belongs to him, and the people all over the world are his children.[3] Africans, as a part of the children of God, need to hear the clear voice of their Father speaking in their different contextual situations.

One basic means by which God speaks to the African peoples today is through the Bible. African preachers, therefore, should fashion out how the Bible can be preached to Africans in such a manner that it becomes comprehensible and relevant to their contextual lived experiences and needs. Preachers are responsible to properly interpret and relevantly apply the Bible so that Africans can hear and understand its message in their unique contexts. When this happens, the African persons will gain a better understanding of their Creator whom they address as "the God of our ancestors." Such fuller understanding will also improve their direct personal relationship and fellowship with him.

THE PROBLEM AND THESIS STATEMENTS

The church in Africa has obvious problems requiring quality exposition of the biblical text. The quality of Christian spirituality in Africa today is on a downward spiralling decline despite the many churches and preachers in the continent. The transforming Christian gospel should be reflected in changed attitudes, behaviour and life-

---

3. J. N. K. Mugambi, *Christianity and African Culture* (2002; repr., Nairobi, Kenya: Acton Publishers, 2009), 74.

styles, and actions. However expectations for such do not match the growth in numbers of professing Christians in Africa. Consequently, vices such as crimes, corruption, ethno-tribal sentiments, hatred and bitterness, sexual immorality, are on the increase, not only in society but also in the church. The life of nominalism, the practice of syncretism, and a massive return to certain practices of African Traditional Religion by a growing number of professing Christians are also on the increase in Africa.

These problems arise because not many of Christian preachers preach the real gospel of Christ preaching instead another gospel. The Bible has not been given its right of place in many of the versions of African Christianity today, much less expository preaching of the biblical text. Additionally, not many preachers in Africa possess the requisite skills to preach in such a way that the Gospel message takes firm roots in the lives and souls of Africans. Even among the few who have received training, some of them do not sense its responsibility and feel a sense of guilt and restlessness when they fail to expound the Scriptures. Hence, the exposition of the Scriptures is impoverished. Yet, the clear, adequate and in-depth preaching of the Scriptures, contextually articulated, relevantly and appropriately applied to the life situations of the African audience, still remains the means that brings about the needed true transformation of lives that by its outcome, also transforms society.

THE MOTIVATION FOR THIS BOOK

Stott had asserted that, "True Christian preaching . . . is extremely rare in today's church. Thoughtful people in many countries are asking for it, but cannot find it."[4] Stott is right. I have observed over the

---

4. John Robert Walmsley Stott with Greg Scharf, *The Challenge of Preaching* (Carlisle, Cumbria: Langham Preaching Resources, 2011), 13.

years with dismay, the departure of expository preaching in the pulpit, as I listen to a number of African preachers. I argued elsewhere,

> A major lacuna in much of contemporary African Christian preaching is the gross lack of adequate exegetical hermeneutics and explanation of the ancient sacred text before its application. The lack of balance makes application to always dominate preaching. This inability poses a great threat not only to the authority and integrity of the Bible and its message, but also to the faith and confidence of the contemporary audience in the power of its message. This unfortunate detour robs the contemporary audience of the beauty of experiencing the feel of the original contextual import of the biblical text. Since the act of preaching is communicating a biblical truth to contemporary contexts, the preacher should allow the ancient text become meaningful to its contemporary audience.[5]

Jumping from the mere reading of a passage from the Bible to application rarely, perhaps, even glosses its meaning. This should be corrected so Africans hear the voice of God in the pulpit.

Secondly, I was quite excited when the seminary where I teach asked me to teach homiletics and expository preaching both at the undergraduate and graduate levels. But of the many books in the school's library on preaching, I could hardly find any that speaks particularly to the African contexts written by Africans. This book in your hand is the result of the courage I reluctantly summoned to fill in this gap to make my contribution to the field of expository preaching in Africa.

---

5. Joel Kamsen Tihitshak Biwul, "The Challenge of Pastoral Hermeneutics in Africa: Suggestions for Effective Preaching by Nigerian Pastors," *TCNN Research Bulletin* Number 59 (September 2013), 28.

THE PURPOSE OF THIS BOOK

This book is primarily intended to assist African preachers and teachers to adequately lead out the voice of God from the divine text so it can be heard in the African contexts. It encourages preachers to move away from predominantly topical to expository sermons. It is also aimed at helping theological teachers and students to use it as a resource material in their instruction and learning in the class of homiletics and expository preaching.

The task of expository preaching should be text-grounded and audience-centred. The purpose of the task is to ensure that the meaning of the ancient text is clearly expounded and its message is adequately and relevantly applied to the contextual life situations of the audience today. The goal of this task is to make the message of the Scriptures transform lives so they become change agents in society.

Expository preaching should motivate African Christians to appreciate the grace of God in their lives, and thus, live out such testimony in their day-to-day life. Like the Ephesians to whom Paul said, "although you were dead in your transgressions and sins, God made you alive with Christ because of his great love and rich mercy," so should the African Christians (Eph 2:1-13). Such appreciation of God's work of salvation and his sustaining power is to cultivate in them the resolve to consistently live in total obedience and service to him. When African Christians acknowledge the Person and work of God, they will love Him unreservedly; seek to serve and live for Him no matter their difficult experiences; and they will consistently have reverence for His holy name and glory.

But not everyone who claims to preach the Bible can lead Christians in Africa to this kind of deep appreciation. The one who can assume such enormous responsibility is that person whose life is transformed by the power of the message of the cross; who is filled and controlled by the Holy Spirit; and one whose consistent loyalty is to Christ and to God, the owner of the Bible that he or she preaches. Only such a person can truly motivate and guide the Africans toward finding their Creator in his written Word.

Therefore, the purpose of this book will have been achieved when African Christian preachers go about the task with zeal, honesty, devotion, conviction, and commitment. The challenge of the task is as Dr. Tim Palmer expressed, "The center of gravity of the Christian church has now shifted from Europe and America to the global South, including Africa. It is now Africa's turn to take a lead in doing responsible contextual theology."[6] Palmer has just re-echoed what Kwame Bediako had said, "By any account, Africa has become a heartland of the Christian faith in our time."[7] When African preachers take up the responsibility of expository preaching seriously and pursue it vigorously, they would have been contributing, in part, to what Palmer calls "doing responsible contextual theology."

THE PROCEDURE OF THE BOOK

The main concern of this book centres essentially on three poles. First, it attempts to explain the necessity of expository preaching and how African preachers can make the meaning of the biblical text understandable to Africans so they can hear God speaking clearly to them in their own contexts of *Africanness*. Second, it demonstrates how the preacher can adequately translate the message of the text to

---

6. Timothy Palmer, *Christian Theology in an African Context* (Bukuru, Nigeria: Africa Christian Textbooks, 2015), 174. Dr. Palmer has been a Western missionary and a Professor of theology who has lived and taught Christian theology in Africa at the Theological College of Northern Nigeria (TCNN) for over thirty years.

7. Kwame Bediako, *Jesus in Africa: The Christian Gospel in African History and Experience* (Carlisle, Cumbria: Paternoster Publishing, 2000), 3.

the modern African context in such a clear way to be acted upon by its hearers. Third, it discusses how expository preaching can facilitate Christian spirituality in the church in Africa.

To achieve its desired purpose, the book is developed in three parts. The first part, written in seven chapters, focuses on the necessity of expository preaching for the church in Africa. It addresses the question whether expository preaching in Africa today is necessary.

The second part has six chapters. It centres on a more practical level by presenting certain steps regarding how the biblical text should be expounded and presented to the African audience. It begins with the need to prepare the expositor and weaves into the sermon itself.

Lastly, the third part, with three chapters, introduces some of the areas that are considered to be fundamental to an effective expository preaching. It draws attention to the crucial need of understanding the background of the biblical text as well as that of the receiving context. Of similar importance is the necessity to know certain obvious obstacles to expository preaching in Africa so the biblical text can be effectively translated to the African audience.

When an African mother cooks food, she is happy when her family members eat the food. If African pastors, preachers and teachers of the Scriptures, and theological institutions in Africa find the whole or some aspects of this book useful, the goal of its endeavour will have been achieved; and for this, I am deeply thankful.

UNDERSTANDING THE NATURE OF EXPOSITORY PREACHING

In most, if not all ancient African societies, the message from the community head (the village head, chief or traditional ruler) was passed from one house to another in specific ways. One of the ways was through the services of the town crier. This is the person who received a message from the community leader and went from house to house to deliver it orally.

Similarly, a preacher of the Word of God assumes the role of a town crier as God's mouthpiece while the act of preaching itself is the oral communication of that Word. Two concepts are fundamental for readers to understand: These are preaching and expository preaching. Expository preaching has purpose and glory that expositors of the Biblical text should understand.

PREACHING

The idea of preaching began in the Old Testament when God sent angels with messages to people. For example, an angel came with a message from God to Hagar with specific instructions regarding her predicament (Gen 16:6-11; 21:15-19). Angels also went on a revenge and rescue mission to Sodom (Gen 19:1-25). However, in the case of Abraham, Moses, and Job, God related his messages directly to them in their different conditions. He covenanted with Abraham when he promised to make him great through his descendants (Gen 12:1-7; 15; 17). After the dramatic call and commission of Moses as a leader of his oppressed people (Ex. 3:1-21), God subsequently spoke with him face to face during the events of the Red Sea (Ex. 14:10-29); the presentation of the Ten Commandments at Mount Sinai (Ex. 19:1-20:21); the consecration of the priesthood (Ex. 28:1, 41; 29:21); and a lot more. Similarly, God dramatically preached to Job when he engaged him in a series of questions Job was unable to answer (Job 38:1-42:6).

After the era of the sermonic preaching by angels and God's direct address to individuals, the preaching tradition expanded during the ministry of the Old Testament prophets. This redefined method of communicating the divine message became necessary as the prophets took on the status of being God's messengers, acting as his mouthpiece. The practice of preaching continued into the New Testament, beginning with the preaching of John the Baptist, the announcement of the virgin conception by the angels, and the preaching of Jesus, and later the Apostles. Preaching developed from simple to complex forms as the history of the church progressed vis-à-vis ancient civilization and globalization. So, what is the act of Christian preaching?

Christian preaching, which is Biblical preaching, in general, is defined by Vines and Shaddix as, "The oral communication of Biblical truth by the Holy Spirit through a human personality to a given audience with the intent of enabling a positive response."[1] Here, what qualifies as *Biblical preaching* involves five factors – it should be an oral communication; it is the translation of Biblical truth; the process involves the Holy Spirit; it is done through a human personality, and it anticipates a positive response. The content of the mes-

---

1.   Jerry Vines and Jim Shaddix, *Power in the Pulpit: How to Prepare and Deliver Expository Sermons* (Chicago, Illinois: Moody Press, 1999), 27.

sage every true expositor seeks to communicate in a sermon is the truth from the Bible. Thus, the Biblical text is central in preaching. The reason for this centrality is as explained by John Piper; preaching "... deals with the Word of God. True preaching is not the opinions of a mere man. It is the faithful exposition of God's Word."[2] Or as Stott puts it, "Preaching is indispensable to Christianity because Christianity is based on the truth that God chose to use words to reveal himself to humanity."[3] Preaching, of necessity, involves oral activity. It is translating truth from the Bible to its hearers in their contexts. Its core, then, is the verbalization of truth from the written Word of God to people.

EXPOSITORY PREACHING

Expository preaching is an aspect of Biblical or Christian preaching. According to Vines and Shaddix, it is,

> A discourse that expounds a passage of Scripture, organizes it around a central theme and main divisions which issue forth from the given text, and then decisively applies its message to the listeners. . ... [this way, it is] the process of laying open a biblical text in such a way that its original meaning is brought to bear on the lives of contemporary listeners.[4]

---

2. John Piper, *The Supremacy of God in Preaching* (rev. ed., Grand Rapids, Michigan: Baker Books, 2004), 11.

3. John Robert Walmsley Stott with Greg Scharf, *The Challenge of Preaching: Abridged and updated* (Carlisle, Cumbria: Langham Preaching Resources, 2011), 3.

4. Vines and Shaddix, *Power in the Pulpit,* 29, 28. Chapell's understanding of an expository sermon, too, is helpful. Such a sermon is "... a message whose structure and thought are derived from a biblical text, that covers the scope of the text, and that explains the features and context of the text in order to disclose the enduring principles for faithful thinking, living, and worship intended by

The act of 'laying open' a Biblical text means exposing and laying the content bare to public view.

Let me illustrate. In most parts of ancient Africa, clay jars, in addition to other uses, were used for storage. Grain such as beans, rice, corn, sorghum and locust beans were stored away in them. Some people also stored away coins, cowries, and other valuables in them. Such storage jars were sealed with clay; they were opened only when they were needed. The content of a jar could only be known by opening the jar, and not just by looking at it.

Similarly, the Biblical text, which is ancient to the modern reader, is *exposed* from its original context by *expounding* its meaning to achieve better understanding. To this extent, expository preaching, then, is the art of explaining the meaning of the Biblical text and applying, adequately and relevantly, its message to the modern context. This way, modern readers can participate in the benefits of the message of the text as its first readers.

But expository preaching requires the explanation or exegesis of the text. Richard L. Mayhue captures this point aptly, "Exposition presupposes an exegetical process to extract the God-intended meaning of Scripture and an explanation of that meaning in a con-

---

the Spirit, who inspired the text." See Bryan Chapell, *Christ-Centered Preaching: Redeeming the Expository Sermon* (2nd ed., 2005; repr., Grand Rapids, Michigan: Baker Academic, 2007), 31. As Richard explains the concept further, biblical exposition expounds, expresses, and exposes the Bible to an audience and the audience to the Bible. Expository preaching is bridging the gap between the biblical and modern contexts. The expositor takes the modern audience into the world of the ancient biblical text and walks them through it, then brings them back to where they are, and shows them how its message affects them in specific ways. See Ramesh Richard, *Scripture Sculpture: Do-It-Yourself Manual for Biblical Preaching* (1995; repr., Grand Rapids, Michigan: Baker Books, 1997), 17, 19.

temporary way. "[5] The task of extracting the God-intended original meaning out of the ancient text seeks to understand, as closely as possible, that meaning embedded in its usage of language structure and expressions. Preaching from the Biblical text without adequate explanation and proper application of hermeneutics almost robs it of its true meaning.

The exegetical method suggested in this book is the literal-literary, historical and grammatical approach to understanding the entire Scriptures. Trailing after this method, Haddon Robinson submits, "Expository preaching is the communication of a Biblical concept, derived from and transmitted through a historical, grammatical, and literary study of a passage in its context, which the Holy Spirit first applies to the personality and experience of the preacher, then through the preacher, applies to the hearers."[6] While we admit that there are other approaches to interpreting the Biblical text, we affirm that the text remains an ancient religious document. The appeal here is to encourage preachers to deal with the text from its original context.

Expository preaching emerges from within and revolves around the Biblical text. If this text is not the nerve centre and the driving force for expository preaching, then something is fundamentally wrong. It is also clear that the way in which the preacher handles the Biblical text is crucial; for it can either impede or inspire its message. Consequently, the burden of proof in translating meaning is placed on the expositor who excavates, explains, and contemporises its meaning and message. This helps the audience to reflect on the

---

5.   Richard L. Mayhue, "Rediscovering Expository Preaching," in *Rediscovering Expository Preaching*: John McArthur, Jr. and the Master's Seminary Faculty (eds., Richard L. Mayhue and Robert L. Thomas, Dallas, Texas: WORD Books, 1993), 3.

6.   Haddon W. Robinson, *Expository Preaching: Principles and Practice* (2001; repr., Leicester, England: Inter-Varsity Press, 2004), 21.

essence of the cross and to behold the heavenly throne for the radiating glory of the God of the Word being preached (see Isa. 6:1-5; Ez. 1:1-28; Rev. 1:9-18; 4:1-11).

WHO IS THE EXPOSITORY PREACHER?

Nigerians are easily identified by one obvious mark. They love to be noticed and recognised. You can always recognize a Nigerian wherever you see one. For this reason, they love titles such as Chief, High Chief, Elder, Your Royal Highness, Your Majesty, Princess, Professor, Dr, President and Founder, General Overseer (GO), Man of God (MoG), and many more. Because of Nigerians' quest for titles, some use all means possible to look for such positions, all for the sake of public recognition. Most of them, in fact, take offense when they are improperly introduced on special occasions. For their identity is caught up in these titles.

The identity of the expository preacher is essential. Such a person is a *herald* of God because he or she represents God before the audience in the pulpit. The preacher derives authority from God to preach his Word, yet at the same time, stands with the people to share in the benefits of it. Donald R. Sunukjian captures it succinctly: The preacher understands himself or herself ". . . as standing, not over the congregation, but among them, holding open a Bible, showing its pages to them, saying, 'This is God's Word – inspired, inerrant, authoritative. It tells us what we need to know – what to think, how to act, what's ahead. It gives us truths. . ..'"[7] Though a *herald*, the preacher does not claim superiority over the audience but equality; both are sinners saved by grace, equally subservient to the authority of the Bible.

---

7. Donald R. Sunukjian, *Biblical Preaching: Proclaiming Truth with Clarity and Relevance* (Grand Rapids, Michigan: Kregel Publication, 2007), 9.

The expository preacher is also a *representative* of God who wields no personal authority except that from God. He or she recognises that they are sent with a specific message for a particular human context. Stott explains what this means, "…the preacher is a servant under someone else's authority, the communicator of someone else's word. The preacher's task is to contextualize this message, relaying it in such a way that listeners can relate to it."[8]

Still, the preacher is a *messenger* sent by God. In old African societies, town criers had one significant function. They were sent on errands by the traditional head of a community with a message for his subjects. The preacher has a similar role to that of the king's or traditional ruler's town crier who relates the ruler's message to the subjects. The preacher as a *messenger* is under obligation to deliver precisely what the owner of the divine Word says. He or she has no warrant to modify or relax the intensity of the content of the holy Word. Like the Old Testament prophets, such a *messenger* declares, "Thus says the Lord." Yet, like Moses, he or she pleads for mercy and forgiveness where divine wrath looms over the hearers (see, for example, Ex. 32:1-4; Nu. 16:41-49). Such a dire and weighty responsibility does not give the preacher room for laxity, laziness or arrogance. The preacher dares not ascribe self-deification in place of the owner of the divine Word. This status calls for awe and the utmost sense of responsibility and accountability in the discharge of the given task.

The expository preacher, in the discharge of his or her role, is to act like the Old Testament prophets who brought a word from God to people. They did not delay in delivering the divine message once received because of its urgency. As Paul charged Timothy as a *herald*, the preacher is to "preach the Word" as one under obligation in season and out of season. Accordingly, the preacher of the divine Word

---

8.   Stott and Scharf, *The Challenge of Preaching*, 30.

wisely does not neglect, negotiate, or abandon this crucial responsibility. The expository preacher is obligated to herald the divine Word as commanded and as charged (2 Tim 4:2; see also 2 Tim 2:15; Luke1:1-3).

THE TASK

Some preachers in Africa are more comfortable with topical preaching to the detriment of expository preaching. Topical sermons, on the most part, only gloss over the beauty of the text. Expository preaching, unfortunately, is not given proper space today because the task is difficult; only a few preachers sense the need to engage in it. Conrad Mbewe agrees that expository preaching is indeed a demanding task. He says, "The people sitting in the pews listening to their pastor sometimes wish that they too could have the privilege of preaching. But very few realize how demanding preaching is."[9]

The task conveys the idea of digging into a tin or gold mine. This kind of digging is not an indiscriminate but a purposeful one, so the miner does not overturn the tin or gold in the process of digging. And this is what the task of expository preaching is – carefully digging into the Biblical text to mine the hidden treasure of the divine Word. The effort is time-consuming because it requires reading and rereading; questioning and re-questioning, and researching into extra-Biblical sources that shed light on the Biblical text under study. Much more, it requires analysing the components of the text, comparing Biblical and extra-Biblical materials, and making a judgement on the meaning of the text and how to apply it to the context of the audience.

---

9. Conrad Mbewe, *Pastoral Preaching: Building a People for God* (Carlisle, Cumbria: Langham Preaching Resources, 2017), 1.

Considerable dedication, diligence and self-sacrifice are required for the task of expository preaching. Sunukjian shows his agreement when he explains that expository preaching is being faithful to the meaning and flow of the original author and to make it relevant in a clear, believable, and pertinent ways to the contemporary listener. In his words, "Biblical preaching takes great pains to present the ideas and sequence of thought of the inspired Biblical author."[10] The preacher goes through such rigors in the attempt to derive from and disclose the thought of the author from within the scope of the passage, so the message is applied to the lives of the listeners.[11]

Expository preachers know quite well that they cannot ignore or gloss over the role of the Holy Spirit in their lives, yet expect to become effective. When the preacher fails to pay careful attention to the quiet voice of the Holy Spirit, the possibility of erring from the truth of the text and, in fact, its correct application to the audience is very likely. Stephen F. Olford and David L. Olford express this very clearly when they state that "Expository preaching is the Spirit-empowered explanation and proclamation of the text of God's Word."[12] As preachers give more space to the Holy Spirit, they learn personal lessons from the Biblical text. Such lessons demand they model the divine Word to the Christian and non-Christian communities by their speech, conduct and lifestyle (1Tim. 4:12; Matt. 5:13-16). Such a requirement is a demanding task.

---

10. Sunukjian, *Biblical Preaching*, 13-14, 10.

11. Bryan Chapell, *Christ-Centered Preaching* (Grand Rapids, Michigan: Baker Books, 1994), 29.

12. Stephen F. Olford with David Lindsay Olford, *Anointed Expository Preaching* (Nashville, Tennessee: Broadman & Holman Publishers, 1998), 69.

THE PURPOSE

The word purpose refers to the reason, intention, or aim of something or an action. When something is done purposefully, it is correctly targeted at achieving a specific goal. Expository preaching has a definite purpose. Grant R. Osborne states, for instance, that ". . . the final goal of hermeneutics is not a systematic theology but the sermon. The actual purpose of Scripture is not an explanation but exposition, not description but proclamation."[13] Osborne's assertion suggests that the specific purpose for Christian preaching throughout history has been that human beings will understand and have the real knowledge of who God is. This purpose is clear from the prophetic, Christological, and apostolic exposition of the Scriptures. As Chris Wright states, it is God who gave us the whole Bible,[14] his divinely inspired[15] revelation written by humans in human words. The primary purpose is so that humanity could know his Person and have a clear understanding of his plans for their benefit. The purpose of knowing and relating with God should be re-echoed clearly through expository preaching.

Such understanding helps human beings know what God requires of them for a functional relationship to develop with him.

---

13. Grant R. Osborne, *The Hermeneutical Spiral: A Comprehensive Introduction to Biblical Interpretation* (2nd ed., Downers Grove, Illinois: Inter-Varsity Press, 2006), 29.

14. Christopher J. H. Wright, *Sweeter than Honey: Preaching the Old Testament* (Carlisle, Cumbria: Langham Preaching Resources, 2015), 4.

15. The subject of biblical inspiration is critical. That God inspired the human authors to write his Word in human language of accommodation presupposes, according to Wright, that Scriptures were "breathed out" by God. This means, ". . . although they were spoken and written by ordinary human beings like us, what was said and written down was as if it had come from the mouth of God." This gives it the stamp of divinity, setting the Biblical texts apart from other literary works. See Wright, *Sweeter than Honey*, 5.

When the Prophet Isaiah gained this type of knowledge about God, he responded to his call thus, "Then I heard the voice of the Lord saying, 'Whom shall I send? And who will go for us?' And I said, 'Here am I. Send me!' He said, 'Go and tell this people….'" (Isa 6:8-9 NIV). Paul also re-echoed this need of knowing what God required of human beings when he said, "How, then, can they call on the one they have not believed in? And how can they believe in the one of whom they have not heard? And how can they hear without someone preaching to them? And how can they preach unless they are sent? As it is written, 'How beautiful are the feet of those who bring good news!'" (Rom 10:14-15 NIV).

The knowledge of God and what he requires of human beings will only come about through a proper exposition of the Bible in which he has revealed himself and his plans. Expository preaching, therefore, should not be a mere address; neither should it be just religious talk. But as George E. Janvier rightly puts it, "Preaching is not a speech, but an encounter with God [through the human channel that] is prepared spiritually to be used of God to speak to people."[16] God has spoken; humanity needs to hear and understand what he has spoken so they can come away with his true knowledge. The accurate and appropriate preaching of the divine Word is inevitable in Africa.

Secondly, apart from the knowledge of God, expository preaching intends to unveil the divine agenda by connecting the ancient text with the modern context. When God spoke, and his spoken words were written by those whom he inspired to do so, it was not only to reveal himself to humans. It was also to reveal the sins of his covenant people and lead them to repentance. Expository preaching is meant to achieve this purpose. To this end, the prophets, as God's

---

16. George Evans Janvier, *Biblical Preaching in Africa: A Textbook for Christian Preachers* (Bukuru, Nigeria: Africa Christian Textbooks, 2002), 7.

representatives and mouthpieces, proclaimed orally the divine Word they had received. They first submitted their credentials to validate their identity using the prophetic introductory formula, "Thus says the Lord" before they announced the divine message. The prophets proclaimed the divine message as guided by the Holy Spirit after they had indicted and rebuked the audience for their sin. They placed the people's guilt before them, charged them with legal facts, and afterwards proposed solutions to the problem where the people showed signs of remorse.

Thirdly, expository preaching presents the ethos of the divine Kingdom with a clear invitation for those listening to become its subjects. John the Baptist's preparatory exposition and the Christological exposition both capture this point when both declared, "Repent, for the kingdom of heaven is near" (Matt 3:1-2; 4:17, see also chapters 5-7 NIV). While John and Jesus, acting as expositors of the divine message, did not always read from any written text to preach about the Kingdom of God/heaven, modern preachers depend on the written ancient text to communicate truths from it to the audience. Hence, "Biblical preaching takes great pains to present the ideas and sequence of thought of the inspired Biblical author"[17] to the modern audience accurately, relevantly, and clearly. All listeners to the preaching of the Bible need to know the rules and principles stipulated in it for Christian living.

Fourthly, expository preaching calls for a fundamental transformation of life. The content of the Bible narrates the history of human failures, disobedience, rebellion, and hard-heartedness against the rule of God in contrast to his expressed love, compassion, mercy, and grace. Stephen's expository preaching indicates this fact (Acts 7) just as the Christological indictment and rebuke of the religious leaders

---

17. Sunukjian, *Biblical Preaching*, 10.

of his day (Matt. 23: 13-39) equally reveal this point. The Biblical text is expounded primarily to cause a change of heart and lifestyle. Sunukjian asserts, "The purpose of the sermon is not to impart knowledge but to influence behaviour – not to inform but to transform. The goal is not to make listeners more educated but more Christlike."[18] Such transformation should spark up revival and the life of obedience to God in the listeners. Olford and Olford affirm, "We believe that true 'heaven-sent' revival and aggressive evangelism will only come when there is a return to the preaching and obeying of God's inerrant Word."[19] The attempt at exposing the Bible is to bring about a transformation of life that results in consistent obedience to God and his Word.

Fifthly, expository preaching not only develops true conviction in Christians but also encourages their faithful service to God. For instance, Jesus came to serve humanity through his death (Phil 2:5-11). His momentary setting aside of his status and death was a great sacrifice for humanity's good. All people transformed by the preaching of the Bible are expected to sacrifice their lives in service to God by serving humanity. Such service reveals what the transforming power of the divine Word can achieve in a person's life. Paul's transformed life's experience and expository sermons to the churches he planted both validate this truth (see Acts 9:1-31; Phil. 3:1-16; Gal. 5:16-26; Eph. 4:11-32).

Sixthly, good expository preaching enhances the quality of the spiritual growth of Christians. In what Mbewe calls "Pastoral Preaching," expository preaching helps ". . . those who have come to Christ to grow spiritually."[20] People who listen consistently to the correct exposition of the Scriptures and faithfully apply truths from

---

18. Sunukjian, *Biblical Preaching*, 12

19. Olford and Olford, *Anointed Expository*, 2.

20. Mbewe, *Pastoral Preaching*, 9.

it to life will have sustained spiritual growth. Like the Berean Christians, such maturing Christians will always use the Scriptures as the measuring standards for all human thoughts, speech, and actions. Overall, expository preaching is to serve for African Christians as "… a source of strength to live in joy, motivate loving and godly service, encourage [the] worship of our great God, and establish [our] hope and trust in Jesus Christ, who initiates and perfects [our] faith."[21]

UNDERSTANDING THE GLORY

Matthew reported what Jesus told his listeners about the importance and glory of the Kingdom of God/heaven. Jesus expressed the glory in vivid imagery likening it to a hidden treasure in a field and beautiful pearls. He said,

> 'The kingdom of heaven is like treasure hidden in a field.
> When a man found it, he hid it again, and then in his joy
> went and sold all he had and bought that field. 'Again, the
> kingdom of heaven is like a merchant looking for fine pearls.
> When he found one of great value, he went away and sold
> everything he had and bought it.' (Mat 13:44-46 NIV).

These two images describe the value of the utopian Kingdom which Jesus sought to establish on earth.

We can also liken what Jesus told his listeners about the glory of the Kingdom of God/heaven to the beauty of the glory of expository preaching. As we noted earlier, the Bible is an ancient text that is far remote from the modern reader. We can only understand what it meant to the first readers by going back in time to understand their world.

---

21. John Jusu, Supervising Editor, "Dedication," in *Africa Study Bible* (Carol Stream: Oasis International Limited, 2016).

Discoveries from the Word of God can be fascinating and fulfilling both for the preacher and the listeners. Just imagine for a moment how a miner would feel when gold is found after digging. The excavator will be filled with joy. When truths are discovered through digging them out from the Bible through a careful, devotional and reflective study, the joy can be overwhelming. Such discovery adds to the quality of the spirituality of the preacher. It will also affect the listeners as those discovered truths are shared with them through the accurate preaching of the Biblical text.

We can illustrate this joy from the words of Jesus to his disciples. Jesus had been talking with a Samaritan woman who came to draw water from the well. His disciples had gone into the nearby town to look for food. When they returned and found him talking with the woman, they were surprised that their Master would speak with a Samaritan, worse, a woman. The Jews considered the Samaritans as people from a rejected community. Women, too, were considered as second-class people in Jewish society. Their expressed amazement reveals that they failed to see what Jesus saw. But Jesus had just won the soul of the Samaritan woman and many more Samaritans whom she invited to come to him. So, when his disciples offered him food to eat, Jesus said to them, "'I have food to eat that you know nothing about. . ... 'My food', said Jesus, 'is to do the will of him who sent me and to finish his work.'" (John 4:32-34 NIV). It is apparent that Jesus was full of joy and satisfaction because the conversion of the Samaritans fulfilled the purpose of his coming to the world.

This is the kind of joy and satisfaction that comes from discovering truths from the Bible. Preachers will be unable to discover the glory of expository preaching only when they fail to devote time to studying it devotionally. There is always something new to learn from the Bible when we explore it devotionally and prayerfully for our spiritual nourishment, whether personal or corporate. Joy, satisfaction, and a sense of self-fulfilment are among the crowning glory of expository preaching.

So far, we have said that the expository preacher is God's representative sent with his Word to its hearers. We have explained that the act of expository preaching is digging truths out of the Bible and laying it before people. The object of expository preaching is to transform peoples' lives so they gain a better and deeper understanding about God and his plans for them. The sense of overflowing joy and satisfaction that both the preacher and hearers can receive from expository preaching is unimaginable. But we first need to understand the Biblical foundations for exposing truths from the Bible before we get started on the task.

CHAPTER 2

BIBLICAL FOUNDATIONS FOR EXPOSITORY PREACHING

According to an African proverb often used in Nigeria, "The words of our elders are words of wisdom. The wise person hears and becomes wiser." Leaders in the family, clan, tribe or a community in the African setting are considered to be people full of wisdom and sources of authority. As such, their counsels are never taken lightly; neither are their testimonies ignored because such words are considered to have validity.

Community leaders in Africa, like the case in the Old Testament, are entrusted with public oversight functions because they are seen to be mature and responsible. Their functions augment those of the traditional rulers (the village heads, chiefs, and kings) who are the custodians of the customs and traditions of the society in their various communities. The judgement of an elderly person is accepted as final when he rules on a matter in the council of the elders in a given community. Comparatively, when the African gods and divinities speak on a matter concerning an individual or a community through their representative priests, the oracle is accepted and respected by the people for its assumed validity. The grounds for such acceptance are rooted in the fact that such messages and instructions come from higher authorities whose validity is not in question.

Christian preaching, then and now, is rooted in the Bible as an ancient religious document accepted as the authoritative source text. Preachers will always appeal to it as their authority. As J. Daniel Baumann asserts, "To preach is to preach the Bible. . .. To preach is to speak with authority . . . It is the preaching of God's Word that makes the church a unique institution in society. What other right does a man have to speak so brazenly unless he has a word from God?"[1]

People who are called to preach do not preach their own gospel, or even another gospel[2] but the gospel of Jesus Christ and his kingdom. It is in his name that such preachers demand attention to the divine message. This is critical! The African priests in antiquity, like the Biblical prophets, delivered the message of the gods to people. They did not herald their own message; neither were they at liberty to modify the message. Instead, such representatives of a higher authority were under obligation to deliver the message exactly the way it was given. They dared not even assume diplomatic negotiation or political lobbying over it.

The Bible is the Word of a higher authority, serving as the foundations and motivation for expository preaching in Africa. No preacher can confidently preach from it without belief or deep conviction in it. A preacher of God's Word must believe in its inspiration and infallibility; in the authority of its content, validity, integrity and its transforming power. Expository preaching is preaching the Bible; the whole of it, the facts of it, and the truth of it.

---

1. J. Daniel Baumann, *An Introduction to Contemporary Preaching* (1972; paperback ed., 1988; repr., Grand Rapids, Michigan: Baker Book House, 1990), 93.

2. Femi Adeleye has written an excellent book on the need to preach the gospel of Jesus Christ and his Kingdom rather than preaching a different gospel as is the case with most contemporary African Christian preachers. See Femi Adeleye, *Preachers of a Different Gospel* (Nairobi, Kenya: WordAlive/Bukuru: ACTS/Grand Rapids, Michigan: Zondervan Publishing House, 2011).

THE DIVINE REVELATION MODEL

Knowledge is construed as "power" because it creates awareness and increases the level of a person's understanding. The narrative of the Biblical account of divine revelation in creation is so that people can know God. Preaching is to achieve the purpose of divine revelation. God revealed himself generally in creation, then through the preaching of the Old Testament prophets and sages, through the incarnation of his Son, Jesus Christ, and in his written Word (the Old and New Testaments). He chose these routes to reveal himself with the aim that the whole of humanity would come to the actual knowledge of him, and therefore, by their obedience through his enabling grace, would live to serve and worship him.[3]

Expository preaching seeks to explain the essence of God's self-disclosure to listeners today. People are told this truth orally by preachers without ambiguity so that they will come to the full knowledge of the truth about God. As Bruce Shelley states, "Clarity is the first law of learning."[4] Particularly, when the message about God's self-disclosure is correctly and clearly presented, it helps the listeners to distinguish the voice of God from other competing voic-

---

3. Christian theologians explain general revelation to mean all the things God created, whether visible or invisible objects in the galaxies, the earth, and in the sea (see Acts 4:24b).

   On the other hand, they explain special revelation to mean Jesus Christ as God's special revelation to humankind. The primary import here is knowability – God wanted, as he has always desired, humankind to know him, to know his plans and purposes for them, and for them to seek to know their place and responsibility in life. Critical to this knowability, framed by obedience, is humanity's experience of a functional relationship with him, and by extension, in human society.

4. Bruce Leon Shelley, *Church History in Plain Language* (2nd ed., Nashville, Tennessee: Thomas Nelson Publishers, 1995), xvi.

es. Consequently, it leads them to believe, follow, obey, and live in service to him in truth and righteousness.

THE PROPHETIC MODEL

Expository preaching is also anchored on the prophetic model of proclamation. In the progressive development of Israel's history, the prophetic office and function were added to those established institutions such as the priesthood and the monarchy. The Biblical prophets were people who came from God with a message from him to their fellow men and women. They were convinced that they were under divine directive and compulsion to deliver the divine message to the human context. As such, the prophets had a straightforward yet potent and compelling sermon theme – "Thus said the LORD." This is the heart of prophetic preaching – the Lord says.

This theme motivated the prophets; hence, they spoke mainly about the religious, moral, and social vices of the society of their day. To rebellious hearts, they offered indictment and rebuke; but to remorseful and repentant hearts, they offered divine forgiveness and hope. The prophets preached without mincing words and without fear or favour of personality (see 2 Sam 12:7-12; 1 Kgs 17:1; 18:16-40; Amos 7:10-17). They were not politicians nor were they international diplomats. On the contrary, they were people under directives and compulsion, sent on an uncompromising errand, with a daunting message. Hence, they had no time to waste; neither did they give room for any negotiation with the recipients of the divine message. Unlike some preachers today, the prophets would not give in to human pressure to distort the divine message since they were quite aware that 'human rights' are subservient to that of their Creator. The unapologetic prophetic approach to proclaiming the divine word suggests that when evil is left unchecked, it soon becomes infectious. Equally, when an anomaly is not addressed immediately, it by and large soon becomes a tolerated and accepted norm.

Like the Biblical prophets, the expositor of God's Word in Africa must proclaim the Word with all the conviction, seriousness and the urgency that it deserves. Although the expositor serves in a time and context entirely different from those of the Biblical prophets, the propelling conviction of these Biblical forebears must not be compromised. Preachers should be people of integrity, people who speak the truth, and people who are forthright. Roland Q. Leavell explains, especially where a pastor is called by a congregation, that one key reason why a pulpit committee takes many months searching for a pastor is because, "They are looking for a man of God with a message from God, a man whose heart is ablaze with spiritual zeal to lead men to God."[5] We not only need men who are called by God into the ministry, but also women who are equally called and whose hearts are equally ablaze with spiritual zeal.

My own pastoral experience has shown that some church members do not like a pastor or preacher who maintains an uncompromising stance on Biblical principles and who is forthright in preaching the truths of Scriptures. Ironically, despite their disagreements and dislikes, they appreciate and respect the pastor for the spiritual flavour that such a minister brings to the congregation.

Today, we live in the modern African context where in most societies, many people like to shy away (save face) from standing up for the truth. People who confront what is wrong and speak the truth can be stigmatised as "leftist," "bad", and "wicked." True preachers have no option but to say what God says in his Word. They have no warrant to think or act otherwise than God's Word

---

5. Roland Q. Leavell, *Prophetic Preaching, Then and Now* (Grand Rapids, Michigan: Baker, 1963), 13.

directs. The reason is simple. Preachers assume a prophetic function when it comes to declaring the truth of God's Word to the audience.

Like the Biblical prophets whose preaching was divine-centred, expository preaching should be God-centred to have the desired effects on African society. It should provoke sinners to come to faith, force the rebellious to bow the knee before King Jesus, and challenge Christians to uphold unreserved their loyalty to Jesus Christ. In essence, expository preaching serves as the transforming force of both the converted and unconverted lives. Through clear and correct Biblical exposition, souls are saved. Those already saved are constantly reminded to live earthly life in light of its eternal values. When preachers of the divine Word in Africa maintain God as the centre of preaching as the Biblical prophets did, the message will generate true reverence for God. As descendants of the prophets, standing in their tradition, expository preachers should persuade listeners to encounter their Creator in his Word. They should persuade the African audience to choose life and live (see Deut 30:15-20; Josh 24:14-15) by their own example of walking the narrow path and going through the narrow gate (see Matt 7:13-14).

THE CHRISTOLOGICAL MODEL

When growing up as a young village boy, I had an uncle who was a blacksmith. Usually, I would sit and observe how he carried on with his trade. My uncle taught me how to fan the fire into flames with a specially made animal skin so that the iron became red. I had to be taught how to handle the skin to fan the fire. If I had not left the small village for a bigger one so I could go to school, I probably would have become a blacksmith like my late uncle. What I observed and learned to do from my uncle's trade has never been forgotten. I observed him keenly and tried fanning the fire into flames with great enthusiasm. As it is characteristic of Africa, children learn more by observation and imitation than by abstract theory.

Jesus said to his initial disciples, "I tell you the truth, anyone who has faith in me will do what I have been doing. He will do even greater things than these because I am going to the Father" (John 14:12 NIV). The disciples were to do what Jesus had done through what they had observed and by what he had taught them by practice. Like these disciples, Christians of every generation, as followers of Jesus Christ, are to imitate his life and ministry in all its ramifications, based on the teachings of the Scriptures. One of the significant things the disciples had observed that Jesus did was his preaching and teaching ministry. As he went from village to village and from town to town, he was preaching about the Kingdom of God/heaven.

Christians are reflectors, serving as light bearers to the testimony of Christ's earthly life and ministry. As his disciples, they learn from their Master how to disseminate the message of the gospel of the Kingdom by word and by life. Jesus had instructed his disciples, ". . . let your light shine before men, that they may see your good deeds and praise your Father in heaven" (Matt 5:16 NIV). When the early church began to reflect the message of Jesus by shining the light of the gospel and of the Kingdom by their life and speech, people noticed that they had been with Jesus (Acts 4:4-13). Their close association with Jesus Christ earned them the nickname "Christians" (Acts 11:26c). Christians not only imitate Christ but most importantly, they obey his commands; and through the power of his grace, they seek to carry out his instructions gladly. Apart from the revelation and prophetic models serving as the Biblical foundations for expository preaching today, the Christological model and mandate are another.

The Christological Model & Christian Preaching

Have you ever thought deeply about why Jesus came to the world? Perhaps. All that Jesus Christ said and did were to point people to God for redemption (see John 14:6; 9:1-5; 11:40-45). In Luke's account about the encounter of Zacchaeus with Jesus, Luke draws the attention of his readers to the fact that the core of Jesus' earthly ministry was the salvation of the human soul as well as the total redemption of humanity from the curse of sin (Luke 19:8-10 NIV). Also, in John's Gospel, John says Jesus applied the metaphor of the good shepherd to himself when he affirmed, "'The thief comes only to steal and kill and destroy; [but that] I have come that they may have life, and have it to the full'" (John10:10 NIV). These Christological pronouncements are anchored on yet another claim by Jesus, "'I am the good shepherd. The good shepherd lays down his life for the sheep'" (John 10:11, 27-29 NIV).

The primary purpose of Christ's incarnation has a salvific focus. For this reason, his major sermon theme was repentance that leads to freedom from sin. This type of repentance was crucial for admission into the utopian Kingdom of God/heaven, the one he came to establish.[6] What his forerunner, John the Baptist, had preached, Jesus also preached: "Repent, for the kingdom of heaven is near" (Matt 3:1-2; 4:17). Expository preaching in Africa is to declare this same message of repentance as a requirement for admission into the Kingdom of God ushered in by Jesus Christ. It should carry with it the Christological caution, "unless you repent, you . . . will perish" (Luke 13:1-5). Such caution serves as a motivation to the listeners to decisively

---

6. New Testament scholars inform us that the ethical codes of this anticipated but momentarily suspended utopian Kingdom are mostly conveyed in the Sermon on the Mount found in Matthew chapters 5-7.

make a purposeful decision to follow Christ; for only those that are saved belong to his flock (John 10:27-30) and will enter his kingdom.

The theme of repentance is crucial to expository preaching in Africa given the high levels of all-pervasive moral corruption on the continent. The forces of evil and godlessness loom over Africa. While preachers are to encourage the unsaved to repent and be saved, they must also challenge sinning Christians to repent, wrench their hearts of sin, and return to the Saviour for cleansing and empowerment for Christian living and service.

Yet this endeavour will only achieve its desired effects when preachers carefully and rightly preach the Biblical text, cogently present the message of the Bible, and relevantly apply it to the listeners' various life situations. The African continent is being devoured by various monsters: widespread corruption and poverty because of bad governance; strife and wars; terrorism and robbery because of greed and selfishness, and famine, diseases and poor development for lack of visionary and caring leaders. The monster of self-centredness and the gradual movement to individualism is equally destroying the family institution and community spirit. African peoples in such situations need to hear the voice of God speaking clearly and directly from the Bible to their situations. For instance, the oppressed, voiceless and helpless in the African society – whether they are Christians or non-Christians – should be able to meet with God and find solace from him in their life's situations when they hear his Word preached to them. Expository preaching will make meaning and cause transformation only when it practically addresses the life situations of the listener.[7]

---

7. See the article by Joel Kamsen Tihitshak Biwul, "The Challenge of Pastoral Hermeneutics in Africa: Suggestions for Effective Preaching by Nigerian Pastors," *TCNN Research Bulletin* Number 59 (September 2013): 28-42.

The Christological Mandate & Christian Preaching

The Biblical foundation for expository preaching also draws from the Christological mandate. During the earthly ministry of Jesus Christ, he also assigned his disciples to preach the same message of the Kingdom that he had preached (Matt 10:7; see also Matt 28:19; Acts 1:8). His mission of salvation and restoration on earth are captured both in his deeds and preaching. Jesus gave his followers the missiological mandate to "go and preach" (Matt 28:16-20; John 16:6).

Recent world events prove that there are more sorrows than pleasure and happiness in the life experiences of most people. It appears the world itself is becoming hostile to its inhabitants given growing occurrences of natural disasters and terrorists' activities.[8] Africa is

---

8. The modern world is facing ecological challenges almost on a daily basis. Also, recurrent natural disasters put people in the position of unrest, uncertainty, fear, and insecurity than stability. The experience of epidemic diseases and disasters such as floods, hurricanes and landslides in different parts of the world are occurring in higher proportion and more recurring fashion than before. Also, terrorists' activities have been on the increase ever since the attack on the International Trade Centre and White House building on September 11, 2001, by the Al-Qaida terrorist group under Osama Bin Laden.

    Additionally, recurring suicide bombing reveals that when the International Trade Centre was first attacked, this act captures the proverbial Biblical statement when Jesus told his disciples, "All these are the beginning of birth pains" (Matt 24:8 NIV). Al-Qaida has replicated itself in other terrorist groups such as Hezbollah in Lebanon, Hamas in Palestine, Al-Shabab in Somalia, Boko Haram and Miyetti Allah (Fulani herdsmen attacks) in Nigeria, & ISIL in Syria. Furthermore, starvation is claiming more lives than expected in war-torn countries on the African continent such as Ethiopia, Somalia, Darfur in South Sudan, Democratic Republic of Congo (DRC), Libya, and in some crisis areas of the North-East and Middle-Belt regions of Nigeria. Very recently, the political upheavals and internal wars that have plagued the Arab world unabated, particularly Syria, is life-threatening, far more than the scourge of hepatitis and HIV and AIDS diseases. These frequent attacks are causing more despair than comfort in the hearts of commuters.

consistently being plagued by the scourge of bad governance and underdevelopment. Many Africans are asking the critical question about the real essence of human life and living itself. Some have also raised critical questions as to whether God truly loves Africa vis-à-vis the bad experiences in their life situations.

The response to these almost helpless and endless human challenges is not found in political solutions. Most African politicians have failed the electorates because of their greed and incompetence. The answer is not even found in mere religious expression. Religiosity in Africa largely remains at the level of formalism and nominalism rather than in its transformative and reformative expression. However, the Christian gospel holds the answer, not because it promises to put to end these challenging human conditions, but because of its inherent hope element. While the actualisation of this hope is in a distant future, its effect is a present reality in life for the assurance that these human discomforts have a terminal point. Such an assurance found in the gospel soothes the pains of aching human souls.

THE APOSTOLIC MODEL

Christian preaching follows the example of the apostolic model of the *kerygma* and the *didaske*. During the time of the Apostles, the *kerygma*, the simple message of salvation, was meant to benefit those who were unsaved. It was as simple as it should always be; Jesus Christ is indeed the Son of God, and there is no salvation for humanity elsewhere except in his name (John 3:16; Acts 4:12; Phil 2:9-11). The *didaske* (the necessary instructions for maturity in faith within the Christian community), on the other hand, was for the benefit of those who had already been saved and placed into the body of Jesus Christ, the church or the Christian assembly. It was instructional for the initiates of the new faith community for a continued spiritual growth.

The resurrection of Jesus Christ had revolutionised the worldview, the belief and faith, and the theology of his hitherto timid and frightful disciples who became 'the Apostles.' Before now, even when Simon Peter confessed Jesus as "the Christ, the Son of the living God" (Matt 16:13-19), he did not have the full understanding of the theological implication of that confession. Although the disciples had a close ministry participation with Jesus for about three years, they were still struggling to have a full grasp of his identity, even during the first few days after his resurrection (Matt 26:31-33, 56b; see also John 21:1-14; Luke 24:13-35; Acts 1:6-8). The post-resurrection questions that the disciples asked Jesus are clear indication that they had not as yet fully grasped his true identity (Acts 1:8-11).

However, they gained a better understanding of the theological implications of Peter's confession only much later after the ascension of their Lord. Thomas' post-resurrection confessional statement of faith about Jesus, "My Lord and my God" (John 24:28) suggestively facilitated this understanding. The belief in the Lordship of the resurrected Jesus became the central theme of apostolic preaching (John 20:24-29). Belief in the Christ of faith as a means of salvation and escape from the judgement which is to come became the dominating message of the early Church (see Acts 2:38-39; 10:46-48; 16:30-31). The Apostles and the members of the early Church had at this point accepted, without question, that Jesus Christ of Nazareth was undoubtedly the expected Messiah. The concept of *belief* not only changed their worldview and theological presuppositions about the Person of Jesus but also changed their views about life in its entirety. Life now had a new meaning for them as they saw matters from a Christocentric (Christ) perspective. From this point on, the disciples lived daily in the light of the angelic eschatological assurance preached to them at Mount Olives (Acts 1:11; see also John 14:1-3; 1 John 3:1-3; Matt 6:24-34).

The eleven Apostles had recognised the priority of preaching the Word (Acts 6:1-6). This recognition motivated them to give careful attention to it far above the other sociological needs of the primitive Christian community. After Paul had joined the team, he also commanded his disciples to preach God's Word in season and out of season (2 Tim 2:15; 4:1-2). The preaching of Paul, who sought to promote and propagate the gospel wherever he went, was Christ-centred. Christology was the central theme of the preaching and teaching of the early Church.

In the same manner, the core and rallying point in expository preaching of the Church today should always be Christocentric. Bryan Chapell says, "Preaching, when truly Christian, is distinctive. And what makes it distinctive is the all-pervading presence of a saving and sanctifying Christ."[9] When Christ is not the nucleus of expository preaching, Christianity itself is robbed of its very essence. Leavell states, "Preaching has been and still is pre-eminently vital to the spreading of the Christian faith. In order to build the kingdom of heaven, Jesus established the gospel as the essential message, the church as the promotional agency, and preaching as the principal means of persuasion."[10] Africa needs to hear from the lips of men and women, "Christ is Lord", in their preaching of the gospel.

THE REVIVAL ELEMENT

Those of us who grew up in our different African villages know that farming activities take place at particular seasons. Different farming

---

9. Bryan Chapell, *Christ-Centered Preaching: Redeeming the Expository Sermon* (2nd ed., 2005; repr. Grand Rapids, Michigan: Baker Academic, 2007), 274.

10. Leavell, *Prophetic Preaching*, 13-14.

implements such as the small and big hoes, cutlasses, some specially made digging or clearing implements, and so on are used. Continuous use of these implements, especially the hoe, reduces its sharpness and therefore its effectiveness. A broken or bent hoe is usually taken to the blacksmith to fix while the one with a dull cutting edge is re-sharpened so it can till the ground effectively. A sharpened farm implement works better, faster, and tills more land.

Similarly, effective expository preaching brings about fruitful Christian revival and transformation of life and society at large. When commissioned and empowered men and women, people who are living in consistent obedience to God and his Word, take up the business of serious expository preaching of the divine Word, it will spark a Pentecostal revival. Such revival will cause definite changes in human society. Luke tells his readers in his report of the event of Pentecost, that following Peter's Pentecostal apologetic preaching, his audience was "cut to the heart" and thousands were brought to the faith (Acts 2:1-41). What Peter did was a straightforward historical exposition of the message about Jesus and his Kingdom, at the end of which he simply challenged the audience to action. Luke states very clearly that what accounted for the irresistible conviction of hearts and massive conversion to the new faith in Jesus Christ as the Messiah, was the effective ministry of the Holy Spirit at Pentecost (Acts 2:1-4). Although the Holy Spirit was actively operative at Pentecost, yet it took Peter's simple but clear explanation of the meaning of the event and a simple exposition of the message of the prophets to achieve a result.

Consequently, his hearers understood the simple message and therefore inquired what to do in response to it. The massive conversion recorded marked a paradigm shift in Jewish religious history. The efficacy of salvation hitherto exclusively enjoyed in Judaism had been displaced by the death and resurrection of Jesus Christ of Nazareth.

Expository preaching should be simple but clear and empowered by the Holy Spirit like Peter's. This brings transformation in human lives. As Stephen F. Olford and David L. Olford state, "We believe that true 'heaven-sent' revival and aggressive evangelism will only come when there is a return to the preaching and obeying of God's inerrant Word."[11] Expository preaching should be Pentecostal in its tone and import to stir the hearts; it should be empowered by God's Spirit to lead to an increased understanding of him, and it should be Pentecostal in its clarity to cause the heart to raise the question of action "What should I do?" Let this be the constant prayer of the expository preacher, "Revive us O Lord, fill each heart with thy love; May each soul be rekindled with fire from above." Christianity in modern Africa needs this revival urgently.

The need for Biblical preaching that deals adequately with the text and the quest to understand exactly what the Bible is saying to the modern readers/listeners is ongoing. Scriptural preaching has a longstanding tradition from divine revelation to prophetic proclamation, and from Christological mandate to Apostolic application, leading to an impressive transforming revival. To preach, therefore, is not only to preach the Bible, but importantly, to understand the theology of the Bible and preaching. To this theology, we now turn our attention.

---

11. Stephen F. Olford and David Lindsay Olford, *Anointed Expository Preaching* (Nashville, Tennessee: Broadman & Holman Publishers, 1998), 2.

THEOLOGICAL FOUNDATIONS OF EXPOSITORY PREACHING

When I travelled to Abidjan, Côte d'Ivoire, in 2016 to attend the seminar on 'Institute for Excellence' for theological institutions in Africa, organised by Overseas Council International (OCI), each meal time was a challenge as the stewards only spoke French, whereas I come from an English-speaking country. Many hand gestures were used to cover the language gap, and I was forced to learn some French phrases, one of which was how to say in French, "What is this?" As most of the food was quite different from what is available in Nigeria, I needed to find out what it was before ordering. The question, "What is this?" was my quest for the explanation of meaning. I needed to understand the menu!

Christian theology is a quest that seeks to understand correct meanings. It asks critical questions on issues because it seeks to have a better knowledge of them. Seeking the theological foundations for expository preaching is fundamental so that the preaching effort in Africa will not become aimless and futile. We seek to explain the Scriptures in Africa today so as to achieve a definite purpose – winning souls to Christ, and ensuring that converts are adequately discipled and tutored in the Christian tradition so that they can grow steadily in their faith and consistent obedience to God according to the Scriptures. Accordingly, Tite Tiénou says the kind of theology that makes sense for Africa is that which encourages more missionary proclamation, more discipleship, and more faithfulness to our Lord.[1] This definite purpose frames the clear exposition of the Scriptures by the Christian church.

The subject of the theological foundations of expository preaching asks preaching's *essential* question. Fundamental to this quest in Africa today is that African preachers, as alluded to by John Parratt, rethink the Christian faith in African terms, and do theology in an African context[2] by preaching the biblical text in such a way that the message becomes relevant and meaningful to the African audience. Their beliefs in God, Jesus Christ, sin and salvation, the Christian faith (the church), the Scriptures, and in eternity are some crucial subjects in Christian theology, and for expository preaching as well. Such a deepened theological understanding is crucial because "Our call is to develop a theology in Africa which will be a truly African doxology to God: Father, Son and Holy Spirit."[3]

A proper theology of expository preaching for Africa today is crucial because of the gradual and subtle shift by the present generation of Africans away from biblical Christianity to social Christianity. Christianity is becoming more of a loud entertaining religious experience than a reflective and reverential one. Many seek to walk on the easy road of Christianity and to enjoy its benefits without the cross.[4] Mal Couch captures this shift quite well,

---

1. Tite Tiénou, *The Theological Task of the Church in Africa*, Theological Perspectives in Africa: No. 1 (2nd ed., Achimota, Ghana: Africa Christian Press, 1990), 56.

2. John Parratt, "Introduction," in *A Reader in African Christian Theology*, SPCK International Study Guide (new ed., 1997; repr., ed., John Parratt, Marylebone, London: SPCK, 2004), 2.

3. Tiénou, *The Theological Task of the Church in Africa*, 8.

4. Cleophus J. LaRue, a professor of homiletics at Princeton Theological Seminary in Princeton, New Jersey, USA, has raised a similar concern about missing out

> ... even the basic tenets of biblical Christianity, seem to be
> diminishing from a brilliance that once was ... it seems as if
> more and more churches no longer are teaching the Word of
> God. Many are departing from sound doctrine. Like those in
> the world, many Christians have adopted New Age enlight-
> enment, accepted spiritual liberalism, and are marching to
> the drumbeat of secularism and materialism.[5]

This fast-expanding unfortunate shift in Christianity demands a biblical confrontation with a crafted and communicated message of the Scriptures. This should start with adequate knowledge of God.

GOD IS

While the Western world has mainly been influenced by the philosophy which does not subscribe to a belief in the existence of God, Africa does have a strong belief in the existence of God.[6] However, there is a problem; God's existence is transcendent. Because he is far removed from humans, he can only be approached through available intermediaries.

---

on the essence of preaching in the case of African American preaching. He raises a clarion call to African American preachers to rethink the aims and ends of preaching which should instead focus more on the substantive content of the sermon than on its celebratory emphasis. He argues that there is inherently more to Christian worship and preaching than jumping up and down, shouting, waving the hands in the air, and clapping of the hands. Cleophus James LaRue, *Rethinking Celebration: From Rhetoric to Praise in African American Preaching* (Louisville, Kentucky: Westminster John Knox Press, 2016), ix.

5. Mal Couch, gen. ed., "Introduction," in *A Biblical Theology of the Church* (Grand Rapids, Michigan: Kregel Publications, 1999), 9.

6. A negligible minority of Africans and Nigerians, probably influenced by some Western atheists, claim not to believe in the existence of God. Ironically, some of them visit their ancestral shrines. Indeed, some of them will cry, "God, help me!" when some life-threatening danger engulfs them. See www.atheist.org.ng for further information.

It is entirely accurate that if one stands for nothing, the possibility exists that one will fall for just anything. Not many preachers make the effort to preach the Scriptures, either of its content or of its power, from deep personal conviction and with a passion for God. Preachers, who are entirely convinced of the integrity and power of the Scriptures and God will, like the Prophet Isaiah, answer the call to expose the Scriptures, "Here am I. Send me!" (Isa 6:8; see Jer 1:6-10). John Piper says,

> People are starving for the greatness of God. However, most of them would not give this diagnosis of their troubled lives. The majesty of God is an unknown cure. There are far more popular prescriptions on the market, but the benefit of any other remedy is brief and shallow. Preaching that does not have the aroma of God's greatness may entertain for a season, but it will not touch the hidden cry of the soul: "Show me thy glory."[7]

Piper's observation is an urgent call for preachers to reveal the real God of Christianity to humanity. Here is a call for preachers to rightly, adequately, and honestly preach the Word so that the real God of the Word could be known (see 2 Tim 2:15).

So many professing Christians today in Africa only have a shallow understanding of the Being of the God of the Bible. They know about God; they sing about God; they pray to God, and they may even preach to others about God. They do not, however, have a full grasp of his Being. Such Christians will find it quite difficult to give the right answer when confronted with the question about who God is.

The Christian God, in reality, is known by the heart, not by the head. He is known by faith, not by reason. Because God is an unseen spirit, only his presence is felt when he acts through events. However,

---

7. John Piper, *The Supremacy of God in Preaching* (2nd ed., Grand Rapids, Michigan: Baker Book House, 1990), 9.

the agent that causes the heart knowledge about God is expository preaching from his Word, preached by people who truly know him and whose lives have been transformed by him. The power of such preaching lifts the soul to the fountain of living waters; it cleanses the soul from societal debris; it helps to clear the Christian mind of the theological cobwebs of the roadside and marketplace theological presuppositions prevalent in Africa today. The expository preaching of the Scriptures is all about declaring the authentic message of biblical theology about God, Jesus Christ his Son, the Holy Spirit, anthropology, sin and its consequences, and about Christian ethics and the Christian life. Authentic expository preaching flows from the heart with full conviction and passion.

Good expository preaching helps to restore the lost glory of God both in the pulpits and in the lives of pious men and women. In the 1950s, Merrill Unger expressed significant concern about modern preaching: "To an alarming extent the glory is departing from the pulpit of the twentieth century."[8] This danger is even more conspicuous in many pulpits today in Africa. Only a few preachers in Africa are resolved to restore this lost glory by honestly preaching the Scriptures with all the conviction and the seriousness that it deserves. True Christian preaching exalts the glory of God in the pulpit; it seeks to declare the whole counsel of God to men and women. It is the kind of preaching that moves the listeners to pray for God's Kingdom to come and his will be done on earth as it is in heaven (Matt 6:9-10).

Because of the loss of God's glory in the African pulpit, many Christians, unfortunately, even some preachers, relate to him as a casual friend rather than as a reverential Father who deserves re-

---

8. Merrill F. Unger, *Principles of Expository Preaching* (Grand Rapids, Michigan: Zondervan, 1955), 11.

spect. Gone are those days when African converts used to sing the hymn, *"Revive us again, fill each heart with thy love; may each soul be rekindled with fire from above."* Instead, the song today is, *"Abraham's blessings are mine; I am blessed in the morning, blessed in the evening; Abraham's blessings are mine."* Some Christians in Africa today seek blessings without obedience; they seek rewards without the cross. The reason for this shift is as simple as it is obvious – the glory of God has departed from the pulpit, and more and more worshipers are becoming spiritually impoverished.

Despite such an unfortunate shift, we believe that biblically centred and forceful expository preaching in Africa will restore both the knowledge and the departing glory of God to the hearts of Africans. First, when a life that is filled with the presence of the Spirit and with awe for the glory of God steps into the pulpit to preach, revival will occur. Second, when preachers who have sensed the importance of the transforming power of the Word, carefully expose it with all seriousness and fervour, the Scriptures will cause repentance and re-dedication in the lives of the listeners. The goal of the theology of expository preaching is reverence for God in the hearts of people. It is respect for him and unreserved obedience to the stipulations of his Word.

What Africa needs today are preachers who will preach Christ and him crucified. Preachers who will continually pray that Christ will increase, but that they will decrease (John 1:26-30; 3:23-31). Africa needs preachers who, when they stand in the pulpit to preach, will expect that Christ will be lifted high so he could draw men and women to himself. God and his glory must be restored to African pulpits.

WHO IS CHRIST?

Matthew reports that when Jesus came to the region of Caesarea Philippi in Galilee, he asked his disciples two critical questions about his identity. First, he sought to know what people were saying about his identity; and second, he sought to hear from the disciples what they knew about his person (Matt 16:13-17 NIV; see also Mark 8:27-32). Who do Africans, particularly African Christians, say that Jesus is?

When the foundation of a building is weak, that building stands the risk of collapse. Similarly, when our understanding of the Person of Christ as African Christians is blurred or weak, our faith is at the risk of deterioration and diminishing. Matthew Michael correctly asserts to this when he says, "THE CENTRALITY OF JESUS Christ to the Christian faith cannot be overstated since the Christian faith derives its essence from the person of Jesus Christ. Without the right emphasis on the centrality of Christ, the Christian faith loses its essence and hence becomes truly meaningless."[9] As he also admits, "African Christianity is in every aspect Christocentric in profession."[10] However, such expression ends only at the level of a profession without adequate knowledge of the real identity of Jesus Christ and without a genuine commitment to him. Visitors to Africa should not be surprised to discover different perceptions about Jesus in African versions of Christianity.

African scholars variously describe the identity of Jesus Christ in metaphoric terms. For instance, he is understood as a priest and prophet; as a chief and king, and as an ancestor and elder brother. He is also understood as a master initiation and healer; lastly, as a lib-

---

9. Matthew Michael, *Christian Theology & African Traditions* (Eugene, Oregon: Resource Publications, 2013), 129.

10. Michael, *Christian Theology & African Traditions*, 130.

erator and sacrifice.[11] Palmer says, "African Christian theology often uses contextualized metaphors in its Christology. These metaphors or images frequently describe functions of Jesus Christ"[12] without his real identity.

> The true identity of Jesus Christ, as revealed in the Scriptures, should be expressed to Africans through expository preaching. However, preachers, first, . . . need to know more about what ordinary Christians believe and confess about Jesus Christ . . . to get a fuller picture of what is going on in African reflection on the meaning of Jesus.[13]

Such knowledge will help to correct any misunderstandings and so implant the actual knowledge of Jesus Christ in the hearts of African Christians.

A correct knowledge of the real Jesus is critical for the Christian gospel and Christian theology in Africa. Like Peter, John understood Jesus as the Saviour and Master. As an eyewitness and a participant in the ministry of Jesus Christ, John expressed his experience of him thus,

---

11. See Robert J. Schreiter, gen. ed., *Faces of Jesus in Africa*, Faith and Cultures Series (1991; repr., Maryknoll, New York: Orbis Books, 2002). Also, see Rosino Gibellini, gen. ed., *Paths of African Theology* (Maryknoll, New York: Orbis Books, 1994). Again, see the work by Diane B. Stinton, *Jesus of Africa: Voices of Contemporary African Christology* (Maryknoll, New York: Orbis Books, 2004; repri., Nairobi, Kenya: Paulines Publications Africa, 2007). Lastly, see S. O. Agbogunrin, J. O. Akao, D. O. Akintunde, and G. M. Toryough, eds., *Christology in African Context*, Biblical Studies Series Number 2 (Nigeria: Nigerian Association for Biblical Studies, 2003).

12. Timothy Palmer, *Christian Theology in an African Context* (Bukuru, Nigeria: Africa Christian Textbooks, 2015), 73.

13. Robert J. Schrieter, "Introduction," in Diane B. Stinton, *Jesus of Africa: Voices of Contemporary African Christology* (Maryknoll, New York: Orbis Books, 2004; Reprint, Nairobi, Kenya: Paulines Publications Africa, 2007), 9-10.

> That which was from the beginning, which we have heard,
> which we have seen with our eyes, which we have looked at
> and our hands have touched – this we proclaim concerning
> the Word of life. The life appeared; we have seen it and tes-
> tify to it, and we proclaim to you the eternal life, which was
> with the Father and has appeared to us. We proclaim to you
> what we have seen and heard, so that you also may have fel-
> lowship with us. And our fellowship is with the Father and
> with his Son, Jesus Christ (1 John 1:1-3 NIV; John 1:1-4, 14).

Expository preaching seeks to create and cultivate this kind of in-depth knowledge and personal encounter with Christ by his disciples in African Christians. Such knowledge helps them to also testify about Jesus as both their Saviour and Master. God allowed his Word to be written so it could not only be read and understood, but also obeyed. It is the responsibility of expository preachers to make this achievable; for this is what they were called to do. This way, genuine Christian faith will be cultivated and nurtured in Africa.

THE CHRISTIAN CHURCH

Despite the challenge from Western individualism on Africa today, Africans still cherish family relationships, a strong bond that can hardly be broken. In the extended family system in Africa, someone is always related to someone, no matter how distant the gap of the relationship.

Such a concept of strong family ties should be carried over into the understanding of the Christian church. This transferred understanding is expected to strengthen the belief and commitment of African converts to Christianity. The church is a new family or community of faith in Jesus Christ. Jesus refers to his followers as a community of faith when he prayed for their unity (John 17:6, 20-22). Paul also describes the Christian community as the body of Christ that is to be sustained by the bond of oneness (Eph. 4:1-6). This aspect of unity connects quite well with the African belief in family relationships. The church is one big united family.

Despite the presence of sporadic schism in some families within the extended African system of family relationship, the family bonding does not disintegrate. Similarly, the church should value her family bonding far more not to allow factors that can bring disintegration. The tie of the family of Christ is much stronger than blood relationships. This understanding of the nature of the Christian community by African Christians should facilitate a stronger stand against the encroaching practice of tribalism and ethnicity in the church. While they cannot separate from their tribes and ethnic bonding, these sentiments should not be allowed to cause disintegration of the church as a higher family of Christ.

Expository preaching, then, can help to deemphasise tribal and ethnic sentiments in the church in Africa by emphasising the unity of the Christian family brought about by a common faith. This needs to become more significant because no tribe or ethnic group will have any space in heaven; only the family of God, consisting of men and women from different tribes and kindred from different nations, will inherit the Kingdom of heaven (1 Cor 12:13; Gal 3:26-28; Rev 7:9). The Christian faith suffers loses when it fails to uphold this theological principle. One area of such loss is the absence of true Christian worship. The church exists primarily to worship through obedience and service. No meaningful worship takes place in the midst of disunity because of certain sentiments.

THE CHRISTIAN SCRIPTURES

According to Stott, "Our understanding of God naturally influences our belief about the Scriptures."[14] Such belief also influences preaching the Scriptures. For instance, a preacher who does not believe in the full inspiration, infallibility, and inerrancy of the Scriptures; and who does not accept without question the authority of the Scriptures as the final rule of faith, will not give it the emphasis it deserves in the pulpit. Palmer reports that throughout the centuries of the church's existence, it has confessed that the Bible is the Word of God.[15]

The Scriptures are the primary source material for expository preaching upon which the preacher's authority resides to demand the audience's attention. God chose to use human beings to write the Scriptures, giving them literary freedom to use their vocabularies, linguistic expressions, and the mark of their personality as he guided them in the process. So, when we read the Scriptures, we hear the voice of God speaking to us in human words. Every expository preacher in Africa must have a clear understanding of what the Scriptures are, and how their testimonies should be taken seriously. Byang Kato said it is only when ". . . the Bible is taken as the absolute Word of God can it have an authoritative and relevant message for Africa."[16]

The need for expository preaching in Africa is increasingly apparent. Biblical literacy is at a very low level in Africa today. There is an increasingly poor reading culture among the younger generation of modern African societies. Sound biblical knowledge is fast depreciating in Africa in part because many other competing demands are

---

14. John Robert Walmsley Stott with Greg Scharf, *The Challenge of Preaching* (Carlisle, Cumbria: Langham Preaching Resources, 2011), 15.

15. Palmer, *Christian Theology in an African Context*, 18

16. Byang Henry Kato, *Biblical Christianity in Africa*, Theological Perspectives on Africa: No. 2 (Achimota, Ghana: Africa Christian Press, 1985), 43.

requiring people's attention. Many African Christians today seem so preoccupied with other concerns such as the pursuit of vocation/business, education, and so on, so that they hardly devote time to personal and corporate Bible study. Some even have great difficulty in keeping up with their daily devotional schedules.

This growing lack of interest in and serious attention to the Scriptures poses a significant threat to Christian spirituality in Africa. It sends an urgent call for honest and faithful expository preaching to rise to the challenge. Christians are expected to love God and his Word. They are also expected to be anxious to listen to the preaching from his Word. Sound expository preaching helps to create this awareness, to resuscitate this consciousness, and to motivate the desire to love the Scriptures. Motivational expository preaching will challenge African Christians to adopt the Berean practice of searching the Scriptures to confirm if these things are so (Acts 17:10-12). This need to search the Scriptures is urgent; particularly as heresy is vigorously competing for space in African Christianity today.

Expository preaching which clearly explains biblical theology is extremely useful in defusing and preventing heresy. Today in the church in Africa, the in-depth, authentic knowledge of biblical theology, alluded to above, is fast eroding from the hearts of many African Christians. Many are quick to quote the Bible in any and every discussion. They are also quick to appeal to it in defence of their theological or denominational beliefs and traditions when challenged. Such apologists, however, have a poor grasp and clear understanding of what the Scriptures actually teach and their meaning. Such scriptural impoverishment makes such Christians become easy prey for false African prophets and preachers. Of course, when they are fed with biblical and theological chaff, they will perpetually live under a distorted theological worldview and false theological understanding. These are likely candidates for breeding heresy themselves.

A sound exposition of the Scriptures will prepare the listeners to sift falsehood with ease. While falsehood disguises itself and may look like the truth, the two are quite remarkably different in the eyes of those that are correctly taught the truth. For instance, although the African pear tree (avocado) bears fruits that look like that of the British pear, yet, it tastes different. Also, the Nigerian *pidgin* English sounds like the English language, yet, it is a distinct form of English from the official English language, whether British, American, or Canadian in origin. For example, while the Nigerian *pidgin*, "I no go gree" means the same thing as "I do not agree," yet, these are different in linguistic structure and their tonal sound.

The presence of deceptive heresy that distorts the Scriptures means only one thing for expository preaching in Africa; it puts the expository preachers on their toes. They have no option but to be very knowledgeable in the Scriptures. Its content must imprison their conscience; and they must make themselves subservient to its power and authority so as to declare it without fear or favour. They must teach their congregants to weigh every thought, word, action, and teaching against the teachings of the Scriptures to ascertain their validity. Kato affirms, "The Bible is the Word of God. Even if all men become liars and unfaithful, God remains faithful (2 Timothy 2:13). Christians may fail and have failed, but biblical Christianity has not failed because Jesus never fails."[17]

ETERNITY

When I was a young Christian convert, the song, *"Are you going there? Everybody talks about heaven"* was a theme song for the Christian community. The principal guiding subject of Christian preaching then was on preparation for eternity. Many Christians made fran-

---

17. Kato, *Biblical Christianity in Africa*, 47.

tic efforts at evangelism because of the need to warn others about the implications of eternity without Christ. However, such a theme receives less emphasis in Christian preaching today in Africa. It appears the consciousness of eternity has fallen into oblivion in the hearts of many African Christians, most likely, because of their pursuance of the cheap theology of physical material blessings.

The concept of eternity in Biblical perspective, though substantially blurred to Africans, is expected to be understood with less difficulty. African Christians, hopefully, should understand this idea better because of the African belief in the ancestral spirit world. Dead African ancestors are believed to be existing in their world where they exercise oversight as well as protective functions over their living relatives. As Samuel W. Kunhiyop explains such belief, "Though the ancestors are dead, their spirits are constantly watching and guiding their descendants through life" as they serve as mediators for their descendants. He adds, "This belief is linked to the belief that when people die, they do not cease to exist but continue to live a meaningful life."[18] Such an African understanding of life after death presupposes the reality of eternity in Christian perspective.

The Biblical teaching on the certainty of eternity is assured. Jesus has already given Christians a hope beyond this earthly life. He says,

> 'Do not let your hearts be troubled. Trust in God; trust also in me. In my Father's house are many rooms; if it were not so, I would have told you. I am going there to prepare a place for you. And if I go and prepare a place for you, I will come back and take you to be with me that you also may be where I am' (John 14:1-3 NIV).

---

18. Samuel Waje Kunhiyop, *African Christian Theology* (Nairobi, Kenya: Hippo-Books, 2012), 136.

Paul re-echoes this eternal hope for Christians in his Corinthian and Thessalonian epistles. He explains the proof of the resurrection to eternal life to the Corinthians,

> I declare to you, brothers, that flesh and blood cannot inherit the kingdom of God, nor does the perishable inherit the imperishable. Listen, I tell you a mystery: We will not all sleep, but we will all be changed – in a flash, in the twinkling of an eye, at the last trumpet. For the trumpet will sound, the dead will be raised imperishable, and we will be changed. For the perishable must clothe itself with the imperishable, and the mortal with immortality. When the perishable has been clothed with the imperishable, and the mortal with immortality, then the saying that is written will come true: 'Death has been swallowed up in victory.' (1 Cor 15:50-54 NIV).

Also, Paul had preached in Thessalonica that Jesus Christ was coming back soon, raising the expectations of the Christians. Consequently, some of them had ceased to work and some others were already selling off their property in anticipation of the return of Jesus as taught by Paul. However, instead of the return of Christ, some members of the church were instead dying. In response to their concerns about this situation, Paul, in a consoling and reassuring epistle, says,

> Brothers, we do not want you to be ignorant about those who fall asleep, or to grieve like the rest of men, who have no hope. We believe that Jesus died and rose again and so we believe that God will bring with Jesus those who have fallen asleep in him. According to the Lord's word, we tell you that we who are still alive, who are left till the coming of the Lord, will certainly not precede those who have fallen asleep. For the Lord himself will come down from heaven, with a loud command, with the voice of the archangel and

with the trumpet call of God, and the dead in Christ will rise first. After that, we who are still alive and are left will be caught up together with them in the clouds to meet the Lord in the air. And so we will be with the Lord forever. Therefore encourage each other with these words. (1 Thess 4:13-1 NIV).

Both Jesus and Paul affirm the reality of spending eternity in heaven. Luke also affirms this reality in his story of Lazarus and the rich man. Both died and went to different places of abode – Lazarus to heaven at the bosom of Abraham and the rich man to hell (Luke 16:19-31). The thought of heaven in the minds of many Christians paints the picture of an uneroded hope. So, when Christians have an evident understanding of the biblical teaching about eternity, the fear of the uncertainties of earthly life and death will be minimised. This is very crucial for African Christian spirituality in the face of frequent deaths as a result of disease, terrorists' attacks, and those blamed on witches and wizards. The teaching on the heavenly reward for Christians will also facilitate faithful service by Christians. The consolidation on such assurances is the task of expository preaching in Africa today.

A proper Christian theology naturally leads Christians to right thinking, good behaviour and an infectious Christian lifestyle. While understanding the nature, biblical and the theological foundations of expository preaching are essential for the task, certain requirements are inevitable for expository preaching in Africa. So, what are these requirements?

CHAPTER 4

THE NEED FOR EXPOSITORY PREACHING

Marriage in Africa is highly valued, not necessarily for the husband - wife intimate relationship, but for the procreation of children, especially boys. A person who is married but remains childless is considered as not yet married, and not yet a full human person. A married woman who only gives birth to female children is said not to know how to give birth. Childbearing plays a significant part of life in Africa because children, who will perpetuate the family lineage and the parental name, are highly valued. Consequently, childless couples in the African context can go to any length to have children. Hence identity status or one's biological lineage is crucial for acceptance and respect in one's community/society. Children who are borne out of wedlock were seen as vagabonds in ancient Africa. Even today, children who have no paternal lineal identity are still considered vagabonds in most communities. Such persons gain no public respect and cannot usually hold any family rights or privileges.

Similarly, if Africans place a high value on children so too should a high value be accorded good quality expository preaching in Africa given its importance for Christian maturity. To ask, then, whether expository preaching is necessary for Africa today, given her many churches and almost uncountable numbers of preachers, is to miss the point. The need is quite evident as it has always been—number is not quality, neither does outward religious expression necessarily explain spiritual maturity.

The necessity of something means it is inevitable and indispensable. The church in Africa cannot do without expository preaching. Vines and Shaddix bring this fact to light more clearly, "Like the powerless Israelites without the ark, the church without strong preaching will have to welcome the new millennium defenceless and weak."[1] This statement sets the tone for this chapter and fundamentally attempts to answer the question of why expository preaching is necessary for Africa today.[2]

BACKGROUND

It is evident that the entire world is grappling with numerous challenges that have significant effects on human society. Africa, is often at the epicentre of these challenges. A catalogue of such challenges includes political, social, and economic degeneration, and poverty and diseases resulting in high mortality rates because of inadequate and poor medical facilities. Ethnic and tribal conflicts and war over land disputes and marginalisation in governance never go away in many African countries. The list also includes corruption and high rate of crimes, and acts of illegality such as flagrant violation of hu-

---

1. Jerry Vines and Jim Shaddix, *Power in the Pulpit: How to Prepare and Deliver Expository Sermons* (Chicago, Illinois: Moody Press, 1999), 17.

2. In an earlier book, I addressed the area of the need of reviving Christian spirituality in Africa and reviving African moral values as some reasons why biblical preaching is needed in Africa. I also drew attention to the fact that such preaching is also needed because African Traditional Religion (ATR) is being revived and a godless generation is emerging in modern Africa. See my book *Preaching the Scriptures* (Bukuru, Nigeria and Carlisle, UK: HippoBooks, 2018), 15-21. However, in this chapter, I divert focus to other areas of need that also require an exposition of the biblical text.

man rights and abuse of human dignity. In some cases, poorly managed internal conflicts have degenerated into genocide.

Additionally, Africa also suffers from such health issues as the scourge of HIV/AIDS, malaria, hepatitis, polio, and many more. Very recently, the continent has been confronted with the challenge of growing numbers of refugees, described as Internally Displaced People (IDPs), because of terrorists' onslaught. Governments, sadly, poorly manage such IDP camps.

Human challenges such as these raise the question of any hope for the future. The magnitude of these challenging issues in Africa also affects the preaching of the Christian gospel and on Christian spirituality as the church is overwhelmed by them. As a consequence, it gives so much attention to these sociological issues that good exposition of the Scriptures that can serve as an antidote to these social vices tends to be neglected.

Although sound expository preaching is an antidote to such anthropological and sociological issues, the content of what most African preachers preach only addresses the momentary and peripheral needs of the people. The reason for this is apparent – African preaching is distinctive in style in contrast to Western and European preaching. As Danny McCain rightly observes, a ". . . distinctively African style of preaching [has] more emphasis on storytelling and parables than on exposition and logic."[3] Unfortunately, much of preaching in Africa today remains at this level without textual exposition.

---

3. Danny McCain, "THE CHURCH IN AFRICA in the Twenty-first Century: Characteristics, Challenges, and Opportunities," in *Africa Journal of Evangelical Theology* 19.2 (2000): 110.

DIVINE REQUIREMENTS

Everyone needs to hear the voice of the Christian God who created them, no matter their ethnic or political background. They need to know his requirements for life in human society including issues such as truth and honesty, justice and fairness, equity and respect for the dignity of human life, compassion and service to humanity, and reverence and obedience to his laws. The application of such laws will restrain and dispel greed, selfishness, tribal and ethnic sentiments, segregation and favouritism. Instead, it will allow for the equal treatment of people in society.

However, these requirements make the exposition of the Scriptures in Africa a necessity. As we expressed earlier, when scriptural exposition is well articulated, it helps people have a better understanding of God and their relationship to him. It also helps to root the fear of God in their hearts thus enabling them to live according to his requirements. The transforming effects will naturally advance the Kingdom of God/heaven here on earth.

Ironically, however, today in Africa, Christian worshippers mainly hear *noise* from the pulpit. The actual transforming voice of God that should be heard from the lips of transformed preachers of the divine Word is absent. So, how will worshippers know God's requirements for life?

The main difference between the God of the Bible and the gods of Africa is God's love presented in his Word. The African gods' requirements are strictly followed out of fear of punishment. Although the Christian God punishes sin, he is worshipped in an atmosphere of tranquillity, reverence and hope for the expression of his love, compassion, mercy and forgiveness to sinful humanity as a gracious Being. In Christian worship, the grateful worshippers come into the presence of God, seeking to know more about him and how to live in a consistent existing relationship with him. What the African gods cannot do for their worshippers, God does, and what they cannot offer to their worshippers, God has offered to them.

It is the quality exposition of the Scriptures that explains the requirements of God to humanity. When God-called preachers help Christians in Africa to discover these requirements, it helps them to obey and worship the God of their Creation in truth and Spirit (John 4:24).

MISPLACED PRIORITIES

People treasure what they consider valuable and whatever is treasured is difficult to part from. In modern African societies, temporal things such as the quest for a vocation, money or wealth, and material possessions are given more attention than things that have eternal benefits. So too are the quest for positions, status recognition or success and achievements. Misplaced values in life are another critical reason why quality expository preaching is necessary for Africa. The necessity for clear Spirit-filled biblical preaching was expressed by Roland Q. Leavell many years ago:

> The importance of preaching cannot be exaggerated: God-
> called preachers must fulfil their sacred missions in the
> pulpit if the kingdom of God is to be advanced. . . . [Because]
> There is an ever-increasing displacement of God through
> the idolatry of money-worship and materialistic greed.
> The nation is suffering from secularism in education, from
> the decay of home life and tragic divorces, from increases
> in delinquency and crime, from the fearful ravages of the
> age-old demon of alcoholic drinking, from the sordid sins
> of sensuality and sexual promiscuity, from mere formality
> or gross negligence of worship of God . . . The antidote for
> these social and spiritual diseases is the same as it was then;

namely, God's gospel preached by holy men under the direction of the Holy Spirit.[4]

Although Leavell's submission was specific to the Western context decades ago, the modern African context is little different. Most African societies and communities face almost similar, if not the same challenges.

In the modern era, technological advancement is on the increase, and Information and Communication Technology (ICT) is also moving on the fast lane of information dissemination. While we benefit from the greater exchange of information, its adverse effects are that not many people care anymore about upholding good virtues and moral values in life and society. For instance, the values of the lifestyle of godliness, integrity and a good moral character, or that of trust, truthfulness and honesty are no longer upheld. Even the principle of good neighbourliness is diminishing in many African societies today. Instead, loose morality, relaxed integrity, and degraded humanity are increasingly common.

Also, the values of diligence and dedication to national causes and the value of upholding personal and corporate integrity are no longer commonplace. Equally, the value of respect for the dignity of the human person and human life; of rendering good corporate services to society; of good governance to advance society's good, et cetera, are all gradually being displaced by the projection of human self and ego. These are perpetuated to the detriment of the rights and comfort of the other members of a given human society. To idolise, deify and worship self instead of God is a misplaced priority!

Most worrisome is the manner in which quite a sizable number of Christian men and women practice their faith. They subscribe

---

4.   Roland Q. Leavell, *Prophetic Preaching, Then and Now* (Grand Rapids, Michigan: Baker, 1963), 7.

to Christianity only in form rather than fact. Such Christians argue that Christianity is in the heart; therefore, they contend, like the Gnostics, whatever is expressed on the externals does not matter as it does not affect the internals. Some would not bother to sin against good moral conscience provided, they claim, they repent and confess their sin to a merciful and compassionate God. But religiosity is not Christianity. Many of such religionists do not keep to the tenets of the Christian religious beliefs and practices (see 2 Tim 3:1-5; 2 Cor 2:17).

The Christian faith is a transforming one (Matt 5:13-16). It transforms a person's worldview and values. No one whose life is transformed by the power of Christ's resurrection ever remains in his or her former state. When freedom from sin is gained in Christ through personal saving faith (John 3:3-6; 8:31-32), the benefiting individual willingly sets out on an irreversible journey. His or her life also is set aglow with an unquenchable fire of Christian witness and spirituality. The life of Paul and the hitherto timid disciples serve as a good case study (Acts 9; Phil 3:1-14; Acts 3:11-20; 4:8-12, 18-20). Spiritual transformation does not allow for a life of sinfulness or spiritual slothfulness. What makes a transformed life effectual is the quality of exposition of the Scriptures.

RIGHT PATHS

Modernity is gradually redefining the world around us. Actions that were previously associated with honourable living and right conduct are being redefined. The things that were hitherto accepted as normative of a given society are being questioned. For instance, not many people today care to walk on the right path of social relationships and social justice, or to uphold the principle of vocational ethics, stewardship, and good governance and accountability. Several distortions are crossing the waves of everything normal in the world today.

Like a viral infection, so many African Christians have been infected by such quests for a redefinition. The adverse effects of the globalised world have blurred the moral vision and religious conscience of many African Christians, causing them to see less and less of what is right and morally good according to the Scriptures. Prevailing distortions are forcing them to approve sinful thoughts, attitudes, actions, speech, conduct, and lifestyles that stand against a good moral conscience.

The essence of Christian preaching is to present the divine requirements to the human context. It also serves as a reminder that obedience to divine laws is rewarded but acts of disobedience and disloyalty are repudiated and punished. The unusual turn of events in modern Africa is one of the reasons why expository preaching is necessary. For expository preaching refocuses the human eyes on the right path. Distorted values can be corrected and redirected towards living lives according to divine principles.

God will not negotiate his standards for correct human behaviour, actions and moral ethics. He has made available to all humans the ability and the freedom to make the right choices. For instance, we read that Enoch "walked with God" (Gen 5:22, 24) and Noah "walked with God" (Gen 6:9). Later when God ratified his covenant with Abraham, he said to him, "I am God Almighty; walk before me and be blameless" (Gen 17:1 NIV). Also, when King Solomon had built the Temple and dedicated it, God told him, "'. . . if you walk before me in integrity of heart and uprightness . . . and do all I command and observe my decrees and laws, I will establish your royal throne over Israel forever'" (1 Kgs 9:4-5; see also 1 Kgs 8:25). God also said to him, ". . . walk before me as David your father did, and do all I command, and observe my decrees and laws" (2 Chron. 7:17-18). The intended meaning of the divine imperative invitation to "walk before me" is to express the idea of the embedded freedom of human choice either to do right or wrong. Human beings are individually responsible for their wrong actions when they fail to walk on the right path in life. For Christians, the examples of the saints in the Bible motivates us to walk on the right path (Heb. 11:13-16; see Ezek 18:2-4, 20).

ALLEGIANCE

In Christianity, adherents to the faith believe without question, in the existence of a creator God, and in Jesus Christ, his Son, who is both Saviour and Lord. They equally believe that the Bible is the revealed, inspired Word of God, written by inspired men in human language. This belief in the Bible subscribes entirely to its teaching as the rule of faith, as a guidebook for life, and as the searchlight that shines and guides worshippers in their daily walk through life. By this, every committed Christian places his or her complete trust in the Bible as the final arbiter in matters of faith and the final authority in personal decisions.

However, the concept of Christian allegiance is threatened today by many factors. The ideology of humanism and the quest for human freedom that stand against traditional cultural, ethical norms and Christian beliefs are gradually dislodging the spirit of religious allegiance in Africa. Such morally impoverished people only crave to satisfy the flesh rather than upholding an excellent moral conscience that should be responsibly exercised for the good of society as a whole.

The misplaced concept of individual rights in Africa today is a fight against allegiance. It is not only a fight against Christian moral ethics, but it is contesting the biblical claims about what a morally good human society is and how it should function. For instance, the clamour for same-sex rights stands directly against what their Creator has prescribed for the good of society and the health of human spirituality. If bestiality and incest are considered grievous evils then so is homosexuality (Lev 20:11-17; Ex. 22:19). The cities of Sodom and Gomorrah were put to the flames by God for the sin of sexual immorality and the evil of same-sex (Gen 19:4-9, 24-25). Paul, drawing attention to the efficacy of the Jewish law, says,

> We also know that law is made not for the righteous but for lawbreakers and rebels, the ungodly and sinful, the unholy and irreligious; for those who kill their fathers or mothers, for murderers, for adulterers and perverts, for slave traders and liars and perjurers – and for whatever else is contrary to the sound doctrine (1 Tim 1:9-10 NIV).

These acts are committed by godless people (Rom 1:18-32) who have dead consciences even when they hold to some form of religiosity (2 Tim 3:1-8). Is it not intriguing that humans, created as rational beings, and expected to act by reason, can go to the extent of doing absurd things that even animals, which act by instinct, will not do?

From time immemorial, various institutions in Africa have regulated morality and respect for authority in society while restraining excessive conduct. For example, children are taught to respect and obey their parents as an obligated moral duty. Wives have traditionally been brought up to respect and submit to the authority of their husbands. Wise African women have helped their husbands who are in some form of leadership, to transform both family and society, by their wise counsel and submissive attitude. Nor is this concept of child or wife submission in Africa synonymous with slavery or the deprivation of human freedom. As the author argued for the dignity of the Miship womanhood,

> The Miship woman, both traditional and modern, just as her female counterparts elsewhere, is a fully human person with a life, blood, feelings, emotions, self-worth, intelligence and competence. The Miship male counterpart and those in both patriarchal and patrilocal societies must admit this reality.[5]

I argued further that society is incomplete without women; therefore, they are to be treasured by society. Accordingly, I contended that, "... the woman is a 100% human person, created in the image and likeness of God, just like the man. She must, therefore, be treated fairly and justly, be valued and given her rightful place to function in society."[6] However, modern life in Africa is fast turning against this paradigm. Children are rebelling against the authority of their parents while wives are equally rebelling against the authority of their husbands in the home. Their argument is premised on the need for personal freedom and equality with the male folks. These recent mishaps dull the heart and make it resistant to allegiance to God and his Word.

These increasingly opposing scenarios make quality expository preaching more compelling in Africa. In the midst of all these growing challenges launched against Christian allegiance, the message of the Scriptures remains the antidote. The emerging distortions and opposition to what is godly in human society presuppose the need for people to return to their Creator and seek truth from him.

---

5. Joel Kamsen Tihitshak Biwul, "Reading the Virtuous Woman of Proverbs 31:10-31 as a Reflection of the Attributes of the Traditional Miship Woman of Nigeria," *OTE* 26/2 (2013):287.
6. Biwul, "Reading the Virtuous Woman of Proverbs 31:10-31," 295.

PRESERVING A GODLY HERITAGE

Missionary presence and activities on the African continent have greatly benefited Africans. Before the advent of Christianity African peoples worshipped the supreme God indirectly via intermediaries. However, with the arrival of Christianity in Africa, a positive change took place redirecting them to commune with their Creator through Jesus Christ. Thus, many Africans believed the gospel and abandoned their ancestral religious worship. Since then, Christianity has become synonymous with the lifestyle of most African converts. The first generation of African Christians (the African ancestors/forefathers) bequeathed to the subsequent generations of Christians a rich tradition and heritage of the faith. This religious heritage was first handed down by Jesus to his initial disciples, then from them to the Apostolic Fathers, to the Church Fathers, and henceforth, to subsequent generations of converts to the Christian faith all over the world.

The African ancestors/forefathers of the Christian faith found in Jesus Christ a new faith worth dying for. Because of this, they treasured and preserved the faith and its message and handed it down to their offspring to perpetuate. The Supervising Editor of the *Africa Study Bible* affirms, "Their resilience, fortitude, and faithfulness has handed us a faith that is authentically Christian and authentically African."[7]

The preservation of the Christian faith and heritage in Africa, in the face of global changes and the challenges encroaching on the foundation of the Christian faith, unavoidably necessitates the need for expository preaching. Paul told Timothy to "Guard the good deposit that was entrusted to you – guard it with the help of the Holy

---

7. John Jusu, Supervising Editor, "Dedication," in *Africa Study Bible* (Carol Stream: Oasis International Limited, 2016).

Spirit who lives in us" (2 Tim 1:14 NIV). The prevalent distortion of the gospel necessitated this imperative. There is a similar distortion taking place in modern Africa. The quest to uphold the heritage of biblical Christianity, to sustain the authentic Christian confession, and to attain quality spirituality as was the case in the past, is increasingly rare. Those once-cherished Christian traditions such as one's thirst and fervour for God, living the life of godliness and holiness, living earthly lives in anticipation of eternity via the principle of self-denial, treasuring moral purity, honesty, and truth are fast becoming old fashioned. Christian heritage can only be preserved through sound expository preaching.

The spiritual climate in Africa is not as encouraging as expected with the presence of growing nominalism and syncretism. It seems the experience in the religious history of Israelite society is repeating itself in the Christian religious history of modern Africa. There was a downward spiral in the religious experience of Israel after the death of Joshua. During the period of the Judges in Israelite history, a new generation that did not know Yahweh, the covenant God of Israel, emerged. This new generation became godless (Judg. 2:7, 10-13). Like this biblical case, the younger generations of Christians in Africa today are becoming more westernised than African. They are fast becoming more secular than sacred, more social-centred than religious-centred, more self-centred than people-centred, and more individualistic than communalistic in their orientation. Their morality and spirituality, to a considerable extent, is loose and distorted, making them vulnerable to societal vices.

Indeed, there must have been some point of disconnect in religious commitment and devotion in-between the time of the African Christian ancestors/forefathers and those that handed the faith to this young generation. This lapse and lack of spiritual fervour and commitment to preserving Christian traditions and its rich heritage by the church in Africa today opens up African Christians to relax Christian commitments and biblical requirements for life. Worldliness grows within Christian circles. For instance, many contemporary Christians have almost lost out on the Christian tradition of patience and endurance. To wait for God's time to grant what they need in life seems an "orthodox" rather than a contemporary approach to religious expression. Their interpretation of the biblical concept of faith is something other than its biblical meaning suggests (see 2 Tim 2:3; 4:5; 2:22).

Unfortunately, the Church in Africa appears helpless in the face of these encroaching challenges. Not many of the Christian congregations, both in the orthodox mainline and Pentecostal circles, are well prepared to counter the effects of the challenge of global change on church members. Only a handful appear to be addressing the situation. In the midst of the multiplicity of churches on almost every street, and the many preachers in Africa, many Christians still live with unanswered ethical, doctrinal, theological and social questions. The vulnerability of such people to falling into the dens of spiritual predatory crooks and the traps of theological robbers is quite apparent.

This serious matter facing African Christianity today calls for quality expository preaching. The church needs serious and godly preachers who are convinced about the transforming power of expository preaching to help such Christians find their spiritual focus. The church needs truly transformed preachers who are surrendered to Christ and will raise their voices to talk about God from his Word to his world. It is only this kind of preachers who can ensure that the message of the cross is always the pivot for expository preaching so Christ will draw men and women unto himself, and so our Christian heritage in Africa is preserved. However, such needed servants of God are not many in Africa today.

THE VALUE OF RESPECT

The Bible teaches the value of respect for constituted authorities, for parents, for the elders in society, for the rule of law, and respect for human dignity and the sanctity of life (see Ex. 20:12; Lev 19:3, 32; Est 1:20; Mal 1:6; Rom 13:7; 1 Tim 3:4). One of the essential values that Africa, since antiquity has been known for, is her culture of respect, which adds beauty and colour to Africa.

However, this well-cherished treasure is fast fading away from the African soil. Respect and obedience to laid down rules for the good of the family and society in Africa today are being challenged and replaced by the encroaching foreign ideology of individual freedom. Civil Society groups and humanist organisations that promote individualism and personal freedom attract large numbers of followers in Africa. These same groups, while not questioning the decisions of the gods of Africa are questioning the authority and integrity of the Bible. Some of these critics, ironically, are the very people who benefited from the Western education brought by Christian missionaries. Worst still, some of them even lay claim to the Christian faith.

Careful expository preaching of the Christian Scriptures can confront such men and women with its authoritative power. Any freedom that stands against laid down rules for cohesive human good, ceases to be true freedom. If the humanists, modernists, and liberal feminists challenge the integrity of the Scriptures and question its authority, those whose lives have been transformed by the content of the Scriptures should in turn respect and defend the orthodox claim of Sola Scriptura (the Scriptures only are the final rule for faith and practice).

God must be respected; his Word must be respected, and his church must be respected as well. True freedom is found only through complete obedience to God's Word and by making oneself subservient under its authority. The power of God's Word, preached by men and women under divine mandate and empowerment, cultivates the attitude of genuine respect in an individual. The compelling message of Scriptures forces people to their knees in compliance with its demands. Bryan Chapell states that the exposition of the Word presents the power of the Word, the authority of the Word, and the work of the Holy Spirit. He argues, ". . . the power for spiritual change resides in God's Word . . . [and it] binds the preacher and the people to the only source of true spiritual change."[8] He argues further that in a system and culture where despairing subjectivism and radical relativism lead men and women to question the source of authority over their lives, the Bible's claim of authority because God has spoken, is the answer.

Expository preachers in Africa must be ardent in fighting hard to recapture this gradually departing culture of respect for people and God. Robinson cautions, when preachers ". . . fail to preach the Scriptures, they abandon their authority. No longer do they confront their hearers with a word from God. That is why most modern preaching evokes little more than a wide yawn. God is not in it."[9] Consequently, he adds, "Preachers should pour out the message with passion and fervor in order to stir souls. . . . When preachers speak as heralds,

---

8.   Chapell, *Christ-Centered Preaching*, 30. Chapell's priority is on the exposition of the divine Word, yet he has not overturned the value of other types of biblical preaching. He admits, "Other types of preaching that proclaim biblical truth are certainly valid and valuable, but for the beginning preacher and for a regular congregational diet, no preaching type is more important than expository. [This is particularly so] Because hearts are transformed when people are confronted with the Word of God."

9.   Haddon W. Robinson, *Expository Preaching: Principles and Practice* (2nd. ed., 2001; repr., Leicester, England: Inter-Varsity Press, 2004), 20.

they must cry out 'the Word.' Anything less cannot legitimately pass for Christian preaching."[10]

Respect for God and his Word is crucial for life. Both the cultures of the Old Testament and that of Africans uphold the value of honour and shame. The attitude of disrespect for people and God and his Word is shameful. Expository preachers are not only to teach what the Scriptures teach on the subject of respect, but they should be models of it by their lifestyle. When people respect the preachers of the Word for their godly lifestyle, they will also respect God and the Bible. Note that this is crucial. The attitude of disrespect for people and God in favour of individual freedom challenges the very foundation of African morality. It also challenges the principles of the Scriptures of loving one's neighbour as oneself (see Ex.20:17; Lev 19:18; Mark 12:33; Luke 10:30-37; Rom 13:9-10). Such a situation can be confronted by a clear and uncompromising heralding of God's authoritative, inspired Word, forcing even hardened hearts to submission.

When the Scriptures are preached by the life that is set aglow for God, a life filled and controlled by the power of the Holy Spirit, change happens. The message will, unavoidably, bring God's irresistible power upon the listeners; it will convict the soul of the listener, demand total allegiance to its commands and directives; and it will compel such individuals to submit unreservedly to the rule and authority of God. Africa today needs this type of preaching; it yearns for it. Oh God, give Africa good expository preachers who genuinely know and have your Word to deliver.

---

10. Robinson, *Expository Preaching*, 20.

SEEKING SPIRITUAL SECURITY

Children in my village were taught not to walk through a forest in the night. Most ancient African societies considered forests as the abode of evil spirits. Children were also taught not to whistle in the night. Doing so, just like pounding at night, would invite evil spirits. Even today in Africa, the idea of the spirit world is a present lived reality such that it does not require either a definition or an explanation. Hence, witches and wizards and demons are dreaded. Some particular geographical locations and sites such as bodies of water, forests, rocks and caves, individual trees, and the graveyard are equally dreaded because of the belief that evil spirits use such places as their abode.

Evil forces and human agents are believed to cause harm to people through various diabolical means.[11] Such spiritual insecurity makes some Christians to consult soothsayers, witchdoctors and diviners for protection. Some also carry amulets and charms for protection against harm. The fear of spirits and the need for spiritual protection by Africans explains the practice of religious syncretism in African Christianity. One of the fundamental reasons responsible for this type of practice is the failure of the Christian gospel to transform the core of the African person. When the socio-psychological and theological needs of the converted African person is not adequately satisfied, it leaves room for a relapse into traditional religion. Yusufu Turaki clearly explains,

---

11. Satanic attacks on Christians is a reality, but their divine protection from such harm is also assured. If, for instance, demons could bow before Jesus (Matt 8:28-34; Mark 1:39; Luke 4:41), if also Jesus himself affirms that he has overcome the world, and of his continuous presence with his people (John 16:33; 14:19), and if lastly, his resurrection has earned for him an authoritative name above all other names (Phil 2:9-11; Eph 1:19-23; 2:6; Col 3:3), then, as Paul affirms, "If God is for us, who can be against us?" (Rom 8:31-39; 2 Cor 4:7-11).

> Any introduction of a new religion to Africa must have
> to bear in mind these social and psychological needs. A
> theology of needs is necessary, especially given the tradi-
> tional background of the African religions. The traditional
> religious system will persist if a new religion fails to both
> address and assuage such needs. To do so effectively, it
> requires (1) knowledge of the theological foundations of this
> traditional religious system and (2) how to apply the mes-
> sage of the new religion to meet the social and psychological
> needs of individuals and communities in Africa. Whatever
> new beliefs are introduced to traditional Africa, whether
> Christian or Islam or modernity, they are often confronted
> by the African traditional theology of needs.[12]

When the traditional and cultural orientations and the core of a person are not completely transformed, old habits and practices will always persist, whether explicitly or implicitly.

Here, accurate and adequate exposition of the Scriptures plays
this transforming role. The Scriptures give sufficient grounds for
the Christian's insulation from satanic and demonic harm. These
grounds guarantee absolute assurance for the Christian's total victory over the forces of darkness, even the devil himself. Expository
preaching should always reaffirm and remind frightful African
Christians of this fact. It should stress that the assurance of divine
protection from Christ against all evil forces is a finished matter. It
should also stress that divine power is already given and the victory that was won at Calvary is still effectual to the African Christian
believers.

A sustained Christian maturity of African converts necessitates
quality expository preaching. This will enhance believers' allegiance
to the Lordship of Christ and the principles of the Christian faith.

---

12. Yusufu Turaki, *Foundations of African Traditional Religions and Worldview* (Nai-
    robi, Kenya: International Bible Society Africa, 2001), 11-12.

It will also help them to develop proper priorities by choosing the right path in life, and thereby, preserving the heritage of their faith, depending fully on the protective power of the resurrected Christ in the face of demonic intimidations. Such growth better prepares the African Christian converts to face the challenge of changing cultures in modern Africa.

CHAPTER 5

AFRICAN CULTURES AND EXPOSITORY PREACHING

Africa is a continent that is blessed by God in every respect. Among such blessings are the peoples' cultures. There are numerous cultures and traditions in Africa just as there are many tribes and ethnic groups. Every culture has its assumptions about reality, some similar while others are distinct.

Expository preaching in Africa may not be entirely effective without a good understanding of the peoples' cultures, customs and traditions. The essence of scriptural preaching is to influence positively the cultural and behavioural patterns of a people, so it aligns with Scriptures. To this extent, a preacher should seek to understand both the biblical text and the different African contexts. Such a dual understanding is helpful in preaching the biblical text as its message is appropriately, relevantly and effectively applied to the Africans in their different lived experiences. The goal is to enable them hear the voice of God speaking to them in their unique individual and corporate contexts.[1] Yusufu Turaki makes this point clearer,

---

1. Stott captured this subject quite aptly in his principle of double listening – listening to the Word and equally to the world. See John Robert Walmsley Stott, *The Contemporary Christian* (Nottingham, England: Inter-Varsity Press, 1992), 24-28.

> The religious and cultural dimensions of Africa's traditions
> affect all aspects of African life, Christian presence and
> witness in Africa. A meaningful and effective Christianity
> cannot flourish well within the African context without
> a serious theological and practical engagement with the
> African traditions. . . . Christian theology must engage, or be
> in dialogue with the African traditions as a prerequisite to
> transforming Africa.[2]

The knowledge of what makes the African person should be taken seriously by the preacher. The pre-conversion religious and cultural contexts of the African Christian largely affects their sociology, psychology and ethics, even their public life. Mbiti emphasises, "To ignore these traditional beliefs, attitudes and practices can only lead to a lack of understanding of African behaviour and problems. Religion is the strongest element in the traditional background, and exerts probably the greatest influence upon the thinking and living of the people."[3]

Africans are unique in their worldview, cultural traditions and customs. Also unique are their ethical norms and values, and their belief systems and mythologies. Even the socio-religious expressions of African Christians is unique to their contexts. Consequently, expository preaching would have the desired effects on the Africans in their various contexts – individual and corporate, only if the preacher first maps the African contours. These contexts of their *Africanness*[4] should be clearly understood to avoid miscommunication and misrepresentation of the Scriptures to them.

---

2. Yusufu Turaki, "Forward," in *Christian Theology and African Traditions* by Matthew Michael (Kaduna, Nigeria: Yuty Graphics, 2011).

3. John Samuel Mbiti, *African Religions and Philosophy* (2nd ed., 1990; repr., England: Heinemann, 2008), 1.

4. What is cooked or brewed, or planted by Africans and germinates on the African continent, is understood as African, even when it is exported. Anything

TRADITIONAL AFRICAN RELIGIOUS BELIEFS AND WORLDVIEW

The African peoples of various cultures and customs, living in various locations within the continent, and speaking different languages and dialects, have their worldview and belief systems that differ significantly from people living elsewhere. The Kenyan scholar, Mbiti, points out, for instance, that the whole of human life in traditional African belief is immersed in a religious phenomenon and this starts before birth and continues after death. However, he observes, "Failure to realise and appreciate this starting point, has led missionaries, anthropologists, colonial administrators and other foreign writers on African religions to misunderstand not only the religions as such but the peoples of Africa."[5] Turaki agrees that African traditional religious beliefs, practices and worldview have a profound and enduring influence on the African person. Their beliefs in impersonal powers, spirit beings, divinities, Supreme Being, and the hierarchy of spiritual beings and powers are very foundational. He states, "Any meaningful and effective approach to the study of the traditional religions and worldview must begin with these foundations of beliefs."[6]

Every African child grows within a specific socio-religious context. Like the Asian child who grows up within the religious context of Buddhism; or the Jewish child who grows up into the Judaic religious tradition; or lastly, the Arab child who grows into the Islamic

---

grown and hatched by Africans, particularly by those who are born and nurtured on the African soil, is also construed as African. These elements constitute part of the concept of Africanness – that which is African in its orientation and expression.

5. Mbiti, African *Religions and Philosophy*, 15.

6. Yusufu Turaki, *Foundations of African Traditional Religions and Worldview* (Nairobi, Kenya: International Bible Society Africa, 2001), 16.

religious context; so is the African child who grows up to live and speak the African religious language and practice its tenets as well. The core theological and philosophical foundations of African Traditional Religions (ATR) is hardly erasable; it has been homogeneous to the Africans since antiquity. As Mbiti asserts, "Africans are notoriously religious, and each people has its own religious system with a set of beliefs and practices. Religion permeates into all the departments of life so fully that it is not easy or possible always to isolate it."[7] The blend of religion and cultural traditions give Africans the unique stamp and mark of the identity of their Africanness. Kunhiyop corroborates this quite well,

> . . . religious beliefs and the African worldview are not lost when Africans become Christians. . . . They affect everyday life, whether in terms of marriage, farming, career choices or even such mundane matters as travelling. Dreams, for example, are not thought of as merely arising from psychological causes but are understood as a real way by which God or the gods reveal themselves.[8]

Religion and culture, then, guide the communal ethics that characterise the socio-religious lifestyle of African societies. Worship is corporate and religious shrines are corporately owned and used by a community or clan. We quote Mbiti mainly on this point,

> Traditional religions are not primarily for the individual, but for his community of which he is a part. Chapters of African religions are written everywhere in the life of

---

7. Mbiti, *African Religions and Philosophy*, 1. Despite the influence of the philosophy of atheism on some Africans who studied in the West, their core religious belief will intuitively come to the fore when pressed to the wall by trying circumstances.

8. Samuel Waje Kunhiyop, *African Christian Theology* (Nairobi, Kenya: HippoBooks, 2012), xv-xvi.

the community, and in traditional society, there are no irreligious people. To be human is to belong to the whole community, and to do so involves participating in the beliefs, ceremonies, rituals and festivals of that community. A person cannot detach himself from the religion of his group, for to do so is to be severed from his roots, his foundation, his context of security, his kinships and the entire group of those who make him aware of his own existence. . . . to be without religion amounts to a self-excommunication from the entire life of society, and African peoples do not know how to exist without religion.[9]

Their corporate worship has at the centre a belief in God as the Supreme Being who is worshipped through intermediaries.[10] Mugambi says, "Among African peoples, it is a common belief that no one can hide from the presence of God"[11] because they strongly believe that he knows all things, hears all uttered words, and sees all human actions. Mbiti corroborates this point, "One should not . . . expect long dissertations [by Africans] about God. [For] God is no stranger to African peoples, and in traditional life, there are no atheists."[12] Idowu is very assertive about Africans' religious belief about the Supreme Deity and other deities. He states that God is real to Africans; God is unique; God is the absolute controller of the universe, and God is One; the only God of the whole universe.[13]

However, the critical point for expository preaching in Africa against such background is this; it is a grievous error to assume

---

9. Mbiti, *African Religions and Philosophy*, 2.

10. Aylward Shorter, *African Culture, An Overview: Social-Cultural Anthropology* (1998; repr., Nairobi, Kenya: Paulines Publications Africa, 2001), 45.

11. J. N. K. Mugambi, *Christianity and African Culture* (2002; repr., Nairobi, Kenya: Acton Publishers, 2009), 75.

12. Mbiti, *African Religions and Philosophy*, 29.

13. E. Bọlaji Idowu, *African Traditional Religion: A Definition* (1973; repr., England: SCM Press, Nigeria: Fountain Publications, 1991), 149-165.

that since Africans assert and affirm the reality of the existence and the *Being* of God, therefore, they have a fuller understanding of the Christian God. Their belief in God may best be equated with that of the religio-philosophical Athenians who had a temple to an unknown god (Acts 17:18-32). African Christian converts believe in the existence of a Supreme Being whom they describe differently, yet they do not know exactly who he is. The preacher can purify and refine such belief to align it with biblical teaching on the Christian God. In doing so, the preacher needs to have a firm grasp on how African worldview and religious belief systems operate and how these have affected the core of the Africans. Such understanding helps to make the communication of God's truth effective by transforming the embedded beliefs in the African convert. A proper peeling off of the traditional religious-worldview allows the divine Word to get to the core of such an African person.

This is quite significant! The goal of biblical preaching is first, to ensure that the biblical text makes sense to the modern readers or listeners in their contexts; and second, as a consequence, that the same message causes transformation of the listener's life situation. The endeavour of expository preaching in Africa, therefore, is to explain the biblical text and its message in a clear contemporised term, vis-à-vis the context of the listener, using all the requisite knowledge of biblical background, hermeneutics, exegetical analysis and homiletics. It is to seek to make plain without complexity, the original intended message of the biblical text, first given to its original recipients, and now being relevantly applied to the contemporary readers or listeners in their unique situations so that the same message can also make meaning to them.[14] This must be the motivating factor

---

14. Kunhiyop is quite correct in asserting that, ". . . the basic task of theology is to help Christians make sense of the Bible." As such, he argues that Christian theology, to be relevant to the African peoples, should avoid abstraction. "Thus

and primary purpose for exposing truths from the divine Word to every cultural and social context of the African peoples.

AFRICAN CULTURAL TRADITIONS AND CUSTOMS

People all over the world differ in their behaviour and lifestyle, primarily because of their different cultural worldview, traditions and customs. In his definition of African cultures during its early development, Walter Rodney says, "A culture is a total way of life. It embraces what people ate and what they wore; the way they walked and the way they talked; the manner in which they treated death and greeted the new-born."[15] Kato agreed when he said, "Culture is what makes a people a homogeneous community. . . . Culture is what binds a people together and gives them a sense of identity as a community . . . . Culture is the whole system of living made up of what

---

theology from a purely conceptual perspective has no essential value to most African Christians. . . . The point is that for most Africans, abstract thinking should be situated in concrete reality and should be productive and relevant. Theology must, therefore, speak to the real issues of life." See Kunhiyop, *African Christian Theology*, xvi. When Scriptures are exposed to an elite African audience, yes, academic abstraction is meaningful as they will be able to resonate with the message. However, for the generality of the Christian congregations in Africa, a simple exposition that speaks to the needs of the market woman — the tomatoes seller, the vegetable seller, the grain seller, the fruits seller and the food seller is what matters. Elite theology and by extension, elite expository preaching, should be reserved for the elites but an embedded expository message with popular theology is to be given to the poor, afflicted, oppressed and deprived, and to the hungry and lowly in Africa.

15. Walter Rodney, *How Europe Underdeveloped Africa* (2nd impression, London: Bogle-L'Ouverture Publications/Dar-es-Salaam, Tanzania: Tanzania Publishing House, 1973). 41.

society knows and does."[16] Culture, traditions and customs are very often deeply intertwined. These are the total value of what makes a people, regulates their behaviour and guides their holistic lifestyle. It depicts the engraved mark or stamp of identity in the mind of a people that gives them a sense of self-worth, and that acts as a binding force for communal belonging. The cultural traditions and customs of a people are the characteristic elements that distinguish communities, societies and a group of peoples as they are learned habits and traits that make individuals adapt to their environment.[17]

Although the corporate identity of *Africanness* binds the African peoples, each tribe and ethnic grouping has some distinctive features as per the expression of their cultural traditions and customs. These distinctive features act similarly to a family where children are born. Each child is given birth with his or her unique characteristic personality different from the other children. While some apparent similarities may exist in their characterisation, yet their personalities remain distinct. This analogy holds for the cultural and traditional understanding of the African peoples. Just as these Africans have different ethno-tribal affiliations and speak different languages and dialects, so are existing cultural and traditional variations.[18] For example, the customary requirements for contracting marriage

---

16. Byang Henry Kato, *African Cultural Revolution and the Christian Faith* (Jos, Nigeria: Challenge Publications, 1976), 5, 6, 7. Shorter says "Culture is the whole way of life, material and non-material, of human society. It is essentially social, the product of a society's tradition and its interaction with other societies. . . . It is also the product of human history." See Shorter, *African Culture, An Overview*, 22.

17. Keith N. Schoville, "Canaanites and Amorites," in *Peoples of the Old Testament World* (Alfred J. Hoerth, Gerald L. Mattingly, and Edwin M. Yamauchi, eds., Grand Rapids, Michigan: Baker Books, 1994; paperback ed., 1998), 176.

18. John Mbiti's discussion on this is helpful. See Mbiti, *African Religions and Philosophy*, 101.

among the tribes in Ghana, Zambia, and Kenya are not necessarily the same. The mourning and burial customs of the tribes in Nigeria, Gambia, and Democratic Republic of Congo are not the same. So are the interpretations of events, seasons or the appearances of certain bush animals in the community.

When Africans became converts to the Christian faith, they, like the Jewish converts to the same faith in Paul's day, still maintained some of the elements in their cultural traditions and customs (see Gal 1:6-10; 3:1-5; Phil 3:2-9). They did not, in no small extent, sever themselves from their pre-Christian cultural and traditional practices. Consequently, culture and traditions are quite active in Africa, so much so that even many professing Christians insist that they and all other Africans are obligated to such norms. For instance, in one part of Africa, one finds that when a wife dies, her corpse is buried in her father's house, not in the husband's home. This practice is in obedience to the requirement of the culture, even if the deceased and her living husband are Christians. Also, one finds in another part of Africa certain practices of traditional and cultural demands on women who are widowed. Since according to the African worldview, the cause of death is always blamed on someone, when a husband dies, the wife becomes the first suspect. As such, she is subjected to some inhumane cultural and customary conditions in order to prove her innocence. Further, often the personal effects of a deceased husband are confiscated from the widow and her children by his relations. Although such practices are completely contrary to the African ideology of corporate communal existence, yet, they exist, because this is culture.

Also, in ancient Africa, even today, although a woman is married to a man, she is also figuratively married to his family, to his clan and to the whole community in which he is a part. Hence, she is addressed as "our wife." This ideology guarantees her security and the expression of love to be extended to her. It also explains why the husband's family and clan settle marital issues. However, soon after the demise of her husband, the woman who hitherto was addressed as "our wife" suddenly becomes a total stranger in the same family and community. These are the contradictions of some African cultures and traditions where such practices still obtain.

The preacher of the Bible, of necessity, is obligated to have adequate knowledge of these variations for expository preaching to become meaningful to such a multicultural audience. It helps to apply the message of the biblical texts to specific situations of the audience. Kunhiyop wrote his *African Christian Theology* to articulate a theology that originates from an authentic search for the meaning of Scripture in order to apply it to African life today.[19] This is the challenge of expository preaching in Africa – to correctly translate the biblical text, to adequately articulate the meaning of the Christian faith and practice, and to relevantly and appropriately relate its message to the contemporary life experiences of the African peoples in their different contextual societies and life situations. This is critical! Here, making the message of the Scriptures relevant to the Africans and appropriate to their individual as well as corporate needs is essential. This effort makes them clearly hear the voice of their Creator through a human voice and to precisely understand what he is saying in their unique life experiences. When this understanding is achieved, the Africans, like the Ethiopian eunuch, will not only ask to be baptised into the water of the divine Word but will also ask to be guided on how to have an existing relationship with him in their Christian walk as well (Acts 8:29-39).

Put another way, the urgent need for a sound biblical exposition on the continent is self-evident. Some professing African Christians

---

19. Kunhiyop, *African Christian Theology*, xiii.

are only haphazardly or partially transformed by the message of the gospel of Jesus Christ. As a result, they quickly fall back to their traditional and cultural practices when life's threatening situations call for a deciding choice between culture and faith. Where converts are not well rooted in the Scriptures and grounded in the faith through proper discipleship, this reversal becomes inevitable. Even then, those of them who are seen to be transformed can easily fall prey, when they lack the personal, rooted conviction in the authority of the Scriptures, and the moral will and courage to take a stand and confront any traditional and cultural demands that impede on their biblical worldviews and values. Where they fail to maintain their stand to defend the cause of their faith in Jesus Christ, they can easily be overwhelmed and overpowered by those cultural demands placed on them. Quality expository preaching that is relevantly and adequately applied will serve as an antidote.

Christianity is not a congregated religion but a religious practice that operates on the pivot of personal religious belief and conviction. When deep personal Christian conviction is developed, the transformed African Christian will then be able to willingly and happily say like Joshua, ". . . choose for yourselves this day whom you will serve, whether the gods your forefathers served beyond the River, or the gods of the Amorites, in whose land you are living. But as for me and my household, we will serve the LORD" (Josh 24:15 NIV). A Christian with such transformed conviction will also say like Paul,

> I want to know Christ and the power of his resurrection and the fellowship of sharing in his sufferings, becoming like him in his death, and so, somehow, to attain to the resurrection from the dead. . . . I press on to take hold of that for which Christ Jesus took hold of me. . . . I press on toward the goal to win the prize for which God has called me heavenward in Christ Jesus (Phil 3:10-11, 12, 14 NIV).

A deep conviction of faith in Christ against culture is the sustaining force for the Christian against ridicule, rejection and possible ostracisation from his or her community. Such conviction of faith comes about only through a thorough exposition of the Scriptures. A total transformation and a deep-seated personal conviction in the sustaining divine power that cultivates a decisive personal choice to stand alone for Christ is the kind of spiritual maturity that expository preaching is expected to achieve in Africa (Eph 4:14-15 NIV).

However, as we pointed out earlier, one of the obstacles to experiencing the transformed Christian life and practice in African Christianity is the lack of adequate discipleship of converts. On the other hand, where such an effort is made, the method used to disciple converts is contextually inappropriate. It follows a structured Western method, forgetting that Africans have their unique pattern of training or mentoring. This weakness accounts for both the life of nominalism and carnality noticeable in contemporary African Christianity. O'Donovan observes, "One reason for the need for biblical Christianity in modern Africa is the presence of a large number of nominal Christians in the church."[20] This is a significant threat to Christian spirituality and the survival of true biblical Christianity in Africa. The redress is that expository preaching should be replete in all aspects of church life – in the pulpit, Sunday School class, during mid-week prayers/services, during Fellowship Groups' meetings, and in the catechism class. Every Christian convert requires proper induction into the tradition of religious beliefs, doctrines, ethics, culture, values and precepts, and the worldview of the Christian faith.

---

20. Wilbur O'Donovan, *Biblical Christianity in Modern Africa* (Cumbria, UK.: Paternoster Press, 2000), 218.

AFRICAN ETHICAL NORMS AND VALUES

Societal norms are standards of acceptable behaviour and conduct, and their values are those essential aspects of life that are highly treasured. Such ethical systems exist among African communities which act as the determinants for their lifestyle and actions. African ethical norms and values are found in African religion, proverbs, oral traditions, ethics and morals of the society where these communities are located. They are rooted in the people's philosophy which has to do with ". . . the understanding, attitude of mind, logic and perception behind the manner in which African peoples think, act or speak in different situations of life."[21] The principles and rules of conduct found in different African communities have been preserved over the ages in various customs and traditions that provide explanations of the reasons, motivations, values and purpose of behaviour.[22] The young of each society are born into and grow up with these ethical norms and values of morality embedded in their traditions and customs.

The African peoples, whether at home or abroad, carry along with them their traditional and cultural beliefs, values, ethics and worldviews as they move from place to place. Such mobility becomes unavoidable because it has been embedded in them since antiquity in their different localised contexts. These norms and values play out naturally in their corresponding religious practices, behaviour and feelings because of the traditional worldview of the Africans.[23]

How Africans behave and why they behave the way they do is an inquiry that is extremely significant for the presentation of the Word

---

21. Mbiti, *African Religions and Philosophy*, 2. See Turaki, *Foundations of African Traditional Religions and Worldview*, 75.

22. Samuel Waje Kunhiyop, *African Christian Ethics* (Nairobi, Kenya: Hippo Books, 2008), 9.

23. Turaki, *Foundations of African Traditional Religions and Worldview*, 36-37.

of God. The expository preacher, then, is faced with two critically similar challenges – the need to understand what Africans think (their norms and values) and what the Bible says (the principles of biblical ethics). A clear understanding of these two orientations helps to make the presentation of the biblical message effectual. Such understanding ensures adequate connectedness of the biblical text with the different contexts of the African peoples. An expository preacher who can stand between these two poles will be able to achieve a proper interface with the objective of achieving a transformative outcome.

THE INFLUENCE OF EURO-AFRICAN WORLDVIEWS

The changes that the period of the Enlightenment impacted upon global history and human society were not without negative challenges. Such changes affected the hitherto traditional understanding on issues, the manner in which certain things were done in society, the lifestyle of people, even some hitherto held beliefs, and so on as those areas experienced gradual shifts.

The Enlightenment also brought positive and negative changes in Africa. These changes were transported by the colonial masters and the Christian missionaries. Particularly, when many Africans began to travel overseas, and peoples from other parts of the world also came to Africa, visible changes became unavoidable as cultural and traditional practices, ideological expressions, educational exchanges and lifestyle influences began to interact and pollinate. From this period onwards, the purely traditional African worldview, beliefs, and ethics no longer remained purely African. Idowu observed, ". . . with the shifting scenes in regard to the knowledge of the universe, we are continually finding that established forms of beliefs are undergoing changes either radically or in their formulations."[24] The days of the African past, since then, have never remained the same.

Significantly, the influence of civilisation, and more recently, globalisation and modernisation, alongside interactive socialisation with the peoples from other parts of the globe, have forced changes on the African mindset. What was *African* in the days of the African ancestors/forefathers is certainly not what is African today. Chinua Achebe captures these changes in his *Things Fall Apart*. In it, he expresses the effects of a changing culture through the frustration of the main character of the book, Okonkwo. Okonkwo had fought against the encroaching culture on his traditional culture without success.

Social and moral changes in many African societies today are becoming resistant to traditional values. Africa largely has become a mixed grill of cultures, moral and social lifestyles. The youths in most African societies are more susceptible to these socio-moral changes. For instance, it is becoming normative for people in a relationship to have sex before marriage. Cohabitation of unmarried people is a growing phenomenon. Social vices such as gangsterism and rape, armed robbery and kidnapping, and alcoholism and drug abuse, committed largely by the youths against the principle of African communal brotherhood, is becoming commonplace. This is a negation of the traditional moral ethics of most African societies. The youths stand at the centre of the clash and resulting cultural confusion of two opposing paradigms – the African culture of morality and the non-African. Their changed social culture, language and vocabularies, style of music, and grooming indicate such influences and are a departure from what used to be uniquely African in orientation. Like the picture painted by Chinua Achebe regarding the

---

24. Idowu, *African Traditional Religion*, 142.

clash between ancient and modern Africa, things have indeed fallen apart in Africa,[25] and the centre of traditional African cultures and values can no longer hold together.

The scenario presented above has more negative changes in African societies. For instance, such changes are being forced upon the treasured family relationships and community social ethics that African societies were known for; the hitherto well-cherished values of the communal discipline of children for good behaviour is fast giving way to individualism. Also, the hitherto cherished African culture of respect for elders and submission to authority is gradually being overtaken by the quest for personal freedom, human rights and self-expression. Only a few youths today would offer to help carry the load for an aged person or greet them as was the case in generations past. When understood in its entirety, it is all a negation of valued cultural relationships in Africa. As O'Donovan points out,

> ... people and relationships between people are much more important in Africa than almost everything else. . . . The high value placed on human relationships in Africa is the reason why extensive daily greetings, even between close relatives, is so important.[26]

---

25. Albert Chinualumogu Achebe, an African novelist, was born in Ogidi, Nigeria, on November 16, 1930. *Things Fall Apart* is Achebe's first novel wherein it he portrays the critical effects of cultural paradigm shifts brought about by the interaction between Western and African cultures, following the advent of colonial and missionary presence in Africa. Okonkwo, the main character, was not only oblivious but bastardised by the new trend. He struggled hard to comprehend the new order after the collapse of the old, yet everything appeared to him a mirage and a nightmare. He was no longer at ease in the face of these changes as things had indeed fallen apart and the centre could no longer hold. See Albert Chinualumogu Achebe, *Things Fall Apart* (Jordon Hill, Oxford: Heinemann, 1958).

26. O'Donovan, *Biblical Christianity in Modern Africa*, 7-8.

However, the church appears helpless and unprepared to address these challenges. It is more reactionary than tolerant in some areas and accommodating in some others. Since society is dynamic, changes are bound to occur. Therefore, the quest for freedom, human right, self-expression, equity, fairness and justice is a welcome development in society.

None the less, so long as such a quest does not uphold good cultural, moral values, it will, by and large, ruin an individual as well as a cohesive African society. A growing number of Africans today, in their struggles for such rights for the good life, are projecting the human self in place of God; a worrying trend when Christians are involved. Yet it is having a godly fear of the Creator and living in a right relationship with him by living life to his glory that will achieve authentic individual and corporate freedom for the African peoples and societies. The Hebrew *Qoheleth* (teacher, preacher, philosopher and wise man) concludes, after a long search for what truly satisfies, "Now all has been heard; here is the conclusion of the matter: Fear God and keep his commandments, for this is the whole *duty* of man" (Eccl 12:13 NIV; see Mark 8:36-37). It is the *fear* of the Creator that can help African leaders and the African peoples to make themselves subservient to the principles of his universal laws. It is the *fear* of the Creator that makes for a good African society where the guiding principles of good moral conscience in governance, upholding moral rightness and selflessness, and ensuring the application of justice, equity and fairness bound by love and unity for corporate existence are not a matter of rhetoric and semantics but are seen to function practically. It is also the *fear* of the Creator that propels people within human society to respect human dignity, right and life.

The negative changes affecting the youths stand as a challenge for expository preaching in Africa as the younger generations of Africans make up the bulk of the audience. Preachers face the uphill task of understanding the younger generation of Africans and of adequately articulating the biblical text to address their needs. The preaching of the biblical text to Africans should be sandwiched with love for the people no matter what they are or how they behave. This way, expository preaching will be able to stress and insist that only by a return to the Creator and living in obedience to him will Africans experience the full life. Expository preaching to the new generation of Africans should be engaging, interactive and persuasive, distinctly explicating the superiority of Christianity and the Christian God.

Such an approach to presenting the message of the biblical text would be more appealing because of a more significant challenge in Africa today. While some unserious older Christians are falling back to a life of nominalism and carnality, everything Western is being thrown at the young African generation. For example, "Beauty Queen" and "Big Brother Africa" contests are not culturally African. Also, heavy makeups and a dress style that exposes one's physique and nudity seem socio-culturally foreign to Africa. Yet the youths easily buy into these. In their naivety, such intrusion is being embraced by them without critical questions and evaluation.

However, there is an even more significant challenge: the youths, being inquisitive explorers, are susceptible to internal heresies and the presence of wolves in the church in modern Africa. The devastating effects of their wrong teachings not only attempt to redefine or replace God and distort the gospel but lives on in African Christian spirituality doctrinal and theological debris and ethical dross. The younger generation of African Christians is mostly the target of these wolves. Expository preachers should, therefore, assume the urgent task to educate these young ones to contend for the true faith. The presence of dislocated, infectious, and poisonous theology in the church in Africa today will have to be confronted biblically in order to save the next generation of Christianity in Africa.

A good knowledge of the socio-cultural and moral ethics of both ancient and modern African societies facilitates the able handling of the Biblical text in conversation with the contexts of the contemporary recipients. Like literary genres, such knowledge aids the preacher to adequately explain and apply the Biblical message to the battered human contexts.

CHAPTER 6

BIBLICAL GENRES AND EXPOSITORY PREACHING

African oral traditions include folklore, tales, stories, proverbs, oracles, songs and dance, and narrated history. When a story is expertly narrated, both children and adults enjoy listening to it. When people speak in proverbs, the adults easily decode the message; but children have to learn to decode the meaning as they grow into adulthood. Again, when the oracles of the gods are delivered to an African community, the people wait for the interpretation of the message. When the drumbeats begin to roll in the village square, the singers and dancers know precisely what song and dance steps are expected. African proverbs, songs, stories, and religious oracles are not the same in form, even when they are separately used to convey the same meaning within a specific communication situation. In the African context, these communicative modes automatically form different genres by their oral composition. Songs, for instance, take different forms, depending on the occasion, whether it is that of lamentation, wailing, funeral, celebration, a war cry or victory in war. Such differences can be understood as genre.

Not all preachers in Africa recognise the presence of literary genre in the Bible, not to talk of their lack of understanding its influence on Bible interpretation. Many Christians in Africa take the Bible as a completely holy book without any human influence. They accept it as if it dropped directly from God without any human participation. This way, they read every aspect of the Bible as the same, not minding if any different way of expression does exist. All they know is that God is speaking to them from his Word. However, the Bible is a book like any book that is written to be read. The difference, however, as R. C. Sproul points out, the Bible is the Book of books because it is sacred and holy. As a result, ". . . it transcends and stands apart from and above every other book."[1] Yet, the Bible should be read as a religious book that has different types of literary materials written in different styles. These different materials should be understood as genre.

The biblical text, as a sacred text, possesses different literary genres. The expository preacher needs to understand these genres and how they function in order to accurately and properly communicate the message of the Scriptures to the audience. A failure to do so can so easily lead to misunderstanding, error, fraud and ultimately heresy. As the interpreter approaches biblical genres, their unique sacredness should be kept in perspective, as should also be the uniquely defined rules for interpreting them.

DEFINING GENRE

The term genre is primarily a French term meaning *type* and *category*. It is used about artistic and literary works. The term also comes from the Latin *genus* which means *birth, kind*. *Genre*, then, refers to *the type* of literary material, or a group of texts classified according to their recognisable and distinguishable type, form, character and style of writing. The undergirding meaning of *genre*, no doubt, calls attention to a group of literary works that have the same quality or quali-

---

1.   R. C. Sproul, gen. ed., "Introduction", in *The Reformation Study Bible* (Orlando, Florida: Reformation Trust Publishing, 2015), xi.

ties by their outlook, structure, style, phraseology and form. Literary genre is a term that describes a group of texts that bear one or more traits in common, such as their similarity in content and structure, in mode of phrasing and style, and in their mood and function.[2] Put slightly differently, they are "a species of literature"[3] that are marked by distinctive recurring characteristics that are recognisable with a coherent type of writing.[4] In brief, *genre* is a literary category or type and style of writing and mode of literary self-expression that invokes a specific emotion in the reader.

Genre understanding should be uniquely applied to the biblical materials. As we pointed out earlier, the Bible is a religious text, highly revered by those who love it for its sacredness. Also, it is an ancient religious text far remote from the modern reader in time and culture. Particularly, the uniqueness of the biblical text lies not only in its theological import but also in its combination of several genres into one book – first, in the whole Bible, and second, in its individual books. The interpreter of the biblical material should consider its Jewish worldview[5] as the starting point. This way, the possibility of errors is minimal.

---

2. Longman III and Dillard, *An Introduction to the Old Testament*, 30.
3. Kevin J. Vanhoozer, *Is There a Meaning in this Text?: The Bible, the Reader and the Morality of Literary Knowledge* (Leicester, England: Apollos, 1998), 336.
4. J. John Collins, "Introduction: Towards the Morphology of a Genre," *Semeia* 14 (1979).
5. The biblical writers did not produce an entirely new collection of literary work, but, as Longman and Dillard submit, they wrote within "a literary context." The biblical authors wrote in an already existing literary tradition, ". . . which they may indeed stretch, but never break." Yet, as a covenant community, Israel produced a literary work that is not only religious but possessing religious characteristics unique to its covenant confession. This confessional conviction also sets the Jewish religious document apart as unique from other forms of literary works the world has and can probably ever produce. See Longman III and Dillard, *An Introduction to the Old Testament*, 30.

GENRE IDENTIFICATION AND DECODING

In the village where I grew up, most social gatherings were coloured with singing and dancing — every song matched with an appropriate drumbeat and a dance style. Those who did not know how to follow the sequence of the drumbeats and the dance style of a particular song were described as *lakar*, meaning, someone who is a misfit in musicology. This forced dancers to see the need first to learn how to dance correctly and well before they would take to the dance floor so as to avoid public disgrace and criticism. An excellent working knowledge of the role of biblical genre for preaching is likewise necessary to help expository preachers to expound the biblical text accurately.

The Bible is accepted within evangelical circles without question as the inspired, infallible, and inerrant Word of God. This belief should be the fundamental guiding frame for genre identification and interpretation of the Scriptures by expository preachers. The author of each Bible book chose and used particular literary genre(s) intentionally to achieve a specific theological purpose. Accordingly, Grant Osborne instructs that readers must first determine the genre of a passage before interpretation can begin. Such interpretation should be made according to its purposes and rules; otherwise, interpreters are at the risk of proclaiming a message alien to the divine intention in the text.[6]

Longman and Dillard suggest a dual purpose in genre identification of the biblical text. First, it helps to determine the reading strategy. A literary genre directs the reading strategy of the reader and therefore triggers in the reader a particular expectation in the

---

6. Grant R. Osborne, *The Hermeneutical Spiral: A Comprehensive Introduction to Biblical Interpretation* (2nd ed., Downers Grove, Illinois: Inter-Varsity Press, 2006), 452.

material. In the second place, it determines the interpretation of a particular text. Since the biblical writers produced their texts in a literary context, genre identification, therefore, provides a secondary literary context. Hence the reader's identification of particular generically related texts of the ancient text will result in the illumination of each text, leading to a clear interpretation.[7]

Leland Ryken clarifies the point further in these words,

> Each literary genre has its distinctive features. Each has its 'rules' or procedures. This, in turn, affects how we read and interpret a work of literature. As readers, we need to come to a given text with the right expectations. If we do, we will avoid misinterpretation.... Knowing how a given genre works can spare us from misinterpretation.[8]

Thus, the reading strategy and interpretive perception of biography, for example, is never the same with that of a parable; neither is that of a purely narrative text the same with prophetic oracle. Readers should not expect to use the same tools that they interpret fiction with to understand a poetic material; neither should they apply the same scheme to understand biblical wisdom with a prophetic portion.[9]

Since Africans already know the differences among proverbs, songs and the dance steps, stories and oracles, an expository preacher should transfer such knowledge to the idea of genre for easy con-

---

7.   Longman III and Dillard, *An Introduction to the Old Testament*, 30-31. As Vanhoozer puts it, "... the literal sense of a text is its literary sense, and this can only be determined by identifying the genre." See Vanhoozer, *Is There a Meaning in this Text?*, 336-7.

8.   Leland Ryken, *How to Read the Bible as Literature* (Grand Rapids, Michigan: Zondervan Publishing House, 1984), 25. Also see Osborne, *The Hermeneutical Spiral*, 26.

9.   Osborne, *The Hermeneutical Spiral*, 26. Also, see Vanhoozer, *Is There a Meaning in this Text?* 336.

nection with the need for biblical genre differentiation and interpretation. This need for a good understanding of biblical genre and the rules for their interpretation should begin with the preacher who will, in turn, relate the message of the text to the audience.

INTERPRETING BIBLICAL GENRES' TYPES

God allowed his Word to be written so humans could understand his expectations of them. This makes the proper understanding of biblical genres and the interpretation unavoidable by the expository preacher. Although the biblical text consists of several genres and subgenres, we consider below only a few of the dominant ones.

Prose Narrative Genre

Narrative discourse and poetry are dominant genres in biblical literature. These also have subdivisions. In the case of the Old Testament literature, prose and poetry are dominant. These also are often divided into five subgenres – prose divided into narrative and law, poetry is divided into psalm and wisdom, and prophecy is a mixture of prose and poetry. Ronald Giese explains further,

> The categories of genres necessary to function effectively in the text of the Old Testament are ten. Prose is best seen as three different genres: narrative, history, and law. Prophecy, which typically is a combination of prose and poetry, is best seen as three different genres: oracles of salvation, announcements of judgements, and apocalyptic. Poetry is best divided into psalms of lament and psalms of praise. Also, wisdom is divided into proverbial and non-proverbial wisdom.[10]

---

10. Ronald L. Giese, Jr., "Literary Forms of the Old Testament," in *Cracking Old Testament Codes* (eds., D. Brent Sandy & Ronald L. Giese Jr., Nashville, Tennessee:

The majority opinion considers biblical narrative as containing both history and theology; both brought together via a 'story' format.[11] Biblical narrative mostly tells the history of God's dealings with humanity. Prose narratives particularly narrate historical events and biographies. The Pentateuch and the historical books are predominantly narrative in form while the narratives of the prophets are sometimes interspersed with poetry. In the New Testament, the Gospels and Acts are dominated by narratives. This analysis leads Kaiser to conclude that, "Narrative is clearly the main supporting framework for the Bible."[12]

Biblical prose-narrative places information in a thematic format, not necessarily in the sequential or chronological order in which these events occurred; nor are they necessarily placed within their historical timeframe. Such narratives report about the occurrence of an event and the participants involved. Sometimes, all characters are reported, and some other times, only crucial characters are reported, based primarily, on the freedom of selectivity of the author. In interpreting biblical narratives, the narrating author, setting of the narrated event(s), the plot, the narrative's timeline, the people involved and dialogue are essential. The climax of a story is to communicate meaning; as such, every biblical narrative has a theologically intended meaning for the reader.

The African expository preacher will find biblical narratives easier to interpret than the other genre classifications because of the story-oriented context of Africa. Unless otherwise indicated or implied

---

Broadman & Holman Publishers, 1995), 19.

11. Osborne, *The Hermeneutical Spiral*, 200.

12. Walter C. Kaiser Jr., "'I Will Remember the Deeds of the Lord': The Meaning of Narrative," in *Introduction to Biblical Hermeneutics: The Search for Meaning* by Walter C. Kaiser Jr. and Moisés Silva (2nd ed.; Grand Rapids, Michigan: Zondervan, 2007), 123.

by the text, narrative portions of the Scriptures are to be interpreted as literal historical events with deep theological imports for the original participants in and readers of the narrative. The meaning of the theological message is what the preacher is to apply to the African audience. For example, an African warrior can only participate in the victory of Israel over Jericho through the application of its theological principles to the African context. Such a warrior cannot make a direct literal application because the warrior was not a direct participant in the war under Joshua's military leadership (Josh 6:16, 20). Also, it is incorrect to relate directly to the divisive issue that Paul addressed in the Corinthian church to the African context of ethno-tribal sentiments except that its theological principles can (1 Cor 3:1-23). Their context is not African. To do otherwise is to make the modern African reader of the Corinthian letter a Corinthian, thereby, risking both its understanding and its benefits to the African who reads the Corinthian text.

Poetic Genre

Poetry is another style of writing that occupies great space in biblical literature. Unlike prose narrative which is a straightforward form of speech or writing, poetry is a more concentrated, compact, and very condensed form of writing.[13] In the Old Testament, for instance, apart from the book of Palms, Proverbs, Lamentations, Song of Songs and Job, considered to be entirely poetic, prophetic books such as Hosea, Joel, Amos, Obadiah, Micah, Nahum, Habakkuk, and Zephaniah are almost entirely poetic in style. Moreover, extensive portions of Isaiah, Jeremiah, Jonah, and Zechariah are poetry. Very likely, only books such as Leviticus, Ruth, Ezra, Nehemiah, Esther,

---

13. Leland Ryken, *Words of Delight: A Literary Introduction to the Bible* (2nd ed., 1992; repr., Grand Rapids, Michigan: Baker Book House, 2001), 187.

Haggai, and Malachi may be said to be without visible poetic elements.[14]

Why is poetry so pervasive in the biblical literature that requires the critical attention of readers? According to Ryken, "Poetry differs from ordinary prose by its reliance on images and figures of speech, and by its verse form. Poetry is heightened speech, far more compressed than prose. . . . the basic unit of poetry is the individual image or figure of speech."[15] Why Hebrew writing consists of poetry is explained by Osborne: "Semitic poetry had its origin in the religious life of the people, both corporate and individual. Prose was inadequate to express the deep yearnings of the soul, and poetry as an emotional, deep expression of faith and worship became a necessity."[16] The message that a literary work conveys affects both the mind and the emotion of the reader. Perhaps the most frequent subject of poetry in the Bible is human emotions. The typical strategy of the Hebrew poets is to picture them as a series of concrete images.[17] Hebrew poets enriched such profound expressions when they ". . . constantly reach[ed] into the everyday experiences of the people to illustrate the spiritual truths they were espousing."[18]

Since biblical poets, for example, employed figurative imageries, as well as comparative, inductive, or indirect language to express the divine Word, the modern interpreter should instead seek the 'intended' meaning in the context of the poem rather than the 'literal' meaning as is the case with prose narrative.[19] To explain further,

---

14. Kaiser Jr., "'My Heart Is Stirred by a Noble Theme': The Meaning of Poetry and Wisdom," *in Introduction to Biblical Hermeneutics*, 139.

15. Ryken, *Words of Delight*, 159.

16. Osborne, *The Hermeneutical Spiral*, 231.

17. Ryken, *Words of Delight*, 160.

18. Osborne, *The Hermeneutical Spiral*, 230.

19. Osborne, *The Hermeneutical Spiral*, 231.

Africans love the Book of Psalms because their cultural and social orientations are deeply embedded by musicology. The Psalms are written in poetry. So, for the African expository preachers to relate well the message of the poetic portions of the Bible to the African audience, "It is crucial to understand how Hebrew poetry functions."[20]

They must, of necessity, "think in pictures", knowing that "Image, metaphor, and simile are the backbone of biblical poetry."[21] This understanding is helpful in achieving a correct interpretation and application of the message of biblical poetry. Several local sources help in this pattern of thinking. In Africa, many existing objects of comparison are inexhaustible. These raw materials can be drawn from animal husbandry, farming and fishing activities, agricultural and hunting activities, and from dance and culture. They can also be drawn from rocks and rivers, from the African mountains and forests, from the type of communal life, corporate existence and traditional leadership, from the various African approaches to rites of passage practised in different communities, and so many more. Even the family structure and relationship can be an excellent source of imagery. Here, expertise is called for on the part of the expositor to carefully and appropriately cull materials from this pool or resources.

However, Hebrew poetry is complex and technical. A more in-depth discussion on it is beyond the intention of this book. The purpose of mentioning it here is to help preachers to correctly translate

---

20. Osborne, *The Hermeneutical Spiral*, 224. Because there are too many variations in Hebrew poetry, Osborne says each poem in Scripture must be studied on its own merits. See pp. 222-241 of Osborne for his discussion on poetry. Also, see Walter C. Kaiser Jr. and Moisés Silva, *Introduction to Biblical Hermeneutics: The Search for Meaning* (2nd ed.; Grand Rapids, Michigan: Zondervan, 2007), 139-156 for poetry types or forms and their functionality.

21. Ryken, *Words of Delight*, 162, 176.

the message of the Bible to the African audience. They should instead use the embedded knowledge of proverbial statements, interspersed with narratives and stories within the context of African oral literary form of communication, to aid the audiences' understanding of biblical poetry. Preachers should apply the poetic linguistic frame of the reading strategy with which Africans use to decode messages from their contextual proverbs in helping the African audience understand biblical poetry. The essence is not primarily the poem itself, but the theological message of God captured in poetic form.

Wisdom Genre

Wisdom material also exists in the biblical text with its subgenres. These include proverbs and sayings, riddles and allegories, admonitions and dialogue, and onomastica (relating to or consisting of name/names, derived from the Gk onomastikos). Wisdom writings present the pragmatic side of life. The purpose of biblical wisdom is the recognition of God as the source of creation and to teach people to live life in God's world by God's rule; hence, the fear of God is wisdom's central theme.[22]

One can confidently say that the African context is very similar to the world of the Old Testament, hence, Africans are at home with the wisdom genre. Biblical proverbs are understood by Kaiser and Silva as ". . . brief sayings that are memorable, embody the wisdom of many, possess a fullness of meaning despite the economy of words. . . . By their nature and form, proverbs are generalized statements with a wide application."[23] Put another way, Osborne says a proverb is ". . . a brief statement of universally accepted truth formulated in such a way as to be memorable." He cautions however that the inter-

---

22. Osborne, *The Hermeneutical Spiral*, 242.

23. Kaiser Jr. and Silva, *Introduction to Biblical Hermeneutics*, 151.

preter dares not read more than what is there as these generalised proverbial statements are ". . . intended to give advice rather than to establish rigid codes by which God works."[24] In Africa, proverbs are specific, not generalised. Unless otherwise indicated, African proverbs always convey a specific message. For example, there is an African wisdom saying that says, "A child that prevents the mother from sleep by its discomforting cry will also not sleep." Also, another African saying states, "The person that fails to give heed to the warning will not fail to suffer the consequence." Africa can rightly be described as the home of proverbs and wise sayings. This already existing proverbial background serves as an excellent bridge to understanding biblical wisdom literature. What remains for the expositor is the proper interpretation of the biblical text so that listeners can make the proper connection between the contents of biblical and African wisdom.

Proverbial sayings in Scriptures are realistic statements based on empirically observed realities in nature and human existence. These may be didactic or merely experiential, describing real-life situations. Riddles also are part of wisdom literature. Kaiser and Silva say they are ". . . designed to puzzle and to perplex the listener or reader in order initially to obscure and hide some parts of its meaning, thereby testing the acuity and skill of those who attempt to solve it."[25] This puzzling and perplexing mode plays out very clearly in Samson's riddle presented to the Philistines (Judg 14:12-18).

There is hardly any African language that is deficient in the use of proverbs in its daily communication. No doubt, there are more proverbs in some African languages than in others; yet, all African languages and dialects are clustered with proverbs, and none can

---

24. Osborne, *The Hermeneutical Spiral*, 247.

25. Kaiser Jr. and Silva, *Introduction to Biblical Hermeneutics*, 152.

be said to be impoverished. The whole of life in the African setting serves as the primary source for proverbs. They are drawn from African anthropology, sociology, psychology, agricultural activities, geography, forestry, zoology, oceanography, ecology, animal husbandry, poetry, architecture, cosmology, and so on. The beauty of various proverbs on the African soil should serve as an essential background for the understanding, appreciation, and interpretation of biblical wisdom materials by the African expository preacher.

Prophetic Genre

Prophecy, is a genre of Jewish literature, because "The roots of prophecy are deeply imbedded in Israel's history."[26] Although various sub-genres exist in the proclamation of the prophetic message, the two basic types are speeches and oracles. Under speeches are judgement and argument speeches, the one proclaiming doom while the other using the people's errors against them. Under oracles also are woe, salvation and legal forms; all these forms are couched in a declarative style. Visions and revelations are also some communicative modes prevalent in Old Testament prophetic literature. This is in addition to God speaking directly to the prophet with specific instructions on what to do. Symbolic actions, war and funeral lamentations, and apocalypse are also aspects of prophetic literature. Every prophetic word has an intended theological import. When such understanding is missed, interpretation and application of prophetic texts, as it is the case in contemporary Africa, will become fraudulent.

It is quite evident that the prophetic literature of the Old Testament seems the most widely used today in Africa. At the same time, it is the most misunderstood and misapplied genre of the Scriptures.

---

26. C. Hassell Bullock, *An Introduction to the Old Testament Prophetic Books* (Updated ed., Chicago, Illinois: Moody Publishers, 2007), 15.

I would refer readers to Dr Michael Kyomya's book *A Guide to Interpreting Scripture*[27] so they learn how to interpret prophetic books. The African quest for protection and blessings makes the hermeneutical import of the prophetic books to lose relevance because of the way in which it is used. Visions and dreams, as well as direct revelation, are some aspects of the prophetic message that are being wrongly interpreted and applied in Africa.

The understanding of biblical prophetic declaration in Jewish society is entirely different from what obtains today in many Christian circles in Africa. Israel's prophets, for instance, neither intimidated nor coerced the people to whom they were sent with the divine message. Equally, apart from the false prophets, Old Testament prophets were never greedy and selfish oppressing the people under the guise of their being messengers of God. On the contrary, they merely delivered the message they had received from God. They were selfless and sacrificial, putting their very lives on the line in obedience to God as his messengers.

African expository preachers of the prophetic texts should do the following: Have a clear understanding of the identity, context, and roles of the Old Testament Jewish prophets. Secondly, they should seek to gain an understanding of the nature of the prophetic message and the context of the people to whom the prophets came with the divine Word. Third, they must seek an appropriately adequate interpretation of the prophetic texts following the principles set for understanding their specific type of genre. Lastly, based upon the preceding, the expositors of the biblical texts to Africa can now try to seek the appropriate, relevant ways to apply the message of the prophetic texts to the modern audience.

---

27. Michael Kyomya, *A Guide to Interpreting Scripture* (Nairobi, Kenya: HippoBooks, 2010).

Gospels, Letters, and Apocalypse

In addition to the above genres, there are also more such as the Gospels, the Letters and the Apocalyptic. The Gospels are not so much of a biography of Jesus as they are concerned to report his ministry among people as God-incarnate. The letters, on the other hand, are personal correspondences to either a corporate group of Christian communities or to individuals. They address specific theological and doctrinal themes. They are also rebukes, exhortations, and appeals. Additionally, these letters contain moral reflections and administrative instructions. Lastly, the apocalyptic materials disclose secret and hidden things that are revealed to some individuals, mostly conveyed through visions, such as we could find in the book of Ezekiel, Daniel, and Revelation.

The place of genre in the Biblical text is as important as the theology of it. This makes a correct understanding of each very crucial for Biblical study and expository preaching. It is the proper decoding of the various forms of genres in the Bible and an adequate teaching/preaching of the Biblical text that makes the Biblical message contextually relevant. This is the subject of the next chapter.

CHAPTER 7

CONTEXTUAL BENEFITS OF EXPOSITORY PREACHING

Most business people around the world know the benefits of investment. Good investments are expected to yield good returns for the investor. Among the places to invest in is what is called the "Stock Market." This is a place where a person buys shares in a company. The shares of successful companies usually yield returns in several ways. First, such companies declare annual dividend pay-outs to their shareholders. Secondly, they also give share bonuses to the investors. Thirdly, shares of successful companies can usually be sold at a profit. Fourthly, share certificates can be used as collateral to obtain loans in the bank. These are the benefits of investing in the "Stock Market."

The maxim which states, "Anything worth doing is worth doing well," holds for expository preaching in Africa. As we discussed earlier in chapter four, we made a case for the role and the necessity of expository preaching for the African context today. In submitting the thesis and the purpose of this book, we contended that because good expository preaching has an immense role to play in the spiritual maturity of African Christians, it is, therefore, indispensable.

Like a good investment that yields good returns for the investor, no doubt, expository preaching holds significant benefits for the church in Africa. In general terms, biblical exposition is beneficial for the growth of the global Christian community. In specific terms, however, expository preaching is exceedingly beneficial to the African continent and in particular, for the church. Africa is a continent that is plagued and exploited by several predators. Some of the cardinal areas and indicators which show that the African church stands to gain from good expository preaching are considered in the following pages.

TRANSFORMATION

When a person's life is transformed, a positive change takes place; and when such noticeable change occurs in a person's life, everything, henceforth, is seen from a new perspective. The transformation of life is one primary benefit of exposing the Scriptures. A transforming gospel presentation through expository preaching in Africa will address, for example, the danger of tribalism.

The existence of clans, tribes and ethnic groups function as a trademark and as a weaving thread in Africa. Ethnic and tribal diversity gives Africa a great strength. It strengthens the bond of unity in the spirit of the brotherhood of the African peoples. According to Barje Maigaidi, ethnicity is ". . . a cultural phenomenon that relates a people to their roots, beliefs and values, providing them with a deep sense of self-identity in the course of their interaction with others. Such self-identity makes the group feel a sense of uniqueness as a people within a larger social context."[1]

Fundamentally, the marks of ethnicity and tribe give people their identity and uniqueness. Ethno-tribal groupings place people into smaller tribes, languages and dialects not only giving them the core of their identity and a closer tie, but they also enable people to relate

---

1. Barje Sulmane Maigadi, *Divisive Ethnicity in the Church in Africa* (Kaduna, Nigeria: Baraka Press and Publishers Limited, 2006), 19.

to other similar groups, enabling all of the ethnic groups to positively contribute to the development of society at large. In this sense, both ethnicity and tribe are right. As Maigadi argues, ethnicity and tribe are a gift from God. According to him, "These cultural elements in themselves are good and essential to the socio-cultural survival of any group, but when they become a means of discrimination against others, then they create . . . divisive ethnicity."[2]

Accordingly, despite the good of ethnicity and tribalism as they serve as a unifying force for a people, they also have a divisive twist to them. Although the homogenous and hospitable nature of Africans is a positive feature, yet, ethno-tribal sentiments can be negative. The individual and corporate expressions of divisive ethnic and tribal sentiments distort the homogenous and hospitable nature of the African peoples. These negative sentiments have encroached on the church as well. However, any African person whose life is transformed by the truth exposed from the Scriptures should perceive life from a different perspective and also interprets issues from a biblical perspective. As such, using the Christian Scriptures as a guide, such a person will fight against these divisions in order to achieve a cohesive existence for the church and African society in general.

The growing sentiment of socio-ethnic and tribal strife and wars has plagued the African continent in recent times. It never really goes away despite the African experience of improved democracy, education, sociological enlightenment, infrastructural development, and so on. Ethno-tribal and social strife in Africa are mostly caused by dominance and deprivation of one tribe or ethnic group by another. It is equally propelled by the quest for liberation and identity by tribal and ethnic groups which feel dominated, oppressed, neglected, and aggrieved. Often in Africa more powerful ethno-tribal or polit-

---

2. Maigadi, *Divisive Ethnicity in the Church in Africa*, 20-22.

ical groupings oppress minority groups. In turn, the oppressed seek to liberate themselves from their oppressors seeking for freedom, personal identity and self-expression. Christians are sometimes involved in ethno-tribal suppression. Acts of dominance and oppression negate the principle of biblical transformation.

Expository preaching helps to counteract these divisions. The Scriptures teach the principle of respect for what is called the *Imago Dei* (the image of God) in every human person (Gen 1:26-27; Ezek 18: 14). Here, expository preaching should emphasise the biblical concept of *oneness* in Christ and the *community* of the saints as antidotes to the practice of tribalism and ethnicity. This brings together the oppressed and the oppressor in line with Christ's priestly prayer for the unity of the Christian community (John 17:11, 20-22). When African Christians honestly apply the biblical understanding of *oneness* within the church, then they will be able to stand in the gap with the message of unity and reconciliation for both the oppressor and the oppressed in African society. As a truly transformed community of faith, then, the church can champion the oppressed in preaching forgiveness and acceptance where hurts exist.

One of Africa's strengths is its communal life. This is the context in which every African child, borne on the African soil, nursed on the African soil, and fed and trained on the African soil, is groomed. The theme of communal unity is also clearly presented in the biblical text. In the Old Testament, we find the concept of Israel as the community of Yahweh. In the New Testament also, we find the concept of the church as the community of Jesus Christ. Christ's 'priestly prayer' described in the gospel of John 17 captures this concept quite vividly. The Pauline discourse in the book of Ephesians 4 also further emphasises this crucial concept of the unitary nature of the church as a new community in Christ. The church is a transformed community. When the biblical text is clearly and correctly taught, it will not only close the gap of tribal and ethnic sentiments but will also strengthen the sense of *oneness* as well in the church in Africa. Hence faithful expository preaching should build on the existing African understanding of the community by reinterpreting it in biblical perspective.

Maigadi believes that when the church in Africa sees its identity as one family of God beyond that of a mere African community of segmented tribes and ethnic groups it ". . . gives the church a relational character." He believes that such perceptions of the connectedness of the church with God as Father and with other ethno-tribal peoples as members of the same one family will cause a definite shift from an institutionalised type of relationship to a relational one. Indeed, this new perception can help to facilitate positive relationships among members of a multi-ethnic church.[3]

Apart from the mistaken practice of tribalism and ethnicity by some members of the church in Africa, there is also the persistent presence of corruption in African society. Corruption in Africa today is a viral infection that has become an attitudinal phenomenon. While its exhibition is less pronounced in certain societies, it is more glaring in some others. As J. A. Oladunjoye points out, "Corruption has become a cancer in the life of nations, and it seems to have defied all treatment. One major reason for this state of affairs is that those saddled with the responsibility of applying the medicine are not sincere in their diagnosis and in dispensing of the prescribed drug."[4]

The Christian gospel can evoke changes in society because of its transformational power. When expository preaching is done appro-

---

3. Maigadi, *Divisive Ethnicity in the Church in Africa*, 194.
4. The Rt. Rev. Dr J. A. Oladunjoye, "Chairman's Keynote Address," in *Biblical Studies and Corruption in Africa: Biblical Studies Series Number 6* (ed., Rev. Prof. Samuel Oyin Abogunrin, Ibadan, Nigeria: The Nigerian Association for Biblical Studies (NABIS), 2007), 1.

priately in Africa, it can attack the viral infection of corruption in society. Its power can kill the infectious parasite of attitudinal corruption. The lifestyles of transformed individual Christians in society should act as change agents, serving as the salt of the earth and the light of the world (Matt 5:13-16). Christians who consistently sit under a qualified and adequate Bible expositor will not only be transformed individually. They will also become transforming change agents in society – bringing positive changes to politics and governance, to civil and public services and in social work. Their presence as employees will bring changes to government parastatals and in private organisations, in the banking industry, in the judiciary and in the academia; and they will also effect changes in the business arena, in the homes, and in the streets. When these transformed Christians carry out their obligations to church and society, they will have been shining the light of the gospel like stars in their dark corners (Phil 2:15-16; Eph 5:11-16). The benefits of such a transformation make the continued practice of expository preaching in Africa an unavoidable necessity.

BIBLICAL LITERACY

A story was told about two friends from a village who went to a local beer parlour one evening to relax as they had always done. On their way home, an argument ensued between them. It resulted in a sharp disagreement. One of the friends had a son who was in secondary school (high school). He wanted to prove to his friend that he knew how to speak some English. Therefore, out of annoyance at the way the argument was going, he said to his friend, "What do you mean?" His friend was furious. Why was he angry at his friend who spoke to him in English? Well, the word *wat* in their language means, "a thief". For him, his friend had accused him of being a thief. He was furious; and therefore, demanded an explanation about what his friend meant by addressing him as *wat* (that is, accusing him of stealing). His poor grasp of English resulted in his failure to understand and his anger.

The literacy level of the Bible by many African Christians is similarly low. Some can even quote a particular passage of the Bible but often without a proper understanding of what it means. One primary reason that explains this deficiency is the lack of adequate exposition of the Scriptures. No truly-called biblical preacher can deny that sound expository preaching has numerous benefits. One of these is a higher level of growth in biblical literacy. Ramesh Richard explains that expository preaching helps the hearers/congregation to become biblically literate, resulting in the growing lifestyle of godliness. He states, ". . . expository preaching helps the preacher promote God's agenda for his [or her] people."[5]

A recent development in urban areas in Africa raises a greater need for expository preaching in the churches. There is a gradual shift from a deeply rooted oral African culture to a literary culture. More people are becoming educated and learned as they pursue further studies, although they give no space to reading the Bible. Scripture expositors should use this welcome development to their advantage. The West has always been construed as a literary-based community and Africa as an orally-oriented community. Today, more Africans are becoming more and more literate. The fast drift from rural to urban settlement is mostly responsible for this shift. A more compelling reason for such increasing literary level is the increasing repertoire of literate Africans who have excelled in their various fields of profession, whether at home in Africa or abroad. This is a good

---

5. Ramesh Richard, *Scripture Sculpture: A Do-It-Yourself Manual for Biblical Preaching* (1995; repr., Grand Rapids, Michigan: Baker Books, 1997), 16-17.

development as it prepares grounds for the reception of the biblical message. Hopefully, literate African Christians, and even inquisitive non-Christians will give more space to the careful study of the biblical text. To meet this growing need, careful expository preaching is ideal.

When the biblical understanding of church members increases through quality expository preaching, it will enhance submission to divine authority as it keeps both the preacher and the listeners subservient to the authority of the divinely inspired written Word. Haddon Robinson says, for instance, that, "The type of preaching that best carries the force of divine authority is expository preaching."[6] When the biblical text is adequately taught through exposition, it will certainly always draw attention to the authority of the text. Richard agrees when he says that expository preaching helps the preacher to grow personally in knowledge and obedience through a disciplined exposure to God's Word.[7]

As more and more African preachers move away from the simple missionary type of the presentation of the biblical text to its in-depth exposition, there should be an increase in the church's biblical literacy. Biblical literacy will also increase when more African preachers move away from topically-dominated sermons to expository sermons. The elite (educated) class in the audience particularly will not only resonate with the Old Testament biblical text, given its close affinity to African cultures, but will be challenged a lot more to learn from the entire biblical material through careful and objective study.

Consequently, the aspects of polygamy, childbearing and women subjugation, for instance, will be given a better understanding when the biblical text is carefully and appropriately interpreted. With such

---

6. Haddon W. Robinson, *Expository Preaching: Principles and Practice* (2nd ed., 2001; repr., Leicester, England: Inter-Varsity Press, 2004), 19.

7. Richard, *Scripture Sculpture*, 17.

an increased level of biblical literacy, even African Christian women will be able to acquire an added understanding of the reasons and purposes for their divinely mandated submissive function to family headship as stated in the biblical text. When such increased knowledge and understanding are embraced free of any form of biases, there will be an improved family relationship. Furthermore, with a high level of biblical literacy in the church in Africa, Christians are less likely to be misled by what they hear from the pulpit or outside it. Instead, they will first test its validity against the biblical text before they commit themselves to believe it like the Berean Christians did (Acts 17:11).[8]

SPIRITUAL MATURITY

African farmers traditionally use organic manure as fertiliser so as to preserve the texture of the soil and increase its nutrients thus improving their crop production. Many African farmers today will have their preference for organic manure against the use of chemical fertiliser. Manure has a more lasting benefit for soil conservation and crop production than chemical fertiliser which only has a short-term benefit. Chemical fertiliser destroys the nutrients of the soil. Similarly, expository preaching enhances lasting spiritual growth compared with topical preaching.

Africans are very religious people. They can fall for anything religious because of their intrinsic religious orientation and worldview. This religiosity springs from African beliefs in the operational presence of the spirits of the gods. It is this deep trust in the efficacy of religion that makes the African peoples a believing community. The

---

8. See a further brief discussion on the subject of biblical literacy in Joel K. T. Biwul, *Preaching the Scriptures* (Carlisle, UK & Jos, Nigeria: HippoBooks, 2018), 26-28.

abode of the African ancestors, as well as that of the divine Being who is unequivocally accepted by all Africans as the Supreme Creator of the whole universe, is perceived to be above the sky. When life experiences become sour, and things are not getting along well, the natural reaction of any African person is to turn to folk religion. He or she is looking for answers from the power above to their problems, some of which are persistent. As a very religious people, therefore, Africans will be more receptive to the Scriptures and stand to gain more from expository preaching.

The intense Africans' religious quest, consequent upon their deeply-rooted religious worldview, serves as a prepared ground for the reception of the message of the biblical text. Adequately explaining the Scriptures, therefore, helps to deepen the quality of their Christian maturity and spirituality. It also helps to strengthen their faith in God in the face of daunting challenges. African Christians have so much to gain from expository preaching. It can help them in the area of building faith in their Creator in the midst of suffering and the uncertainties of life. This is particularly crucial given their sociological and physiological challenges such as poverty, sickness and disease, and even death consequent upon poor medical services. The challenge of terrorists' vandalism and collapsing family values and relationships also stir them in the eyes.

When Africans turn to religious quests in the time of need, their attitude follows in the tradition of the Jewish people. Such religious quests connect well with the words of the Psalmists, "As the eyes of slaves look to the hand of their master, as the eyes of a maid look to the hand of her mistress, so our eyes look to the LORD our God, till he shows us his mercy" (Ps 123:2; 25:15 NIV). Alternatively, again "I lift up my eyes to the hills – where does my help come from? My help comes from the LORD, the Maker of heaven and earth" (Ps 121:1-2 NIV); "Lord, you have been our dwelling place" (Ps 90:1 NIV).

A sound biblical exposition will help to deepen the faith of African Christians in God.

The valued asset of conviction in God and his Word by Christians is gradually declining in Africa today. The influence of modernism and poverty seem to be responsible for such a decline. However, personal conviction and faith in God and his Word is a significant area of the benefit of expository preaching for the church in Africa. Quality expository preaching will grow mature disciples for the church in Africa, people who develop strong Christian convictions. The transforming effect of good expository preaching on both the preacher and the listeners makes for a deep personal conviction in the sovereignty of God, and the power and the authority of the Scriptures as fundamentally significant for the African context.

For example, just as children and youth need to be properly taught and prepared for adulthood so too does a proper discipleship programme help to develop the convert's personal trust and conviction in God. A properly discipled Christian convert in Africa will become a devout follower of Jesus Christ and a staunch defender of the Christian faith. When properly rooted in the Scriptures such a disciple will easily carry this kind of devotion over from his or her previous traditional belief in the power of the gods. A culturally relevant methodology for this discipleship, therefore, is essential. As Bauta D. Motty asserts, the church in Africa ". . . today is in dire need of a relevant indigenous disciple-making model, with methods that are culturally-relevant and biblically affirmed, to mature its members."[9]

---

9.   Bauta Dauda Motty, *Indigenous Christian Disciple-Making* (Jos, Nigeria: ECWA Productions Ltd., 2013), vi.

DOCTRINE & THEOLOGY

Each village in Africa has its specific market day. People move from village to village either to sell their produce or to socialise with other people on the different market days. On the market day of one of the villages, a mild disagreement had ensued between two elderly men who were drinking the local liquor at one of the stands. The disagreement soon degenerated into the exchange of blows. Before long, the fight took on a tribal dimension, and in a very short time, it turned into a free for all fight covering the entire market square.

Like the case of this unregulated market fight, the preaching climate in Africa today is neither censored nor regulated. Every person who claims to have received some revelation or a call starts to preach, and sooner or later, a church/congregation is formed. Those of them that have the finances go on air to sell their product through radio or satellite TV programmes. Moreover, like the flies that follow the smell of rotten mangoes, these preachers always have followers. Some others come up with some named "ministries." The establishment of either a "church" or a "ministry" is a flourishing and often lucrative business in Africa.

Such a preaching atmosphere in the present African context puts the Christians at both doctrinal and theological risk. Given this context of unregulated preaching by these "preachers" and "ministry owners" it doesn't take long for erroneous thinking and heresies to develop in this fertile soil.

There are several reasons for this lack of regulated preaching. One of them is historical ignorance. When the history of the development of the doctrine and theology of the church is either overlooked or not known, errors easily creep into the church. Errors distort and pollute the biblical, doctrinal and theological heritage that has been passed down from the African church Fathers. Bruce Shelley points out the adverse effects of historical ignorance on contemporary Christians and Christianity when he states, "As a consequence of our ignorance concerning Christian history, we find believers vulnerable to the appeals of cultists. Some distortion of Christianity is often taken for the real thing."[10] African Christians who have sensed the calling to preach God's Word must preach well to counteract the activities and errors of these newcomers.

Values are values, and they need to be preserved. Africans have long had cherished values that regulated their communal life. However, today distortions in the cultural, religious, moral and social ethics, and the customs of many African societies are becoming apparent. Some Christian converts unknowingly fall victim to these distortions. Corrective action largely depends on the implantation of the divine laws in human hearts. The Bible, for instance, has traditions and ethical values that are synonymous, in no small extent, with those of some African peoples. This background serves as a suitable connector between the biblical and the African contexts for expository preaching. Therefore, when biblical value systems are adequately explained and appropriately applied to the African context, it will reshape any existent theological and ethical distortion.

We have, so far, argued that when the Scriptures are rightly and adequately explained and properly understood, it holds some clear benefits for both the preacher and the listeners of the divine Word. In summary, John McArthur, Jr. expresses the following five critical features of expository preaching for the global Christian community:

1. Expository preaching allows God himself to speak, because it expresses his glorious Sovereignty; it brings the preacher into direct

---

10. Bruce Leon Shelley, *Church History in Plain Language*, 3rd ed., (Nashville, Tennessee: Thomas Nelson Publishers, 2008), xv.

and continual contact with the mind of the Holy Spirit who authored the Scriptures;

2. Expository preaching frees the preacher to proclaim all the revelation of God, producing a ministry of wholeness and integrity;

3. Expository preaching further promotes biblical literacy, yielding rich knowledge of redemptive truths.

4. Expository preaching carries ultimate divine authority, rendering the very voice of God; and lastly,

5. Expository preaching transforms the preacher, leading to a transformed congregation.[11]

CONSERVATION

In any agricultural community in Africa, the conservation of farmlands and farm produce is essential. Granaries of different types, shapes and sizes are used in storing up what is harvested both for food and for economic purposes. Also, seedlings are stored towards the next farming season. Perishable root crops are also stored in cool places such as under the tree or in a safe location and covered with either grasses or some leaves. The undergirding concept of storage points to the principle of conservation for future benefit.

This conservation principle further resonates well with Africans. The longstanding effort of Africans to preserve their customs, traditions, and cultural heritage protects those elements from either harm or loss. These customs, traditions and cultures, even folklores and mythologies, have been passed from generation to generation almost intact in their original forms. A protective ingenuity by Africans is meant to keep a particular African community from any

---

11. John McArthur, Jr., "Introduction," in *Rediscovering Expository Preaching: John MacArthur, Jr. and the Master's Seminary Faculty* (eds., Richard L. Mayhue and Robertson L. Thomas (Dallas, Texas: WORD Publishing, 1993), xv.

inglorious act. Such an act has a good point of connection with the Christian faith.

With the help of good expository preaching, the protective ability of African Christians will be significantly enhanced at preserving the fundamental beliefs and doctrines of their faith. This is why historical theology of the church, which focuses on the historical development of her theology and doctrines, is critical for the sustenance of her existence. Critical in the sense that it helps the contemporary Christian to have a good grasp of the socio-cultural background of the spread of the Christian faith. It also helps to grasp the changing ethos of the Christian church throughout her history. [12] Further, it helps individual African Christians to trace the doctrinal-theological development of the historical roots and heritage of the church.

The preceding required knowledge is particularly significant because many African Christians seem to be losing their grip on the theological and doctrinal roots of their faith. Such Christians need to learn from Moses' instructions to the Israelites. He instructed them to jealously guard the Law of Yahweh against any foreign religious infiltration. Moses instructed,

> Hear, O Israel: The LORD our God, the LORD is one. Love
> the LORD your God with all your heart and with all your
> soul and with all your strength. These commandments that
> I give you today are to be upon your hearts. Impress them
> on your children. Talk about them when you sit at home
> and when you walk along the road, when you lie down and
> when you get up. Tie them as symbols on your hands and
> bind them on your foreheads. Write them on the doorframes
> of your houses and on your gates. When the LORD your

12. . The word 'ethos' means the distinguishing character, sentiment, moral nature, or guiding beliefs of a person, group, or institution. In the sense of our usage, it refers to the distinctive character and firm guiding beliefs of the church and the Christian faith.

God brings you into the land he swore to your fathers, to
Abraham, Isaac and Jacob, to give you – a land with large,
flourishing cities you did not build, houses filled with all
kinds of good things you did not provide, wells you did not
dig, and vineyards and olive groves you did not plant – then
when you eat and are satisfied, be careful that you do not
forget the LORD, who brought you out of Egypt, out of the
land of slavery. Fear the LORD your God, serve him only
and take your oaths in his name. Do not follow other gods,
the gods of the peoples around you; for the LORD your God,
who is among you, is a jealous God and his anger will burn
against you, and he will destroy you from the face of the
land. Do not test the LORD your God as you did at Massah
(Deut 6:4-16 NIV).

All the successive instructions in the Mosaic statements go to
show the necessity of the preservation of the love and reverence for
Yahweh as well as his Law within the Israelite community.

The church throughout history has had to contend with opposing
forces in an attempt to conserve the testimony and integrity of the
Christian faith. Because of this several Councils convened at different times and in different places. Consequently, African Christians
should not allow the resolutions of the various ecumenical Councils
decided upon in the early years of the history of the Catholic Church
to fall into historical amnesia or disrepute; nor should the signa-
tory ethos of the Christian heritage be eclipsed by the challenging
contemporary demands on Christianity. The content of Hebrews
chapters 11-12 should also serve as a constant reminder to the African Christians today that, "The labour of our heroes' past shall never
be in vain." This commitment should as well always challenge and
propel any such person of faith to proclaim, "Onward Christian soldiers."

Adequate expository preaching in Africa gains for the church transformed people who serve to transform others; increases the literacy level of the members, motivating them to preserve the faith as they become more mature. Nor is it likely that he or she who is properly fed with truths from the Scriptures will become easy prey to doctrinal and theological errors of our time. Yet this is not all. The preacher himself or herself need to be equipped; hence their preparation for the task is expedient.

CHAPTER 8

PREPARING THE EXPOSITORY PREACHER

The practice of initiation as a rite of passage was quite common among many communities in ancient Africa. Some parts of Africa still maintain this tradition. Young boys, for instance, were taken to the shrine and kept there for days during which they would be formally initiated into adult manhood. When a young lad completed the process, he was admitted into the society as a matured man. According to Mbiti, the male child had now grown from passive into active membership in the community physically, socially and religiously.[1] Such membership qualified him to perform certain restricted activities like fighting in a war and participating in those religious activities in the shrine that were performed only by the initiates.

The purpose of African traditional practice of initiation is to prepare the younger individual for admission into adulthood in his community. Such a significant rite ". . . is one of the key moments in the rhythm of individual life, which is also the rhythm of the corporate group of which the individual is a part."[2] Traditional initiation rites of passage in the African cultural heritage is an inevitable stage

---

1. John Samuel Mbiti, *African Religions and Philosophy* (2nd ed., 1990; repr., Gaborone, Botswana: Heinemann, 2008), 118.
2. Mbiti, *African Religions and Philosophy*, 118.

in the social development of the individual, and it is an integral part of the life of the community.[3]

Africans' important traditional rites of initiation are a purposeful preparation of the next generation of a community. This is proper planning to face serious challenges or to assume crucial roles in the future. A person who fails to plan for anything is already planning to fail in everything because planning is essential for success in life. Similarly, the preparation of the expository preacher is essential for a successful and effective preaching ministry.

PREPARATION'S PURPOSE

Preparation is vital in order to achieve success. In old Africa when tribes went to war against one another, the tribal leader, together with the leading war hero of the attacking side, had to first plan before the battle. The battle had to be strategized, and the fighters had to be adequately prepared. Such preparation was necessary for victory.

Similarly, the African farmer studies the ecology, seasons, and the atmospheric condition of a particular environment to accurately determine the time for every agricultural activity. Besides, the farmer has to prepare for the farming season by first clearing the farm before tilling it. Much time is given to preparation for a good yield. Even in villages where there are only streams and rivers, the one who goes out fishing will have to prepare the fishing hooks and the earthworms to use on the hooks.

Just like the war hero, farmer, and the fishing person, adequate preparation is an integral part of the making of an effective expositor of the Scriptures. The need for a very conscious, deliberate, purpose-

---

3. J. N. K. Mugambi, *Christianity and African Culture* (2002; repr., Nairobi, Kenya: Acton Publishers, 2009), 99.

ful, and systematic preparation of the expository preacher is quite apparent if the task of expository preaching is to be successful. Nothing whatsoever should take precedence over such preparation. Vines and Shaddix assert,

> The call to preach is precisely that — a call to preach. The call to preach, however, is more than just preaching. The call to preach is also a call to *prepare*. God gives to those He calls the necessary gifts to preach, and He expects them to prepare as much as possible. In one sense, that preparation involves a man's lifetime. Men prepare sermons; God prepares men. The man [or woman] who would preach, then, has the responsibility of learning to prepare.[4]

The word *prepare* consistently occurs six times in this statement. It is used in relationship to the word *preach,* which also appears seven times. These occurrences underscore the significance of preparation for the task of expository preaching. No one who does not prepare can hope to achieve anything tangible and of any significant value. A person who has a nonchalant attitude towards preparation is considered an unserious person in most African societies where hard work and being responsible in the community are of great value.

Adequate preparation develops the needed mental maturity and conviction to follow through on a task. Jesus drew the attention of his audience to the importance of planning in life. He taught about the need for a builder to first consider if he has sufficient funds to build a house, and about a king who should first consider the strength of his military before launching out to war (Luke 14:25-33). Jesus, drawing inferences from the above, said to his disciples, "'If anyone would come after me, he must deny himself and take up his cross daily and follow me'" (Luke 9:23 NIV). The idea of self-denial here presupposes

---

4. Jerry Vines and Jim Shaddix, *Power in the Pulpit: How to Prepare and Deliver Expository Sermons* (Chicago, Illinois: Moody Press, 1999), 13.

the concept of conscious preparation upon which the acts of "taking" and "following" depend. The preparation to become a disciple of Jesus Christ was not to be haphazardly done; instead, it was a decision that was consciously, willingly, and purposefully taken by counting the cost involved.

The need to prepare the expository preacher as the herald and divine mouthpiece can neither be assumed nor given less priority. As Ralph Turnbull points out, "A significant form of preparation for preaching is the preparation of the preacher. Effectiveness in the pulpit is indeed tied to the life, the integrity, and the Christian character of the man who declares the gospel. Good men are full of their message and will be heard."[5] Adequate preparation achieves more success in preaching the Word.

Honest and called expository preachers in the African context are engaged in a spiritual battle. Their adequate preparation becomes necessary for victory. The preacher of the Word is not merely sent on an errand but is sent into a fierce battlefield to contend with opposing forces against the divine message. Satan is frustrated when souls are saved and when Christians are growing in the faith. The steady maturity of the saints always stands as a stumbling block on his way; hence, he would not stand by and watch but will fight back with all that he has at his disposal. The temptations of Jesus validate this point (Matt 4:1-11). Also, Paul was confronted severally by Satan through various agents to hinder him from succeeding in the ministry. He was attacked, beaten, stoned, imprisoned and denied his rights (2 Cor 11:23-33; 2 Tim 3:10-12).

Expository preaching requires adequate preparation to accomplish because it is quite a demanding and serious task. For instance,

---

5. Ralph G. Turnbull, ed., *Baker's Dictionary of Practical Theology* (1967; repr., Grand Rapids, Michigan: Baker Book House, 1982), 34.

when a country sends its ambassador to another country, such a representative must assume the task with every seriousness in order to give a good impression of the sending country. Similarly, the expository preacher represents God in the pulpit. Stott uses six descriptive metaphors from the Bible to variously describe the expository preacher.[6] The preacher, serving as a spokesperson for God, is described as a herald or town crier who is sent to announce the good news (1 Cor 1:23; 2 Cor 4:5; Isa 40:9; 52:7); as a sower sent to sow God's seed into God's field (Luke 8:4-15); as an ambassador that is sent to a fertile or hostile foreign land to represent his or her nation (2 Cor 5:20; Eph 6:20) and as a steward who is put in charge of God's divine treasure and entrusted to faithfully serve it (1 Cor 4:1, 2; 1 Tim 3:4, 5; Titus 1:7). The preacher is also described as a pastor/shepherd who is assigned the task of shepherding the flock under the oversight of the chief shepherd (Ezek 34; John 21:15-17; Acts 20:28-31) and as a confident worker who serves with all the conviction and dedication needed to achieve the assigned task (2 Tim 2:15, 18).[7] These descriptive terms point to only one fact – that the one who dares to preach the divine Word occupies the position of a representative and a spokesperson of a higher authority. To serve in such a capacity means occupying a noble position that demands deep conviction, utmost seriousness, carefulness, and great humility.

The preceding descriptions indicate that spiritual maturity, preparedness, competence and expertise are required of the expository preacher for the African context. Preachers of the divine Word should approach the task with a voracious attitude, perceiving such a representative role as a rare privilege rather than something bur-

---

6. John Robert Walmsley Stott and Greg Scharf, *The Challenge of Preaching: Abridged and Updated* (Carlisle, Cumbria: Langham Preaching Resources, 2011), 19-30.

7. Stott with Greg Scharf, *The Challenge of Preaching*, 22, 29-30.

densome or as an opportunity to achieve selfish gains. The individual who assumes such an enormous task cannot do so on his or her terms and strength but strictly on those of the one who assigns him/her. The prerequisites to assuming this arduous task of representing God in the pulpit are the necessity of adequate spiritual, theological, socio-anthropological, and ethical preparation.

SPIRITUAL PREPARATION

Expository preaching begins with the spiritual preparation of the preacher. The most vital part of this preparation is the conversion of the preacher—belief and personal saving faith in Jesus Christ is the starting point. It is the transformed life, inspired and guided by the Holy Spirit, who causes the transformation of other people through the preaching of the Scriptures. The presence of the Holy Spirit in the life of a transformed person gives the boldness to declare the given message without being intimidated or deterred. For example, a hitherto weak and frightened band of disciples were able to bring about a great revolution in the world of their day because Christ transformed their lives. Their belief in the resurrected Jesus Christ of Nazareth, who is now their Saviour and Lord, made the difference in their lives.

For us in Africa today, attention is shifting from the core of the message of salvation and maturity in Christ to that of prosperity, miracles, exorcism, and gymnastic power displays. Such growing spiritual jamborees and gymnastics in the pulpit leaves a cautious observer pondering whether disguised African witchcrafts, magicians and traditional medicine actors have not taken over the African pulpit. The content of these publicly displayed jamborees in the name of God or Jesus appears irreconcilable with the content of the ministry of Jesus whom these actors claim to serve. Comparatively, the Gospels' accounts reveal that none of the preaching and teaching and the miracles performed through the disciples of Jesus was fake. Scrutiny of the Gospels and Acts validates their authenticity. Jesus transformed their lives, they were filled and aided by the power of the Holy Spirit, and they put their lives on the line in service to their Lord; nothing fake, nothing dishonest characterised their lives and ministry.

The complete spiritual transformation of the life of the preacher of the Scriptures is a crucial preparation. An expositor of the Scriptures whose life Christ has transformed cannot preach the Scriptures without a deep conviction. The preacher has to develop a firm conviction in the God of the Bible about whom he or she preaches. Such a preacher must also develop a firm conviction in the integrity and authority of the Bible from which he or she seeks to preach. If preaching is to pass the description of being Christian at all, then a robust personal conviction in God and the Bible by the preacher is an inescapable necessity.

All the prophets of the Old Testament and the apostles of the New Testament preached vigorously with a firm conviction in God and in the authority of his Word. Their proclamations were effectual because these preachers saw themselves as transformed men under orders from God. They were deeply convinced about the reality of his Being, sovereignty, and supremacy over cosmic order; as well as of his power, authority, and superiority over the multiplicity of pagan deities. They were entirely convinced in the authority and in the transforming power of the message which he had given them to proclaim as his spokesmen. Such unwavering conviction allowed them no room to waste time in delivering the given divine message or to negotiate the terms of the message with the intended audience.

The African expository preacher cannot overlook the need to maintain a consistent relationship and fellowship with God as an aspect of adequate spiritual preparation for preaching. The preacher's life of total commitment and obedience to Christ is anchored on an intimate fellowship. The prophets and the apostles, as heralds, were adamant to deterring human threats to their mission. This is so because the one who had called them had prepared them individually for the task. Notably, they knew the secrets of consistent walk and fellowship with God. This is the secret of their success in ministry. Richard re-echoes this need,

> An effective sermon is the child of the union of spiritual dynamics with studious mechanics. The dynamics of sermon preparation arise from the preacher's relationship to the Lord of the text. It is a serious exercise that must be bathed in prayer and enabled by the Holy Spirit from the preacher's very first exposure to a text.[8]

Turnbull also agrees, "Today, sermon preparation still must begin with men who are under orders from God and who regularly experience a living, vital relationship with God. Apart from men in dynamic contact with the Lord, there can be no authentic preaching."[9] Still, Baumann stresses this fact further by arguing that there can be no authentic Christian preaching except the preacher has experienced the touch of the power of the gospel to keep him or her in constant fellowship with the Lord of the gospel,

> The fact of a radical commitment to Christ is so essential to service within the life of the church that deep heart searching is not simply recommended; it is imperative. . . . Christ must not only be spoken of; He must be an observable part of the preacher's person. . . . Power in the pulpit is not simply

---

8. Ramesh Richard, *Scripture Sculpture: A Do-It-Yourself Manual for Biblical Preaching* (1995; repr., Grand Rapids, Michigan: Baker Books, 1997), 17.

9. Turnbull, ed., *Baker's Dictionary of Practical Theology*, 81.

a rhetorical art; it arises in part from the recesses of a trans-formed life.[10]

Where deep personal conviction in the Christian God and the power of his revealed Word is lacking, and when the role of the Holy Spirit is absent, the preacher's sermon becomes weak, powerless, and perhaps meaningless. Where the life of consistent commitment, obedience, and fellowship with God is lacking in the one who stands in the pulpit, the message will be emptied of its deserving divine authority, flavour and its desired effects. Gordon D. Fee reminds all preachers of the Word about this need when he states, "Sermon preparation without personal encounter with the word and with-out prayer will probably lack inspiration, and sermons preached by those who have not themselves sat in awful silence before the majes-ty of God, and his word will probably accomplish very little."[11] Again and again, the emphasis is laid on the fact that the spirituality of the preacher is a requirement for effective expository preaching. For ex-ample, Prophet Isaiah was unable to say, "Here am I. Send me!," until he first had a personal encounter with Yahweh of Israel when he saw a glimpse of him in his glory. Isaiah also did not answer the urgent call until he sensed the need for divine cleansing in preparation for the prophetic ministry (Isa 6:1-8).

Listening and understanding are two crucial parts of human communication. In most ancient African communities, the priests received the oracles of the gods and delivered their message to the community. A priest would have no message to deliver if the gods did not speak. Unfortunately, today in the church in Africa, many preachers are neither sensitive to the presence of God nor to his

10. J. Daniel Baumann, *An Introduction to Contemporary Preaching* (1972; paperback ed., 1988; repr., Grand Rapids, Michigan: Baker Book House, 1990), 34.
11. Gordon D. Fee, *New Testament Exegesis: A Handbook for Students and Pastors* (Philadelphia, Kentucky: The Westminster Press, 1983), 134.

voice. The loss of spiritual sensitivity on the part of some preachers in Africa today renders them irrelevant. This explains why some of them have turned into noisemakers and manipulators of the people as spiritcrafts instead of heralding the divine Word. Piper is right, "Genuine spiritual power in the pulpit is not synonymous with loudness. Hard hearts are not likely to be broken by shrill voices."[12] Of course, Christian preaching is standing in the gap between the souls of men and women that are hanging in the balance between heaven and hell. Chapell says of this task,

> When we face real people with eternal souls balanced between heaven and hell, the nobility of preaching both awes us and makes us more aware of our inadequacies. We know our skills are insufficient for an activity with such vast consequences. We recognise that our hearts are too lacking in purity to lead others to holiness. Honest evaluation inevitably causes us to conclude that we do not have sufficient eloquence, wisdom, or character to be capable of turning others from spiritual death to eternal life.[13]

Prayer also must be considered an aspect of the spiritual preparation for pulpit effectiveness. No doubt, "Good preaching is born of good praying."[14] Where the Holy Spirit is not actively involved in the life of the expository preacher, and where his presence is not actively felt in the preaching situation, nothing positive happens in the preaching. In many parts of Africa it is culturally expected that women will kneel to ask a husband or his relations for forgiveness or when making a passionate request or a plea. The expository preacher

---

12. John Piper, *The Supremacy of God in Preaching* (rev. ed., Grand Rapids, Michigan: Baker Books, 2004), 101.

13. Bryan Chapell, *Christ-Centered Preaching: Redeeming the Expository Sermon* (2nd ed., 2005; repr. Grand Rapids, Michigan: Baker Academic, 2007), 26.

14. Piper, *The Supremacy of God in Preaching*, 99-100.

should use the knees beyond what an African wife does. He or she should kneel before God in prayer until heaven's doors are opened in answer to prayers. The knees are used to ask for the permeating power and presence of the Holy Spirit in the preaching process. True transforming expository preaching is not accomplished by the preacher's intellectual ability and ingenuity, or professional competence, though these are important; but through the pervasive power of the Holy Spirit operating in the life of the preacher.

THEOLOGICAL PREPARATION

Both formal education and personal experience have their place in the development of an individual. In any normal human society, formal education is given the priority. When the citizens of a country are correctly and adequately educated, they will, in turn, use their learning to develop the society in all areas such as civil and public services and politics, industry & commerce, religious institutions, and in the field of scientific and technological advancement. In addition, experience helps in correcting the mistakes of the past and in facilitating the attainment of present achievements by an individual or a country. When acquired experiences are appropriately harnessed, they can lead to productive development.

The Bible expositor for the African context inescapably requires good theological training in order to ably minister in the contemporary African society. In his *The Contemporary Christian*, Stott believes that Christianity is an authentic religion because it presents not only a historical figure but also historical events. The expository preacher for the church in Africa is called to sustain the authenticity of the Christian gospel and doctrine, the authenticity of the Christian faith and belief, and the fact that salvation is found only by personal faith in this historical figure (Acts 4:12). If Jesus is a historical figure who proposed a historical religion, then there is a need for proper development of theological conviction about this unique person and his message in order to contextualise him in the contemporary society. Stott presents a double method to this effect:

> How can we develop a Christian mind, which is both shaped by the truths of historical, biblical Christianity, and acquainted with the realities of the contemporary world? How can we relate the Word to the world, understanding the world in the light of the Word, and even understanding the Word in the light of the world? We have to begin with a double refusal. We refuse to become either so absorbed in the Word, that we escape into it and fail to let it confront the world, or so absorbed in the world, that we conform to it and fail to subject it to the judgment of the Word. Escapism and conformity are opposite mistakes, but neither is a Christian option. In place of this double refusal, we are called to double listening, listening both to the Word and the world.[15]

When the disciples of Jesus Christ took over the ministry after his ascension, the religious order of their day recognised them as ignorant fishermen who were not learned in the law of the Jewish religion (Acts 4:13). It is true that the disciples never trained in any rabbinic school nor held any official position in any of the recognised religious circles of the day. However, they were trained for three years by the best teacher, Jesus. Not that such an example removes the need for good theological education today. For when the highly educated Saul (Paul) came on the scene after his dramatic conversion experience (Acts 9:1-19), the course of history for the early church also changed remarkably. The gospel gained global acceptance, and the church took a global outlook with his emergence. Paul's membership of the

---

15. John Robert Walmsley Stott, *The Contemporary Christian* (Leicester, U.K.: Inter-Varsity Press, 1992), 27.

early church facilitated the mobility of the gospel from Jerusalem to the Gentile world. More significantly, although Paul was a newcomer to the missionary enterprise, yet, he has more literary works to his credit in the Bible, far more than any of the twelve other apostles. The remarkable difference lies in his much learning which made him adaptable to the Jewish, Grecian, and Roman worlds.[16]

As a preacher of the way, Paul's presence in Christianity aided the massive spread of the gospel. As Bruce Shelley notes, the rapid growth in the Christian influence of the Gentile Church in Antioch, which at some point, succeeded Jerusalem as the centre of missionary outreach, was primarily due to the work of Saul of Tarsus.[17] His tripartite cultural world (Jewish, Greek and Roman) equipped him to be the greatest of all the missionaries[18] of his time. Paul's in-depth knowledge of the laws, cultures, religious practices and social life of the Jews, Greeks, and the Romans was quite resourceful for his acceptability and ministry effectiveness in his days. His ministry experience attests to the importance of a good theological education for the African expository preacher.

While itinerant missionary activities by lay African evangelists have had a significant impact on the spread of the gospel in Africa, we believe that this impact would have been far more had they been

---

16. Eckhard Schnabel has produced a handy volume on Paul. See Eckhard J. Schnabel, *Paul the Missionary: Realities, Strategies and Methods* (Downers Grove, Illinois: Inter-Varsity Press, 2008). Paul's much learning plays out quite clearly both in his literary works, sociological connectedness and in the quality of his theological prowess.

17. Bruce Leon Shelley, *Church History in Plain Language* (2nd ed., Nashville, Tennessee: Thomas Nelson Publishers, 1995), 19.

18. W. Ward Gasque, "The Challenge to Faith," in *Introduction to the History of Christianity*, (2nd ed., ed., Tim Dowley, 1990; paperback ed., Minneapolis: Fortress Press, 2002), 57-68. Saul was a Jewish name while Paul was a Roman name. His tripartite world refers to his Jewish, Greek and Roman backgrounds.

properly theologically trained. Even the glaring socio-cultural, anthropological, and religious mistakes that the early Western missionaries to Africa made would have been greatly minimised had they been appropriately trained theologically. Formal theological and socio-anthropological training is still unavoidably necessary for expository preachers in Africa. Proper formal training in theological education gives a solid grounding for authentic expository preaching.

This need for a good theological preparation is particularly crucial today. Many more Africans are getting more educated and exposed to the global community than it was in the days of our African Christian ancestors. Many more growing Christian Africans are also becoming more critical about the simple Sunday school lessons they were taught. They are raising critical questions regarding the approach of the seemingly parochial orthodox missionary presentation of the Bible to Africa. They are also asking more critical questions about the Scriptures and the Christian gospel. Even some, because of their much learning, are philosophically inclined and are, therefore, resistant to the message of the gospel until convincing proofs support it. Worst, the influence of the philosophy and ideology of humanism, liberalism, and feminism on some learned African women and some sympathetic men is not helping matters. These agitators are not only fighting for the correction of gender imbalances in both society and church, but much more, they are raising critical queries on the presence of gender bias in the Scriptures. They are equally raising sentiments regarding clerical ordination that hitherto has long been an exclusive reserve for men. Additionally, they are fighting for recognition as co-equals with their male counterparts and to be granted the same leverage also to occupy leadership positions and assume the headship of the denominational churches as well.

Africa is thus more complicated today. The challenges that are confronting the African continent, particularly, those facing the church, cannot be addressed merely by the simplistic "God said it, I believe it, and that settles it" ideology. Neither can it be effectively addressed by simply defending and maintaining the status quo of denominational traditions or orthodoxy. An informed listener to the preaching of the Scriptures will fault any speaker for begging the question at best, and as someone being parochial at worst, where tangible convincing proofs are lacking. Even Peter conceded this when he said, ". . . always have *your answer ready* for people who ask you the reason for the hope that you have" (1 Pet 3:15 NJB; emphasis is mine); or "Always *be prepared to give an answer* to everyone who asks you to give the reason for the hope that you have" (1 Pet 3:15 NIV; emphasis is mine).

Today, more and more people in the world are clamoring for religious or inter-faith dialogue. We think that this is more needful in Africa because of the way and manner in which different religious ideologies are expressed and vigorously compete for space. How, for instance, are African Traditional Religion, Christianity and Islam to dialogue with one another? On what and which religious platform is this dialogue to start and proceed? Dialogue can be defensive rather than a reasoned negotiation given the African experience so far. A good theological education will help the Christian expositor to successfully *engage* with others in apologetics seeking to persuade them of the truth of the Gospel. A well-informed expositor of the Christian Scriptures, having been properly trained, knows that it is religious engagement, not religious dialogue that appeals to both human reason and conscience. The burden of proof, therefore, depends on such a person to prove the superiority of Christianity over other world religions. A half-baked and ill-prepared preacher is simply unable to achieve this task; theological education, therefore, is thus essential.

Much more, a broad-based theological education equips the expositor of the Scriptures with basic foundational knowledge in the area of church history, biblical doctrines, missiological and anthropological studies, and in biblical and theological studies. It also provides knowledge in the area of biblical hermeneutics, Christian spirituality, relationships between church and state, and dialogue with other faiths through Christian apologetics. It is encouraging to note that some theological institutions in Africa go beyond the foundational biblical-theological courses to offer courses in the area of society and law, principles of rhetoric, social service and human development, and health issues. This broad-based curriculum of theological education will help the learner to integrate theology with sociological realities, so they relate better to society. How can the expository preacher in Africa today become successful at the task without a good grounding in theological education?

SOCIO-ANTHROPOLOGICAL PREPARATION

Expository preaching addresses the human context seeking the positive transformation of human souls as its outcome. The expository preacher needs to have proper comprehension, not only of the spiritual nature of the people to whom he or she is preaching but also of the social context within which to present the message. From a theological point of view, humanity is fallen and is in need of divine grace and forgiveness. Even those who are saved need sustaining grace from God for their daily walk and service. The preacher must thus have the ability and skill to balance the divine Word with the human world in the sermon.

The expository preacher requires some socio-anthropological knowledge because he or she needs to interact with other African cultures. Such knowledge helps in engaging the African cultures with the biblical culture. Lingenfelter and Mayers explain that cross-cultural ministry is something thousands of Christians in ministry will have to learn because it involves tension about time, value judgment, self-worth, over the methodology of crises management, goals, and so on.[19] An adequate understanding of the various elements of the cultures of the African peoples' groups who listen to our sermons will greatly aid the effectiveness and the success of the effort in communicating God's Word to his world.

ETHICAL PREPARATION

Naturally, no one wants to suffer. The human body always wants to enjoy the good life. Unfortunately, the demanding desires of the flesh can make the expository preacher relax what is morally 'right' and 'wrong' according to Scriptures. Today in Africa, some preachers have become peddlers of the divine Word by preaching for personal gain when they preach to impress the audience. The philosophy of the business world is brought into the pulpit for this reason. Aware of this danger, Paul calls the attention of the expository preacher to preach the Word based upon the biblical moral principle of integrity (2 Cor 4:5; Phil 1:15-17; 1 Tim 4:12; 6:11-12). In giving the ministerial instructions to Titus to serve as a guide to him as he oversaw the Cretan churches, Paul drew his attention to the presence of heretics among the congregations who had taught false doctrine for personal gain (Titus 1:10-11). Paul asserts that these heretics are "deceivers" who had ruined ". . . whole households by teaching things they ought not to teach – and that for the sake of dishonest gain" (Tit 1:10 NIV).

---

19. Sherwood G. Lingenfelter and Marvin Keene Mayers, *Ministering Cross-Culturally: An Incarnational Model for Personal Relationships* (Grand Rapids, Michigan: Baker, 1986), 11.

Some pastors and preachers in Africa today no longer value ministerial ethics and integrity. Such self-centred and self-seeking people are only greedy for gain and fail to consider preaching as a noble and an important task. Therefore, they pretend to be working for the benefit of the people while they work for their own benefit. Because of their greed, they are very crafty, manipulative, and can smartly coerce their prey to their advantage. These are people Paul describes as trying to please men to win their approval (Gal 1:10) by perverting the truth through preaching a different gospel (Gal 1:1-9). In the Cretan context, Paul explicitly identifies the heretics as Cretans by quoting what one of their respected 16th century B.C. poet and philosopher, Epimenides, a native of Knossos, had said (v. 12-13a; cf. Acts 17:28). It was common knowledge in Greek literature that to "Cretanize" meant to lie.[20] Such a description would suggest an emphasis on the low reputations of the Cretans generally.[21]

Many pastors and church members in Africa today no longer uphold the moral of the means justifying an action. Anyone who tells an original lie or manipulates some persons or financial documents to their benefits is a hero. The fast-growing lucrative business today in Africa is politics and religion. Quick money and publicity are made through these two means. It is easier to make fast money through religion. Sadly, since most Africans do not take time to reason before they act, many of them believe the lies rather than objective truth. Such people can easily be manipulated by religion. The claim to God's call to the ministry has beclouded the contemporary African climate of ministry; hence, many more Africans are turning into

---

20. Kenneth Barker et al., eds., *The NIV Study Bible: 10th Anniversary Edition* (Grand Rapids, Michigan: Zondervan Publishing House, 1995)1851.

21. A. Duane Litfin, "Titus," in *The Bible Knowledge Commentary: New Testament* (1983; repr., John F. Walvoord and Roy B. Zuck, eds., America: SP Publications, 1988), 763.

preachers and founders of churches and ministries. If one were to ask those who own personal churches in Africa, they would quickly affirm their calling by God to the pastoral and preaching ministry. Only by the fruits of such pastors will one be able to validate the authenticity of such claims (Matt 7:15-23).

Another growing moral trend today in the church in Africa is the lifestyle of competition. Pastors, churches, and so-called ministries are competing in the public space for recognition and membership. Most of them do a lot of unethical and bizarre things to maintain their status. Their speech and actions leave observers asking, are these people true Christians? Have they, in the real sense of the term, been called by God to do ministry? Do they understand the weight of the office which they occupy?

Truly called expository preachers are obliged to uphold biblical standards of morality in life and the ministry. The minister and the preaching of the gospel are under close observation by church members and the society because of their high expectation on the minister. Given this reason, Maxey advises that it is the task of the preacher or minister to bring dignity into the ministry. Their life should make people see what worthiness, nobility, repute, honour, and respect should be in a godly person. It should also inspire awe or reverence, the impressiveness, and the stateliness of the minister. Maxey also notes that although we are living in an age in which respect for the ministry has been largely lost, it is still the task of the preacher to inspire in the minds of the people the dignity due to the gospel of Jesus Christ.[22]

Moral preparation rooted in biblical ethics is not an option for the expositor who is a *minister* of God and the gospel of his Kingdom. Ac-

---

22. I. Parker Maxey, *Ministerial Ethics and Etiquette* (Salem, Ohio: Schmul Publishing Company Inc., 1987; Owerri, Nigeria: World Parish Publications, 1990), 55.

cordingly, Gula says, ". . . a moral ministry must be closely related to experiences of God and convictions about God. God is the ultimate centre of value, the fixed point of reference for the morally right and wrong, the source and goal of all moral striving."[23] Everything is lost where integrity is lacking in the pastoral and preaching ministry of an individual. Everything is lost when the glory, respect, and reverence due to God in the preaching of his Word are lacking in a preacher. However, absolutely nothing is lost when Jesus Christ is the core of expository preaching, and when God and his Word are enthroned in their proper place in human hearts.

We have argued that adequate training of the expository preacher for the African context through good education is inevitable for the preaching ministry. Such training helps to develop deep theological and ethical convictions in the preacher. A person stands their guard only when they know what they stand for. So, how does the trained expository preacher build the expository sermon?

---

23. Richard M. Gula, *Ethics in Pastoral Ministry* (Mahwah, New Jersey: Paulist Press, 1996), 9.

CHAPTER 9

BUILDING THE EXPOSITORY SERMON

Building an expository sermon is like building a house. A house has different parts to it and different stages in its construction as well. These parts are carefully put together at different stages of its construction into a shape described as a house. The process begins from its foundation level to the very last aspect of its finishing. Building the expository sermon is also a process that requires mastery, careful attention, intellectual reflections, and critical questioning. LaRue calls the process a "preparatory rhythm" that differs from preacher to preacher.[1] The art, science and discipline of carrying out this enormous task make the sermon process very critical. This process should not be taken lightly.

SERMON CONSTRUCTION'S BUILDING BLOCKS

The expository sermon should be perceived in the imagery of a human body. The body is what the actual sermon is. It elaborates the sermon idea to convey meaning to the listener. It also puts forward

---

1. Cleophus James LaRue, *I Believe I'll Testify: The Art of African American Preaching* (Louisville, Kentucky: Westminster John Knox Press, 2011), 99-122. LaRue is a professor of homiletics at Princeton Theological Seminary in Princeton County, New Jersey, USA, and a leading scholar on African American preaching.

the proposition of the sermon as its point of concern and then moves on to develop it sequentially to achieve the specific purpose of the sermon. In addition, the body of a sermon includes main points and sub-points that form the outline and that structure the sermon's explanation.[2] These parts are sequentially and logically arranged to achieve proper coordination of its primary segments.

Like the human body, every expository sermon has two parts. These essential parts are the skeleton and the flesh of the sermon. The skeleton can be described as the sermon outline, plan, or structure.[3] It makes meaning only to the preacher while the flesh helps the listener to understand the entire message. The skeleton of a sermon acts like its graphic architectural design like in a physical building plan. The flesh, on the other hand, serves as the sermon's actual building like in the case of a house. The skeleton of the sermon consists of the sermon topic and the major divisions concerning the main points as well as the sub-points where applicable. Unlike the skeleton, the flesh has more parts. It consists of the sermon's explanations of the facts, its argument of various points, and illustrations for clarification. It also consists of the sequential and logical reasoning, persuasive ordering of thoughts and rhetoric, factual support by supplying appropriate data, et cetera. The sermon flesh does not only contain the central theme, dominant thoughts, and basic motivating thrust of the sermon[4], but it develops them in a coherent, cogent, articulate and sequential manner. It acts like a fully developed script.

---

2.   Bryan Chapell, *Christ-Centered Preaching: Redeeming the Expository Sermon* (2nd ed., 2005; repr., Grand Rapids, Michigan: Baker Academic, 2007), 132.

3.   We shall be using the terms sermon skeleton, outline, plan, or structure interchangeably since all these synonyms have the same meaning.

4.   Stephen Olford and David Olford explain that, first, the dominating theme of a sermon is the truth that the text proclaims, that is, the central idea, the big idea, and the unifying element of the sermon. Second, the integrating thoughts are what comes out of the text, expressing what the text says about the dom-

These building blocks of the expository sermon should be well coordinated to be meaningful. Samuel T. Logan, Jr. states that a good and useful sermon is that which is well planned, well focused and precise,

> Among the necessities of good, revived preaching (or, indeed, any other worthwhile endeavour), this must be at the top of the list – proper planning. One must know what he [or she] wishes to accomplish and must plan all he [or she] does with this in mind; otherwise, he [or she] will accomplish nothing. What one hits depends upon the care, the precision with which one aims. . . . a sermon, to be great, to be effective, whether it is long or short, must be focused. . . . The aim must be precise and proper preachers recognise this . . . [5]

Precision and focus keep the sermon within its theme, proposition, basic motivating thrust and its purpose. It helps to keep a good transition from the introduction to the body, transition within the various parts of the body, and transition from the body to the conclusion. Proper structuring of the sermon is very necessary because it helps to achieve a definite order and logical flow of thought. It acts as a road map. Glen C. Knecht says proper sermon structure assists the preacher in no small measure as he or she wields the gift of a tongue of fire energised by the Holy Spirit to effectively communicate God's heart to people in a sermon context.

---

inating theme. Also, third, the motivating thrust is more of the application of the message, because it has to do with the challenge, the call, the appeal, the appropriate cumulative application of the text. See Stephen F. Olford and David Lindsay Olford, Anointed Expository Preaching (Nashville, Tennessee: Broadman & Holman Publishers, 1998), 141-143.

5. Samuel T. Logan Jr., "The Phenomenology of Preaching," in *The Preacher and Preaching: Reviving the Art* (ed., Samuel T. Logan Jr., Phillipsburg, New Jersey: Presbyterian and Reformed Publishing, 1986), 129.

Despite the crucial role of a good sermon structure, some preachers fail to give careful attention to it. One temptation is to ". . . abandon all effort at structure in the interest of the free flow of the fiery tongue . . . [to] let the burning heart simply set forth its message without regard for shape . . . If the preacher feels the subject intensely, is that not after all enough?"[6] Some of such preachers could argue that the apostolic preaching was neither formalised nor technical. In as much as this reasoning has some validity, we have long gone past the apostolic age. We are now in the twenty-first century.

The context of modern society is more complicated than in the time of the apostles. We confront more critical minds than probably in their time. Notably, we face more challenging doctrinal, theological, and ethical issues that are subtly heretical. Such modern context calls for a proper articulation, logical presentation and convincing proofs to substantiate biblical propositions. A good structure helps to address in a sermon doctrinal, theological, or ethical issues without faltering.

GOALS OF GOOD SERMON STRUCTURES

Using a structured format when addressing formal occasions is quite normal. Thus, when addressing family, tribal, and community leaders, or addressing communal social gatherings for official occasions, ceremonies, dances and celebrations, speakers are expected to follow certain structures. In some cases, the address of the community leader during a town hall meeting is re-echoed by his mouthpiece so all can hear what is being said. Similarly, every sermon must proper-

---

6. Glen C. Knecht, "Sermon Structure and Flow," in The Preacher and Preaching: Reviving the Art (ed., Samuel T. Logan, Phillipsburg, New Jersey: Presbyterian and Reformed Publishing, 1986), 275.

ly and adequately follow a good structure. A good sermon structure will achieve many clearly defined goals:

First, a well-structured sermon helps the preacher to achieve a systematic and coherent presentation of thought. The risk of zigzagging through the message as a swerving car is greatly minimised;

Second, a good structure gives the preacher clear direction. It not only helps the preacher be precise, but it also helps to achieve confidence in the pulpit. As Knecht points out, "With a solid organisation of his [or her] material he [she] meets his [her] hearers confidently. He [she] knows where he [she] is to go . . . [as his or her] heart can follow the movement of a good order."[7] A preacher will neither have to scout for what to say nor fail to hit the specific sermon target with a good structure;

Third, a good sermon structure helps the preacher keep to time when preaching. Running out of time is a notorious enemy for preachers. Larsen correctly notes, "One of our great problems here has to do with having enough time."[8] Because "Timing is an important part of preaching,"[9] the preacher is able, with a planned-out sermon structure, to appropriately allocate time to all the parts so that none suffers over-flogging or understating in time. Time allocation regulates how the preacher balances between the sermon speed and the material;

Fourth, considered as ". . . the most important part of the sermon,"[10] a good sermon structure helps the listeners to comprehend the sermon with ease as they follow the progression of thought, the

---

7. Knecht, "Sermon Structure and Flow," 277.

8. David L. Larsen, *The Anatomy of Preaching: Identifying the Issues in Preaching Today* (Grand Rapids, Michigan: Kregel Publications, 1999, and Ibadan, Nigeria: CHRIST AND WE PUBLICATIONS, 2000), 120.

9. Knecht, "Sermon Structure and Flow," 277.

10. Knecht, "Sermon Structure and Flow," 278.

development of the parts, and the sequence of arguments in the message. Digressions are seriously reduced with a good structure;

Fifth, since we have already argued that a good sermon structure achieves order, this, no doubt, earns the respect of the listeners for God; for they would have seen for themselves in the sermon that God is a God of order. "Hearing the logical exposition of God's truth according to sound structure reveals to them a system of doctrine that is orderly and self-consistent";[11] and,

Sixth, a well-structured sermon makes for easy remembrance of the sermon, especially its major divisions, by the audience.

We should point out that although a well-organised sermon structure plays an essential role in the expository sermon, its development is not achieved easily. The task requires hard work, good thinking and careful reflection. As Knecht explains,

> If structure is so worthwhile, we should not be surprised that it is also difficult to achieve. To take what one has gathered from his exegetical, theological, and literary sources, and his personal experiences and mould that material together into one coherent and unified thrust is an arduous task. Such labour requires comparing Scripture with Scripture, choosing what is relevant and what is not, weighing the importance of different aspects of the truth, deciding about the sequence of the ideas, and fashioning the remaining elements into a shape that is suitable for its holy purpose and aim. This requires deep concentration and strenuous effort, and sometimes agony. This is the part of sermon preparation that asks the most of the minister.[12]

It takes discipline, faithfulness, hard work, patience, and endurance to go through the process of arriving at a good sermon struc-

---

11. Knecht, "Sermon Structure and Flow," 279.
12. Knecht, "Sermon Structure and Flow," 279.

ture. The preacher's love for the people and God will help motivate him or her to keep going with the structuring.

BENEFITS OF PROPER SERMON STRUCTURES

The benefits of a properly structured expository sermon can be inexhaustible. Both the preacher and the audience stand to benefit from a sermon that is well thought out, well proposed, and well structured. Some of these benefits are discussed below:

The very first clear benefit of a suitable structure is the achievement of a definite order. Knecht says for no reason whatsoever should the sermon structure be neglected or abandoned. He argues, "Because God is a God of order. He did not create everything all at once, but in sequence. . . . [Since] God is also full of order in what He does[,] We must copy God in this order . . ."[13] A proper sermon structuring helps achieve the logical flow of the thoughts and arguments; the harmonious relatedness and makes the sermon comprehensible and applicable to the listeners.

Maintaining a clear focus in the sermon is another benefit of an excellent sermon structure. According to Baumann,

> A well-organised sermon unfolds in a purposeful fashion.
> . . . An outline will aid both the speaker and the listener. It
> prevents the preacher from rambling. It establishes an order,
> a direction for thought. Omissions, digressions, inconsis-
> tencies, misplaced emphases, and unsupported assertions
> will be sharply reduced. Sermons wander without the safe-
> guard of a well thought out structure.[14]

---

13. Knecht, "Sermon Structure and Flow," 275-6.
14. J. Daniel Baumann, *An Introduction to Contemporary Preaching* (1972; paperback ed., 1988; repr., Grand Rapids, Michigan: Baker Book House, 1990), 149.

A clear structure helps to keep focus and maintain balance in the sermon. It equally helps to filter out unnecessary elements in the sermon.

A good sermon structure functions as a microscope or telescope, or even as a road map to facilitate unity. It helps the preacher to tie the parts together to achieve unity in the whole sermon. Also, a good structure helps the preacher not only to detect gaps within the sermon that need filling but those materials that need weeding out as well. Robinson explains this further,

> An outline. . . . Clarifies in the speaker's eye and mind the relationships between the parts of a sermon. . . . The speaker views his sermon as a whole and thereby heightens his sense of unity. An outline also crystallises the order of ideas so that the listener will be given them in the appropriate sequence. Finally, the preacher recognises the places in the outline requiring additional supporting material to develop his points.[15]

Another significant benefit of a good sermon structure is that it helps the preacher to standardise its grammatical structure. Because the sermon structure functions like someone reading a page in a book, bad grammar is easily detected and corrected. For example, inconsistencies in the way grammatical parts of speech are used, either in the topic or the major and sub-points in the sermon, are easily identified and corrected. The wrong use of tenses as well can be easily detected and corrected with the help of a good structure.

The logic of relationship, good flow, and transitions between the topic and the other parts of the sermon can easily be reasoned out with a good structure.

---

15. Haddon W. Robinson, *Expository Preaching: Principles and Practice* (2nd ed., 2001; repr.; Leicester, England: Inter-Varsity Press, 2004), 128.

STRUCTURING EXPOSITORY SERMONS

Preachers do not all follow the same method of sermon structuring. While some prefer the numbers system (I., II., III.) method of outlining, others prefer the letters system (A., B., C.) method. These numbers and alphabets represent the major points/parts in the structure. Some preachers prefer a combination of both or a 1., 2., and 3., approach. Still, there are those that use what Larue calls the horizontal approach.[16] Here, each section of the sermon is placed in a box, like a PowerPoint presentation, progressing from left to right or from top to bottom. Additionally, some preachers use the mental approach. They preach from memory without notes.

In structuring the sermon, the essential graphic content (the leading sectional ideas to be articulated and defended) should be developed following either the main points only or following both the main points and sub-points progression. Either of these two approaches largely depends first, on the nature of a particular sermon, and second, on the length of the biblical text. The sermon occasion, type of audience, and the time available for a particular sermon will also determine the choice of its structure.

While some expository preachers follow mainly a verse by verse or paragraph by paragraph type of scriptural exposition, others follow the sermonised type of expository preaching. A sermonised type of sermon development synthesises the exegeted material extracted from the biblical text and arranges it in a coherent, sequential order. It structures the sermon following the main guiding thought of the synthesised material.

What follows below are four examples of sermon structuring selected from sermons I have preached. The structure follows the sermonised approach. This list is intended to show how an expository

---

16. LaRue, *I Believe I'll Testify*, 118-122.

sermon structure is developed along the line of a sermonised type. It also demonstrates what the goals and benefits of a structure discussed above are like.

1. Topic: The Marks of the Life that is United with Christ
   Text: Philippians 2:1-4
   Introduction
   A. The Life that is United with Christ Possesses Godly Virtues, vv. 1-2
   B. The Life that is United with Christ Seeks Right Living in Christ, vv. 3-4
   Conclusion

2. Topic: Avoiding the Faulty Foundation of Self-Confidence
   Text: Philippians 3:1-9
   Introduction
   I. The Champions of False Self-Confidence, vv. 1-3
   II. Paul's Former Grounds for Self-Confidence, vv. 4-6
   III. Paul's New Ground for Self-Confidence, vv. 7-9
   Conclusion

3. Topic: Dealing with Heretics in the Church
   Text: Titus 1:10-16
   Introduction
   I. Identifying the Characteristics of the Heretics to Deal with, vv. 10-12, 16
      A. Heretics are Rebels Against the Truth, v. 10
      B. Heretics are Hollow People, v. 10, 16
      C. Heretics are Self-centred People, vv. 11-12
   II. Identifying the Heresies to Deal with, vv. 11, 15-16
   III. Identifying the Methodology with Which to Deal with the Heretics, v. 13
   Conclusion

4. Topic: Proper Investment for Good Dividends
    Text: Matthew 6:19-21
    Introduction
    I.   Caution Against the Misplacement of Investment Priority, v. 19
         A. What the Caution Is
         B. Why the Caution Is Necessary
    II. Counsel for Right Placement of Investment Priority, vv. 20-21
    Conclusion

FLESHING OUT THE SERMON SKELETON

We mentioned earlier that the body of a sermon has both the skeleton and the flesh. When the basic frame (skeleton) of the sermon is carefully crafted or structured, the final procedure in the whole sermon process is fleshing out the skeleton. To *flesh out* the sermon means to give form to the structure so that the sermon makes sense to the listener. Just as in the human body, the flesh of a sermon contains the arteries, veins, tendons, nerves, and so on of the sermon. Robinson says fleshing out the sermon outline is filling in the outline with supporting materials that amplifies, explains, proves, or applies the points to make them understandable and appealing.[17]

Words are used to flesh out a sermon so that the sermon outline takes proper shape, makes sense, and conveys meaning. A sermon skeleton is fleshed by applying the *DEICA* principle, an acronym that stands for Definitions, Explanations, Illustrations, Correlations, and Applications. Christian preaching primarily is meant to communicate God's Word to God's world in its purest form, using a method that is non-technical. The DEICA principle is used in order to achieve simple understanding of the simple truth of the scriptural passage being communicated. The Scriptures are preached to be heard and

---

17. Robinson, *Expository Preaching*, 140.

understood. Most importantly, Christians not only preach to be heard and understood, but they preach in such a manner that an understanding of the biblical message should lead the listener to take definite action in response to the message. Consequently, in preaching, ". . . using questions, constantly applying, carefully illustrating, and repeating keywords and truths all help to keep people thinking along with the preacher as the message unfolds."[18] The use of the *DEICA* principle helps in enhancing a clearer and more meaningful pulpit communication. It also enhances an increased level of biblical literacy, thereby achieving a better response from the pews.

Definition

People who stand in the pulpit to preach are there to represent God by heralding his Word and communicating a special message from him. To communicate the truth of divine revelation, therefore, means being clear and straightforward. Bullock re-echoes the point,

> To attempt to communicate is to risk being misunderstood. Thus, one of the challenges of human relationships is to transfer our thoughts and concepts to one another accurately and minimise to every possible degree the risk of misinterpretation. Oral language has the advantage of intonation, emotion, facial expressions, and physical gestures. . . . This is especially serious when the [preacher] speaks for the Creator and Redeemer of the world, and the [listener] needs desperately to hear the voice of God accurately.[19]

In order to ensure the listener properly understands the sermon's message, some clear word definitions need to be made. As Robinson

---

18. Olford and Olford, *Anointed Expository*, 194.

19. C. Hassell Bullock, "Introduction: Interpreting the Bible," in *The Literature and Meaning of Scripture* (eds., Morris A. Inch and C. Hassell Bullock, Grand Rapids, Michigan: Baker Book House, 1981), 11.

puts it, "A definition establishes limits. It sets down what must be included and excluded by a term or statement."[20] When preaching, specific keywords, terms, concepts, phrases, and so on are used in an attempt to make the point of the sermon clearer. These are to be appropriately defined, first, within their original contexts, and then its specific usage within the context of the sermon if a slightly different meaning is intended. The reason for this is so that the audience can be able to follow with ease the development and progression of thought and the arguments advanced in defence of the point of the sermon. Precise definitions are critical, as Baumann says, "Definition is one means of clarifying ideas, words, or concepts that are fuzzy, unknown, or misunderstood."[21]Yet, "Definitions given in sermons need to be accurate but also clear and concise. This means we usually cannot provide a definition that will encompass every nuance of meaning to all people in all places. We are merely trying to define terms in such a way that they make sense for this sermon."[22]

Here is a warning to all preachers, never assume that the audience is already familiar with the key words, terms, and so on that are being used in the sermon. Clear communication of God's truth requires that words and connotations used by a preacher are correctly and clearly defined to achieve clarity of their usage, of their expression, and their specific purpose. For instance, if the preacher is talking about the subject of forgiveness in the sermon, he or she should first and foremost, clearly define the boundary regarding whether the reference is to divine or human forgiveness. Also, it should be evident in the preacher's mind what nuance of the word is in use, whether it is in its noun, verb, or adjectival form. Lastly,

---

20. Robinson, *Expository Preaching*, 142.

21. Baumann, *An Introduction to Contemporary Preaching*, 152.

22. Chapell, *Christ-Centered Preaching*, 123.

the preacher then makes a correct and precise definition of the word along with its usage within the context of the sermon.

Definitions help at avoiding jargons and ambiguity, thereby reducing the risk of confusion on the part of the listener. Preachers rather than confuse, and in some cases, even offend the listeners when they want to impress them by using theological, biblical or our professional jargons. Preaching is not meant to impress the audience but rather to *express* the mind of God to the listener. From personal experience, when I use a word or words in any of the biblical languages, I am always being careful not to intimidate the audience by saying the 'Hebrew or Greek' word. I rather prefer to say, 'in the original language in which the Bible was written,' the word used as translated as so and so means this.

Explanation

Luke narrates the encounter that Philip, the evangelist, had with the Ethiopian eunuch on his way returning from Jerusalem. The eunuch was reading a passage from the Book of Prophet Isaiah. When Philip explained to the Ethiopian eunuch what the Isaiah text meant, he had a better understanding of the text. Such understanding led to his conversion and baptism (Acts 8:27-38).

Accurate explanation in expository preaching achieves good understanding on the part of the listener. This is significant because explanation attempts to respond to an aspect of the question of meaning and workability of the message in a sermon. It is an attempt to clarify what may be fuzzy to the listener or what may be a misrepresentation of the message if not clearly explained.

As mentioned earlier, all words, terms, concepts and phrases, or even proverbs have meanings in their original contexts. Even their nuances convey significant meaning only within the context of their usage. The preacher needs to clearly explain the use of any terms, words, or even general statements if the meaning is not familiar to the audience, or when they are used slightly different from their original meaning in the sermon.

In our example of the word 'forgiveness,' the preacher should, well ahead of the presentation of the sermon, raise these definitive questions to help explain the meaning of the word: which forgiveness is in view here, divine or human? How does God forgive and how do humans forgive? What are the motivating factors behind divine forgiveness and human forgiveness? What are the biblical and theological, even ethical and sociological implications of human forgiveness when rightly used?

Besides the above, the basic idea or leading thrust of the biblical text used for the sermon requires explanation. When a preacher declares that the 'Bible says,' he or she should go beyond this point to explain what it means. We return to the example of Evangelist Philip to clarify the point (Acts 8:26-39). Philip gave a straightforward, clear explanation of what the Isaiah text that the Ethiopian eunuch had been reading meant. The effect of his explaining the text was obvious – it led to belief and the conversion of the eunuch. It is quite doubtful if the Ethiopian eunuch would have had a transformation of life and asked for water baptism if Philip's explanation of the Scripture was fuzzy and ambiguous.

A sermon explanation is done in a number of ways. The principle of comparison and contrast can be used to explain a particular point in the sermon. Here, the preacher either compares what is already known to the audience with what is being explained or uses some available examples from the audience's environment to contrast with the point being made. For example, in Africa, there are myriads of complex human issues and challenges that can be drawn upon and used comparatively to explain certain points in a sermon.

Similarly, as we interact with our environment as well as with other people in our communities, we learn a lot about ecology and human psychology as well as sociology. These lessons are ready explanatory materials.

Also, a descriptive approach can be used to explain the text. Chapell says, "With this form of explanation, a preacher describes a word, a scene, a character, or a situation in such a way that listeners are better able to understand a text"[23] and a sermon. Let us illustrate the point here. In Africa, we farm and grow various kinds of crops. We also have mountains, caves, rocks, hills, valleys, forests, streams, rivers, creeks, and so on. Also, two primary seasons are quite noticeable in Africa – dry and rainy seasons (that is, planting and harvest/resting seasons). These are good reservoirs for a descriptive analysis that the preacher can draw upon when explaining a sermon point.

Again, the use of object lessons or practical demonstration to explain a point in a sermon can also be effectively employed. As Robinson suggests, it is better to define too many terms than too few[24] since the aim of explanation is clarity so that the audience achieves a proper understanding of the point being made. When object lessons or practical demonstrations are masterfully used in the process of explanation, meaning and understanding are grasped with ease and with better clarity.

Illustration

Sermon illustrations have their place in the sermon and should not be neglected. Janvier says of the roles of illustrations, "They can explain something, give a bridge from the world of the Bible to today, give a mental breather to the listener, help people identify with the

---

23. Chapell, *Christ-Centered Preaching*, 123.
24. Robinson, *Expository Preaching*, 143.

point, help to maintain interest in the message, [and] catch the attention of the listener."[25] Illustrations are used in preaching to clarify a particular point. Here, ideas, historical events, life issues that confront people, human behaviour and attitudes, dramatic actions that play out in human society, et cetera, can be used to illustrate a point. Richard stresses its importance when he says, "The impact of a sermon is always connected to the illustrations in it [because] . . . They take the listener from the known to the unknown."[26] Relevant and adequate illustrations clarify in the listener's mind what is being said and they quickly drive home the point in the message.

A number of sources can be used to draw out good illustrations for sermons. For example, events and human experiences, quotes from books, speeches, and biographies, and stories and proverbs are suitable materials. Richard says the only one way to get illustrations is to observe life – use eyes to see, ears to hear, and the heart to understand life.[27] Illustrations should not be done indiscriminately but honestly. For example, stories play a very vital part of life in Africa. They are used to teach morals to the younger generations in every age, to achieve cognitive development in children, and to inculcate wisdom in the mind as well. However, the traditional understanding within most Christian congregations is that stories are just what they are, 'stories'; they do not have to be true. Such perception stands as a negative implication in using stories for sermon illustrations.

---

25. George Evans Janvier, *Biblical Preaching in Africa: A Textbook for Christian Preachers* (Bukuru, Nigeria: Africa Christian Textbooks, 2002), 106.

26. Ramesh Richard, *Scripture Sculpture: A Do-It-Yourself Manual for Biblical Preaching* (1995; repr., Grand Rapids, Michigan: Baker Books, 1997), 125. He notes that the purpose of illustrations is to illustrate and add light to the message. He cautions that they are not meant to lengthen or entertain, but they are instead meant to help the audience understand the content or the claim of what is being said.

27. Ramesh, 127.

African Christians who regularly attend worship services and listen to sermons know preachers for telling stories when preaching. Some listeners may not, therefore, take a preacher seriously when he or she illustrates a sermon with a story. What may likely be going through the mind of such listeners is the perceived conclusion that the story is not true; it is just a story. On this point, the credibility of the sermon is likely to be watered down and its intended message may, therefore, be dismissed.

To avoid this danger, it is helpful to let an audience discriminate between a true and a fake story when either is used. When using a story that is created by the preacher for illustration, it should be masterfully used, so it drives home the point of the message into the listener's heart. In showing his support, Chapell states,

> An account does not have to be real or current, but a preacher must tell it in such a way that listeners can identify with the experience. A preacher tells the what, when, where and why of an occurrence to give listeners personal access to the occasion. Each listener is enabled to see, feel, taste, or smell features of the event as though he or she were involved in the unfolding account.[28]

A preacher's mastery of a story, real life or made up, is crucial so that its intended effect is not missed in the sermon.

Correlation

The basic idea behind the concept of correlation in a sermon situation is scriptural cross-referencing. The whole Bible explains itself and throws much light on its meaning and message. Students of biblical hermeneutics insist that Scripture interprets Scripture. Vines and Shaddix say when the Scripture is allowed to interpret itself, it

---

28. Chapell, *Christ-Centered Preaching*, 176.

enables the preacher to discover what other passages of Scripture say about the subjects being discussed in the sermon passage.[29] This means an appropriate correlation helps the preacher to show from other passages the synergy of the truths being expressed to clarify the point of the sermon.

Correlating Scripture with Scripture in a sermon helps listeners to see the inherent connecting relationship of the Word of God. This will earn the confidence of the listeners in the credibility and power of the inspired Word. Correlation also reveals the unity of the divine thoughts as variously expressed in Scriptural passages. It equally strengthens the development of the thoughts and the arguments of the sermon. One significant effect of adequate and appropriate scriptural correlation is this – it deepens biblical literary and earns more profound respect for God as well as the efficacy of his Word. This will increase the trust of the listener in the credibility and validity of the Christian faith.

In as much as correlation is essential in a sermon, a good knowledge of hermeneutics is required so that various parts of the Scriptures are not taken out of their original contexts and misapplied. Interpreting Scriptures out of their original context and meaning is considered as proof-texting, and proof-texting is not only gross hermeneutical misconduct that breeds terrible theology, but it cultivates dangerous heresies and bad theology for the church. While some preachers in Africa commit this error because of their ignorance of what 'true-text' and 'proof-text' are, some who know what is right intentionally proof-text in order to achieve certain personal gains. This act against Scriptures is equated to a treasonable offence. James cautions, "Not many of you should presume to be teachers, my

---

29. Jerry Vines and Jim Shaddix, *Power in the Pulpit: How to Prepare and Deliver Expository Sermons* (Chicago, Illinois: Moody Press, 1999), 115.

brothers, because you know that we who teach will be judged more strictly" (James 3:1 NIV). Peter corroborates this when he says, "For it is time for judgment to begin with the family of God; and if it begins with us, what will the outcome be for those who do not obey the gospel of God?'" (1 Pet 4:17 NIV).

Application

The maxim that states, "A fool at forty is a fool for life" is critical for human living. The point here is that an adult who fails to learn lessons from the events and the mistakes of life may never learn. The primary goal of preaching the Scriptures is that the listeners learn and apply lessons from them. Here, the sermon application is crucial to the preaching effort. It tells individual listeners that this sermon is for them and that its message is relevant for their lives. As Robinson says, "While it is essential that you explain the truth of a passage, your task is not finished until you relate that passage to the experience of your hearers."[30] Application plants the value of "God's Word to the lives of contemporary listeners" as Jesus himself demonstrated: "He took parables, laid them alongside the issues of life faced by the people, and made practical application"[31] from them to his listeners.

Truths from the text are to be applied to the context of the audience. It is a good application that makes the message meaningful, forceful and personal, requiring definite action on the part of the individual listener. The focus of the application is on achieving the purpose and goal of the sermon. Application answers the "So what?", "What difference does it make?", "How does it concern me?", also, "What do you want me to do?" questions raised in the mind of listen-

---

30. Robinson, *Expository Preaching*, 86.
31. Vines and Shaddix, *Power in the Pulpit*, 20.

ers about a sermon. A good application wrenches the heart and turns on the light so that hearers could see themselves as God sees them[32] (Acts 2:12-41; Acts 6:8-7:60).

Failure to apply a sermon robs the listener of something very fundamental. Preaching is not merely to pass on information but to effect transformation. So, if lives will be transformed by the preaching of the Word, truths from it must be personally directed and applied. Effective sermon delivery requires persuasion on the part of the listener to make the message personal. Preachers should avoid what Stanley observes, "Much preaching today leaves people with the feeling, 'So what?' They listen to a sermon but go away without being persuaded to do anything about what they have heard."[33]

The sermon application can take different forms depending on the purpose of the sermon and the life situation of the particular audience. It can take the form of an exhortation, encouragement, a sharp rebuke, an educating process by way of information, a direction by way of an imperative, a challenge to action as was the case in Joshua's speech to Israel (Josh 24:14-15), et cetera. Preachers need to gain an adequate understanding of both the biblical and contemporary human contexts to be able to appropriately apply the truths of God's inspired Word to his impaired world. The sermon application will become ineffectual and meaningless if the real-life situations of the listeners are not clearly understood and entered into by the preacher during the sermon. Such a situation will be like, for example, serving a Nigerian from the South-East with spaghetti or pizza while what the person needs for food is *gari* or *fufu* — or serving a Liberian with *tuwo* while what the person needs for food is rice.

---

32. Vines and Shaddix, *Power in the Pulpit*, 21.

33. Charles F. Stanley's forward to the book, *A Guide to Effective Sermon Delivery* by Jerry Vines (Moody, Chicago: Moody Bible Institute, 1986), vii.

Unavoidably, a good sermon structure drives the sermon to a specific direction so the purpose of preaching is achieved. But a good structure to a sermon thrives on a well-structured topic or the guiding thrust of it. We examine how a good topic for a sermon is "birthed" in the next chapter.

CHAPTER 10

BIRTHING THE EXPOSITORY SERMON

Automobile companies or car plant factories do not just produce cars. They first design a concept car incorporating various ideas to explore about its design, type of engine, shape, and other necessary components. Only once they have tested their concepts will they proceed to building a car. In the same way, sermon topics are born. Developing a fitting topic for an expository sermon also follows a similar process like building a car. It is carefully thought through so that the topic gives shape to the entire sermon.

A sermon topic has to be carefully developed because of the function it plays in the sermon. In some parts of old Africa, just as it was the case in most ancient cities of the world, villages and communities were heavily guarded for security purposes. Each village and community had both major and minor roads that led into them. The major roads in the African villages led into some key places such as the house, market square, cultural centre, stream or river, et cetera. However, minor roads lead mostly to the various locations of farmlands.

The sermon topic functions as the primary access road that leads into a village or a community. It is the main central leading idea and focus of the sermon. It is the controlling theme of the entire preaching. The topic serves as the main grid that holds the different components of the sermon together, and as the main thrust upon which the whole sermon hangs. It is what Robinson calls the big idea,[1] what Chapell calls the theme or the main subject,[2] and what Vines and Shaddix call the title.[3] Also, the topic is what Olford and Olford describe as the unifying element of the sermon,[4] that is, the dominating and permeating truth[5] of the message. Furthermore, the sermon topic is the main thread that weaves together all the critical thoughts and words in the sermon into one coherent whole. It is the main focus and rallying point of the sermon discourse. Like a good book, the sermon topic is the name tag or the label given to the main sermon discourse.

When a sermon fails to have a clear topic, the entire sermon will be like a person embarking on a journey without a definite destination in mind. Alternatively, let us put it another way. The primary reason why a nation has an organised army is to protect the territorial integrity of the state. When there is an enemy encroachment, the army is expected to first, identify the enemy, its nature and its military might; and second, to plan its strategy of counterattack when its commander-in-chief gives the order. Similarly, a sermon without a clearly stated topic is like an army launching an attack on no specific enemy and without a clearly defined strategy and rules of engagement.

---

1. Haddon W. Robinson, *Expository Preaching: Principles and Practice* (2nd ed., 2001; repr., Leicester, England: Inter-Varsity Press, 2004), 33.

2. Bryan Chapell, *Christ-Centered Preaching: Redeeming the Expository Sermon* (2nd ed., 2005; repr., Grand Rapids, Michigan: Baker Academic, 2007), 129.

3. Jerry Vines and Jim Shaddix, *Power in the Pulpit: How to Prepare and Deliver Expository Sermons* (Chicago, Illinois: Moody Press, 1999), 140-42.

4. Stephen F. Olford and David Lindsay Olford, *Anointed Expository Preaching* (Nashville, Tennessee: Broadman & Holman Publishers, 1998), 141.

5. Olford and Olford, *ibid,* 143.

These analogies necessitate our asking the lead question of how to choose a sermon topic on which to preach. One of the principal questions leading to the choice of the sermon topic should concern a specific aspect of God's revelation. This is crucial because every sermon, at least from an evangelical perspective, must be biblically and theologically centred and Christologically and missiologically oriented. Christ is the centre of the Scriptures, and as a religious text, every part of it has an emerging theology. Another leading question that would help to determine the sermon topic would be to identify what aspect of the human condition the sermon should address. This also is critical as every sermon needs to be relevant to those listening. A centreless and focusless sermon is both goalless and aimless by its orientation. Every sermon is preached to achieve a specific purpose.

DEFINING THE SERMON'S PURPOSE

When we were growing up as children in our African village setting, we used to get out of bed very early at about 5:00 am to go to the farm. The grass grew long during the rainy season and covered the footpaths that led to the fields. The dew would also settle on the grass overnight. The footpaths were also quite slippery in the morning hours as algae grew on them. Because of the dew, we did not like going to the farm early in the morning, yet, we were always forced to go. Going to the farm quite early was a great discomfort to us. The purpose for such discomfort was part of our training so we could become responsible and industrious citizens when we grew into adulthood.

Similarly, every sermon must have a definite controlling purpose. Before choosing an appropriate topic from a given text for the sermon, the expositor must first define the sermon's statement of purpose. The preacher should ask the question, "Why am I preaching this sermon?" or "What do I hope to achieve at the end?" Robinson states, "No matter how brilliant or biblical a sermon is, without a definite purpose it is not worth preaching."[6] The purpose of the sermon is the expected transforming effect on the life of the listener. Whereas the big sermon idea states the truth of the particular part of the Scriptures to preach on, the purpose defines what that truth should accomplish in the sermon.[7]

Let me illustrate. Educational psychology requires that a teacher develops aims and objectives for every lesson to be taught in order to achieve an effective classroom instruction. Such aims and objectives must be those that are realistic: explicitly stated to avoid ambiguity, specific to a clear target; measurable regarding class evaluation and achievable within the class timeframe. This explains why instructional technology is used in addition to instructional materials to facilitate the teaching-learning experience. These materials make the transfer of knowledge easily understandable in the teaching-learning process. Good educational aims and objectives determine the steps to be followed by the teacher in the instruction process; they maintain a clear focus during the instructional session; and lastly, they help in the final evaluation of the learners at the end of the lesson.

The sermon's purpose functions in a similar way. It is the controlling question on the mind of the preacher right from the sermon preparation to the sermon presentation. The purpose helps to guide what material to include or exclude from the sermon. It also regulates what to say during the sermon presentation. Still, the purpose

---

6. Robinson, *Expository Preaching*, 107.

7. This idea is a paraphrase from what Haddon W. Robinson said, 108.

enables the preacher to identify where in the sermon to make specific emphases and relevant applications as well.

In evangelical theology, it is believed that each inspired human author of the Bible had one principal meaning in mind at the time their biblical material was written. That original intention must always be the interpretive grid or cardinal guiding rule. Hence, a good guide to the expository preacher in determining the purpose of any sermon is to first determine the biblical author's original intention and purpose for writing. The true meaning is situated within the ancient text, not in the preacher's contemporary mental assumption. As the preacher prepares the sermon, then, he or she should first find out from the sermon text the situation addressed in the text, the author's purpose for addressing it, why the biblical author made a particular statement, and what he intended to achieve in his original audience.

When we read the biblical text within its ancient interpretive frame, we discover that several things play out in it requiring of us to seek to discover the intentionality of the author for their inclusion in the text. Our careful observation of a text in search of the purpose for a sermon ultimately forces us to ask,

> Why are these concerns addressed? What caused this account, these facts, or the recording of these ideas? What was the intent of the author? For what purpose did the Holy Spirit include these words in Scripture? Such questions force us to exegete the cause of a passage as well as its intents and to connect both to the lives of the people God calls us to shepherd with his truth. Until we have determined a passage's purpose, we are not ready to preach its truths, even if we know many facts about the text.[8]

---

8.   Chapell, *Christ-Centered Preaching*, 48-49.

These questions guide the expositor towards determining what the sermon purpose statement is to be like.

DRAWING UP THE SERMON TOPIC

Choosing a topic for a sermon largely depends on the sermon type, nature and purpose. For instance, in a predominantly expository sermon that aims to educate, its nature and purpose are ". . . designed for the study of the specific details, context, and development of a biblical passage in order to encourage and enable listeners to love God and to help them understand how to apply the truths of his Word to their lives."[9] Such a sermon nature and purpose will regulate the topic.

Also, a careful study of a biblical passage leads to the choice of the sermon topic. When the text for a particular sermon is determined, it should be studied carefully and devotionally to select the dominant theme. A sermon idea or topic from a particular text may well be located in a simple statement, a keyword, a recurring phrase or word, or from the immediate or broader context of the biblical passage. Very rarely will the sermon occasion determine the topic in real scriptural exposition; only in a topical sermon is this possible.

Again, a particular concern on the heart of the preacher, what is called the burden of the sermon, may also serve as a guide to birthing the sermon topic. As a student of homiletics, the preacher should always be a student of his or her society and historical events. Every society has certain concerns that are political, economic, moral and health in nature, or that are social, ecological and legal. Some of such concerns also are religious and educational in nature. A discerning preacher will discover a sermon topic from the topical issues from the society within which he or she lives. The many human concerns

---

9.　Chapell, *Christ-Centered Preaching*, 131.

in contemporary society are sufficient issues to be addressed in sermons by the preacher. Except in the case where the preacher has eyes but cannot see, has ears but cannot hear, and has a mind but cannot think; otherwise, there are, for instance, so many family issues, students' issues, employers-employees' moral issues, acts of unfairness and injustice, and so on begging for attention in society.

Furthermore, in the case of resident ministers, current needs within the congregation or parishioners may well inform the choice of sermon topics. People who walk into the sanctuary every Sunday are real human persons who have real human needs. These needs must be identified and addressed from the pulpit. Many people today are seeking tangible and lasting solutions to their real human problems or challenges in life. They are also searching for correct answers to their real human questions. The solutions to such life-threatening issues are found in the Bible, and the better guide who is looked upon to show how the Bible answers personal questions is the expository preacher. In this case, a sheep-centred shepherd will never lack what area of human needs to preach on.

STRUCTURING THE SERMON TOPIC

When an idea is identified for a sermon, how can it be structured? In my small village, children are tutored on how to create straight ridges when farming using the big hoe. During such tutelage, they are guided on how to place the legs in the furrow, not on the ridge being made, so the ridge is not tampered with. When a farmer is not careful to use expertise in making straight ridges, some will become short and get hooked to the straight ones. Such type of ridge is called *tud* in my village, that is, an abnormal, crooked, incomplete and imperfect ridge. All ploughed ridges are expected to be in straight lines to demonstrate the farmer's excellence and expertise.

As a farmer in an African village, to be able to come up with the topical idea of a sermon is one thing, but to make the topic clear, reasonable and relevant to that idea, and achievable in the sermon is entirely another. Structuring the sermon topic refers to the way and manner in which it is stated, captured, or worded. Let me use the imagery of driving a car to discuss how to structure the sermon topic. People who drive on the highways will undoubtedly come across different road signs. These signs guide them on their journey as they drive along. One of the benefits of road signs is to help users avoid accidents. Like traffic signs, certain guiding principles serve as benchmarks[10] to assist the preacher in arriving at an excellent and well-stated sermon topic.

First, the topic should be structured around a single biblical truth or idea, that is, it embodies a single, all-encompassing concept.[11] A topic that has multiple ideas gives no specific focus and stands the risk of confusing the listener. Olford and Olford agree no less when they say, "Multiple titles, multiple subtitles, multiple subjects and issues to be covered can confuse or blur the focus of the message."[12] The preacher needs the professional expertise and discipline to address only one subject at a time in a sermon. After all a preacher represents God in the pulpit, and is expected to be a good communicator of the divine Word.

Second, the topic of a sermon should capture both its subject and complement. The subject states the big sermon idea to be discussed, but the complement states what is to be said about the big idea. For example, the idea of pain is a subject, but what about pain is a question that begs for its complement. Let me borrow from Robinson. He says the complement answers the stated or implied question of the

---

10. Vines and Shaddix, *Power in the Pulpit*, 141.

11. Robinson, *Expository Preaching*, 36.

12. Olford and Olford, *Anointed Expository Preaching*, 192.

subject and explains with these examples: "If I say that my subject is 'the importance of faith', the implied question is, 'What is the importance of faith?' Also, 'The people that God justifies…' forms a subject because it answers the question, 'What am I talking about?' However, the unstated question is, 'Who are the people God justifies?'"[13] Just as it is the case with the propositional and prepositional statements of a sermon, also, the preacher is to succinctly state what he or she is to say in the sermon and what is to be said about the subject.

In this connection, then, a single word that may capture an idea does not suffice to be a sermon topic. For example, words such as discipleship, witnessing, worship, grief, love, forgiveness, giving, temptation, godliness and righteousness are too vague to qualify for a good sermon topic. The ideas in them for a sermon must be carefully and clearly stated. When a preacher stands in the pulpit and announces that he or she is speaking on the subject of discipleship, this is quite okay. However, this statement cannot be the topic for the sermon. When a listener hears such statement, the natural question that comes to mind will be, 'What about discipleship?' 'What aspect of discipleship is the preacher addressing?' 'What is the sermon going to say about it?'

Let me explain the point further. Structuring the sermon topic is similar to a research topic in academic work. Before approval is given for any research to be carried out, the idea/topic has to be clearly stated. In research, the problem statement says what the concern of the investigation is, and the purpose states what is to be done about it and why. The subject and complement of the topical idea in a sermon both function as what the research problem and the research purpose are in a thesis. For instance, if I were to preach from Mat-

---

13. Robinson, *Expository Preaching*, 41.

thew 8:23-27, I would probably title it "Going through the Storms." "Storms" is my subject and "Going through it" is my complement.

Third, the topic of a sermon must be clearly stated to avoid ambiguity. Words are to be carefully chosen and appropriately used in the central theme of the sermon. This calls for discernment and economy in the choice and use of words in the topic. Olford and Olfrod caution preachers not to misuse words or to waste words when they advise preachers to "Watch out for general words, vague expressions, and dull or technical terms that simply do not clarify or communicate"[14] the key idea of the sermon. This is critical. The caution about clarity begins from the structuring of the topic and weaves through the different major and minor parts, that is, the main points and sub-points, of the sermon. I once preached from Philippians 2:1-4 and titled it, "The Marks of the Life that Is United with Christ." This topic is specific to what characterises the life of a Christian. *Clarity* is key to every sermon presentation. As such, the sermon topic must be clearly stated and appropriately worded; the introduction must be clearly stated; the various parts within the body of the sermon must be clearly organised, and the sermon must be clearly and poignantly concluded.

Fourth, the sermon topic should achieve unity by tying all the parts of the sermon together. The controlling idea in the topic should weave through the sermon's main points as well as the sub-points. The topic should tie together all parts of the sermon as one big whole to be given to the listener like a plate of food. Unity acts as a distinct thread that holds the sermon together: the primary idea, or theme, "glues the message together" to make its features stick in a listener's mind.[15] When clarity and unity are missing in the sermon topic, it

---

14. Olford and Olford, *Anointed Expository Preaching*, 194.
15. Chapell, *Christ-Centered Preaching*, 44.

will not only affect the development of the main and sub-points of the sermon, but it will particularly lead to a subversive disconnect in the mind of the listener. Here is an example:

Text: 1 Timothy 2:9-10
Topic: Preach the Word by Your Lifestyle
  a. Let Your Outward Appearance Preach the Word, v. 9
  b. Let Your Good Deeds Preach the Word, v. 10

You see, the controlling idea "Preach the Word" weaves through the significant parts of the sermon.

Fifth, the sermon topic must specifically direct attention to a definite achievable purpose in the lives of its listeners. Right at the beginning of each sermon, and given that the sermon is focused on the people who are listening to it, the preacher needs to explain what he or she intends to achieve. People are the target of the message in every sermon; therefore, it should address a particular need in the lives of its listeners. While preachers should always stay with the biblical text in preaching, they should not also do so "without considering the spiritual burden of the text for real people in the daily struggles of life."[16] Sometimes, a preacher can easily get excited with a sermon which has no discernible effect on the listener whom the preacher expected to share in his excitement. Preachers should always be conscious of the listeners' participation in the sermon subject, so their real needs in their real-life situations are addressed.

Sixth, the sermon topic should be brief and easily remembered. It should be precise and definite because a good sermon topic should be easy to remember. The topic should be carefully and simply worded; it should capture the full thought of the sermon; it should be well phrased out, and it should be made simple and without any techni-

---

16. Chapell, *Christ-Centered Preaching*, 48.

cal words or phrases. However, despite the attempt at brevity, the topic should neither be too brief and thus not capture the complete idea of the sermon nor too long to capture more than the one main idea to be addressed. I once preached a sermon from Philippians 1:12-18 and titled it, "Good Food Out of a Broken Clay Pot." I used the phrase "Clay Pot" intentionally because of what I was going to say in the sermon. This topic, I hope, is simple and brief enough for the listeners to remember. I preached yet another sermon from Matthew 6:19-21 under the topic, "Proper Investment for Proper Dividends." These examples are to demonstrate the emphasis I have laid on the quality of simplicity and brevity in a sermon topic.

Seventh, the sermon topic is to be structured by adequate and appropriate choice of words. Words can be quite misleading if improperly used. Avoid using words in the sermon topic that say what you do not intend to say, or that mean what is not in the biblical text. As one who lectures in a theological institution, I have always told my students, particularly those that write theses with me, to use a very good English dictionary next to their Bible whenever they write. Words are used in various forms and ways to convey meaning within specific contexts. Words in almost every language have both synonyms and antonyms. This is one key reason why most words have nuances (shades of meanings) and cognates (relationships) as well.

THE FORMS OF A SERMON TOPIC

During my secondary/high school days, my English teacher taught me various forms of letter writing. Like a letter, sermon topics take different forms. A topic can be a phrase that conveys a complete thought or a complete statement that conveys the sermon idea. For example, imperative, interrogative, and declarative statements are used to fashion out sermon topics. Vines and Shaddix explain that,

"... a statement that emphasises an action or command that the sermon will put forth" is imperative; "... a probing question, which the sermon promises to address", is interrogative; and "... a statement of claim, which the sermon proposes to support", is declarative.[17]

Also, a sermon topic can also be structured following explanatory, implicatory, directory, and anticipatory statements. An explanatory statement in a sermon topic tells how the sermon works by a clear response to the question "how? An "implicatory" or implicative statement of a sermon's topic tells the effect(s) by responding to the "then what?" question. Also, a "directory" statement of the title of a sermon supplies guiding principles as it answers the "where?" question. Again, an "anticipatory" statement of a sermon topic has its focus on time as it answers the "when?" question of the sermon. These forms are some suggested guides on how to choose and frame a good sermon topic. We have chosen to give space to them because of their crucial role in the sermon. One among the areas of measuring and evaluating the professional expertise and competence of a preacher is in the area of the sermon topic.

Word order and form in a topic are critical. I have always told and reminded my students in the homiletics class that every topic must have at least a keyword and a key phrase. Also, it should have a noun, verb and adjective as the case may be. Such keyword(s) and phrases take the lead in the whole message as it weaves through the development of the whole sermon. Such components should reflect in all the main and sub-points of the sermon. These should be consistently repeated during the sermon presentation for emphasis and for maintaining focus.

A good topic for a sermon that also has a good structure enhances the positive listening pleasure for the listeners. Yet, a good topic is

---

17. Vines and Shaddix, *Power in the Pulpit*, 142.

only a starting point in the sermon process. The next question would then be, how do I begin the sermon? The next chapter explains how.

CHAPTER 11

IGNITING THE EXPOSITORY SERMON

When I was learning how to drive a car, I understood that there is a difference between cranking and igniting the engine of a car. To 'crank' the ignition is to start the car partially, so only the light shows on the dashboard. However, to 'ignite' the engine of a car is to start or turn on the engine so that it can run before driving it. Some older automobiles cannot efficiently move unless they are first ignited and run for some minutes before driving them. Igniting a car is preparing to drive it over a short or long distance. Like igniting the engine of a car before driving it, an expository sermon also requires igniting. This is called the sermon introduction.

In any good literary work, the introduction sets the pace and tone, because it tells the reader what to expect in the work. This principle also applies to preaching. Every sermon must be appropriately introduced. The sermon introduction should be understood both in its general and specific senses. The general introduction consists of the first few statements made by the preacher. For example, the preliminaries of a sermon cover materials such as the greetings and acknowledgements, announcing and reading of the text,[1] and stating

---

1. Chapell identifies three types of attitudes towards the Bible in the audience as soon as the preacher announces the text to be read. They are those who are eager to read, those who are scared to read, and those calloused to reading it. See Bryan Chapell, *Christ-Centered Preaching* (2nd ed., 2005; repr., Grand Rap-

the topic as well. All these form part of the general introduction to the sermon. An audience that is new to a preacher familiarises itself with the preacher during the general introduction. Robinson notes,

> During the introduction an audience gains impressions of you, the speaker, that often determine whether or not they will accept what you say. If you appear nervous, hostile, or unprepared, they are inclined to reject you. If you seem alert and friendly, they decide you are an able person with a positive attitude toward yourself and your listeners.[2]

However, the specific introduction to a particular sermon directs the attention of the audience to focus on the main idea of that particular sermon. When you introduce the audience to the subject or central idea of your sermon, it sets the pace for the entire message. The specific introduction "should lead the people right to the text, the truth, and the theme of the message."[3]

An introduction serves as the gateway to the sermon by opening the door to it. Such an open door informs the listeners, as they walk

---

ids, Michigan: Baker Book House, 2007), 250. The preacher, therefore, must be careful in managing these categories of people in the audience by the way and manner in which he or she announces and reads the biblical text. If the preacher does it haphazardly, he or she stands the risk of losing the scared and the calloused in the audience.

2. Haddon W. Robinson, *Expository Preaching: Principles and Practice* (2nd ed., 2001; repr., Leicester, England: Inter-Varsity Press, 2004), 165-6. Given the fundamental nature of a well catchy sermon introduction, particularly of audience receptivity, Robinson notes that the introduction, in a real sense, introduces the congregation to the preacher. He explains, "In the final analysis, listeners do not hear a sermon. They hear you. . . Men and women in our culture value relationships, and they will make a judgment about you and your attitudes before they will give their attention to what you have to say." See p. 166 of his work as cited above.

3. Stephen F. Olford and David Lindsay Olford, *Anointed Expository Preaching* (Nashville, Tennessee: Broadman and Holman Publishers, 1998), 192.

through it, about what to expect in the sermon. The introduction lets the "... audience know the central idea of the text and the proposition of [the] sermon.... The introduction lays the big idea before the people and prepares them for its development."[4] This is done by the use of a directional statement that describes the content and focus of the sermon about to be presented. A transitional statement that links the introduction with the body of the sermon usually follows immediately.

The sermon introduction is needed because it has a specific purpose to accomplish and a specific area on which to focus. According to Gordon Fee, your sermon needs focus, or you will not know what you are trying to accomplish, and you will be difficult to follow.[5] As "... the initial part of the sermon in which the preacher is attempting to *buy a hearing* from the audience . . . The introduction, therefore, should be intriguing, gaining listener interest and seizing their attention."[6] One key element that aids focus in a sermon is a good sermon topic carefully couched, either from the primary concern of the sermon as in the case of a topical sermon type or from the text in the case of a textual and or expository sermon type.

Although a sermon, no matter how it is presented, has some form of an introduction, the point here is the need for a clearly defined and a well-stated introduction to a sermon. A sermon without it is like a pilot flying a plane on no clearly defined altitude and to no definite destination. In this regard, a good sermon introduction is structured according to the purpose of that particular sermon. Chapell maintains, for instance, that, "Only the conclusion rivals the introduction

---

4.   Jerry Vines and Jim Shaddix, *Power in the Pulpit: How to Prepare and Deliver Expository Sermons* (Chicago, Illinois: Moody Press, 1999), 220.

5.   Gordon D. Fee, *New Testament Exegesis: A Handbook for Students and Pastors* (3rd ed., Louisville, Kentucky: Westminster John Knox Press, 2002), 133-136.

6.   Vines and Shaddix, *Power in the Pulpit*, 219.

for determining whether listeners will digest the sermon food offered them. No matter how good the meat inside, if these surrounding 'slices of bread' are moldy, we should not expect anyone to take a bite."[7] This re-echoes the dire need for a clearly stated, forceful and robust introduction.

THE SERMON INTRODUCTION'S PURPOSE

First of all, a compelling introduction to a sermon helps to get the *attention* of the audience to what is to follow. The case of Moses and the burning bush in the Midian desert around Mt. Sinai (Exod 3:1-5) is a good example. The burning bush attracted Moses' attention; therefore, he turned to see the unusual sight. A sermon poorly and shabbily introduced is not only awkward and unprofessional but it "forfeits a hearing"[8] because "The introduction is the contract for communication. If the preacher does not gain the attention of the audience in the first two or three minutes, he will probably never get it."[9] This is why "An introduction should present listeners with an arresting thought that draws them away from apathy or competing interests . . . [and] no matter what avenue a preacher takes, the task remains the same: Get their attention! [by making] the opening words count."[10]

Every preacher should remember that not all who are seated on the pews with their eyes glued to the pulpit area are mentally alert and involved in whatever goes on during the worship service. Peo-

---

7. Chapell, *Christ-Centered Preaching*, 239.

8. Chapell, *Christ-Centered Preaching*, 239.

9. Larsen, *The Anatomy of Preaching*, 74. He suggests that the introduction should not exceed 10-15% of the total preaching time.

10. Chapell, *Christ-Centered Preaching*, 239. He emphasises the point when he goes as far as to say, "If the opening sentence does not stimulate interest when it stands alone, reject it."

ple troop into the church every Sunday for different reasons. Some attend church service just because they feel left out or to meet new acquaintances and make new friends or new business partners. Even those who come to church genuinely to listen to the preaching of the Word of God may, during the service and preaching, become distracted. While some may become absent-minded, thinking about how to handle some aching challenges in life, some others may be having side-talks with a friend or some visitor. As Robinson observes, "When you step behind the pulpit, you dare not assume that your congregation sits expectantly on the edge of the pews waiting for your sermon. In reality, they are probably a bit bored and harbor a suspicion that you will make matters worse."[11] Some of them, even just by the sight of you, might have concluded already that you will only waste their time as they assume you have nothing significantly essential for them. Some in the audience may be saying, "Preacher, my time is too precious to be wasted listening to you; you have to convince me that what you have is worth my time and attention." Only people who are desperately seeking some fire brigade approach to their physiological needs or challenges will sit waiting expectantly for the preacher.

The preachers of God's Word should prepare the way for the message by attracting attention like John the Baptist prepared the way for the coming of the Saviour (Matt 3:1-1-12). His unique way of life and ministry attracted attention and people trooped to listen to him. Preachers should get the listeners' attention to the subject matter of the sermon through a friendly, brief and masterfully introduced sermon introduction, then transit gradually and purposefully into the main body of the sermon.

---

11. Robinson, *Expository Preaching*, 166.

Secondly, an effective introduction to a sermon is used to *arouse the interest* of the audience in the sermon. As we see in the example of the burning bush above (Exod 3:1-5), Moses was curious to discover why the bush was burning yet not consumed. Hence, he turned and moved closer to see the amazing sight. When people are not interested in whatever anybody says, they will not care to pay attention to it. When people do not have a stake in what a preacher has, they will care less whatever is said. However, when they know that the message concerns them because it affects them directly, they will do everything possible to give it all the attention it deserves. This underscores the critical role of arousing the interest of the listener to the expository preaching. Chapell captures this well,

> To assume that one's listeners automatically share one's interest in the sermon is a mark of an inexperienced preacher. Such a preacher reasons that because God's people should be interested in God's Word that they will be interested in a discussion of it. Only in a perfect world would such an expectation have merit.[12]

Vines and Shaddix add, "We cannot assume that those who sit in our congregations are automatically interested in what we are going to say. We must create that interest."[13]

Arousing interest in a sermon should be purposefully done. What this means, to use Hogan's words, is that a preacher must enter the audience's world and persuade them to go with him or her into the world of biblical truth, and specifically the truth that is the burden of the sermon.[14] The sermon introduction should be electrifying to graphically arrest the interest, provoke the listeners' thoughts, and

---

12. Chapell, *Christ-Centered Preaching*, 228.

13. Vines and Shaddix, *Power in the Pulpit*, 219.

14. William L. Hogan, "It is My Pleasure to Introduce . . . ", *The Expositor* 1, 3 (August 1987): 1.

generate curiosity in such a way that refocuses their attention from other competing demands and makes each person say, "'Hey! I need to hear this.'"[15] Let me illustrate what getting attention and arousing interest means. If I were to preach on the central subject of escape from death, I would ask a question: "Who among you will answer 'Yes' when death comes to take you in the next two hours? I want to talk to you about how you can escape death."

An introduction in a sermon such as this will capture attention and create interest in it because death is a common, but dreaded, phenomenon for everyone. It has no regard for personality or one's status; neither does it discriminate on the basis of gender, race, and age. Death has no regard for one's material possessions, tribal and religious affiliation, or academic attainment. Death owes no one any advanced notice in regards to when it will come; neither does it owe an apology to the grieving relations of the deceased. Even those people who think they do not care whether they live or die will care when they face the reality of death. The introduction to a sermon to get attention and create curiosity is a critical moment; hence, it should not be done carelessly, shabbily, hastily or haphazardly.

Thirdly, an effective introduction is needed in order to *establish the precise direction of thought* in the sermon. As we explained earlier, the sermon topic should express one single controlling idea that is clearly and aptly stated. This idea is introduced to show the content of the sermon and the expectation in the central subject. J. Daniel Baumann states that the first moments of the sermon may answer one of two questions, that is, either, "What is he going to talk about? [or] What in general is he going to say about it?"[16] Richard also points out that the main introduction ". . . will orient the audience to the

---

15. Chapell, *Christ-Centered Preaching*, 239.

16. J. Daniel Baumann, *An Introduction to Contemporary Preaching* (1972; paperback ed., 1988; repr., Grand Rapids, Michigan: Baker Book House, 1990), 136.

theme that you are going to pursue . . . the main introduction will naturally be related to the theme of the CPS."[17]

In essence, as Chapell maintains, an introduction should signal what a preacher will address so that by the conclusion of the introduction, every listener should know that the message is about a specific and clearly defined subject.[18] The audience should be able to follow the preacher from the start to the finish of the sermon without any doubt or confusion about the subject and its content. They should be clear about what the preacher is saying, why he or she is saying what is being said, and about the 'what' and 'why' of what is being said. The introduction would have set out the road map for the listeners to achieve this understanding. This means that the audience should be able to have a precise knowledge of the central theme of the sermon, an adequate understanding of the thrust of the sermon, and lastly, be able to grasp the purpose of the sermon.

Fourthly, an *effective* introduction is used to *open up the need(s) of the listeners*. So many people in this generation live a life of denial, secrecy, pretence and falsehood, and concealed hurts. Often, just by the simple sermon introduction, it can touch on such areas of hu-

---

17. Ramesh, *Scripture Sculpture*, 108. The CPS refers to the Central Propositional Statement of the sermon. This is the statement of the aim of the sermon that states what the preacher sets out to discuss, explain, and argue. This is the point the preacher intends to convince the audience to accept and act on. "What do I have to say or offer to the listener in this sermon" is a question of the proposition. There is also the Central Prepositional Statement of the sermon which is a statement of purpose or the aims and objectives of the sermon. The prepositional statement looks at the end of the sermon to achieve its anticipated goal. This statement serves as a guide for the preacher rather than the audience. Hence, "Why am I preaching this sermon?" and "What specifically do I want to achieve in the listener by this sermon?" are essential prepositional questions that the preacher must always ask during the period of sermonic construction.

18. Chapell, *Christ-Centered Preaching*, 240.

man need. Opening up needy areas in an introduction is helping the audience sense their need to hear the issues you will address in the sermon.[19] Very early in the sermon, listeners should realise that the preacher is talking to them about themselves because the introduction should raise a question, probe a problem, identify a need, and open up a vital issue to which the passage speaks to bring the grace of God to bear on the agonizing worries and tensions of daily life.[20]

People will always want to listen to sermons that pick on their challenges or areas of need and that promise to offer solutions to them. For example, a poor African parent who is a peasant farmer and is having a hard time sending his or her children to school will be glad to know how to increase his crop yields. Also, an African housewife who is being cheated on and battered by her husband will readily submit to any teaching that could give her some comfort. Again, a poor African widow who has no means of subsistence but has children to cater for and numerous bills to pay, will most likely, fall just for anything that will alleviate her traumatised life. The presence of these important social and physiological realities is one underlying reason why the business of false prophets and false preachers/teachers, spiritualists, and religious merchandisers is flourishing in the market of spiritual deceit in Africa.

A good sermon introduction is intended to raise such needy areas in the audience. However, when it lacks this quality, then the preacher cannot sell to the audience something they do not know they need.[21] Hence, it is absolutely the job of the preacher to so describe

---

19. Richard, *Scripture Sculpture*, 107.
20. Robinson, *Expository Preaching*, 170.
21. Vines and Shaddix, *Power in the Pulpit*, 222.

the problems that people face and the solutions that Scriptures give so that listening to God's Word becomes important[22] to them.

Fifthly, effectively introducing the expository sermon reveals its *relevance,* thereby compelling the listener to listen. "Where does it concern me?" or as Nigerians say, "It is your cup of tea," is a statement of relevance. However, a good introduction should capture Adrian Roger's four magic introductory formula words: "Hey! You! Look! Do!"[23]

Standing in the pulpit means that the preacher, who is the representative of God and a herald of his Word, has a message from him for the listeners. By introducing the sermon, then, the preacher indicates to the listeners that it is for them; that the message from God is quite relevant to their life situations; and that it is very urgent, requiring their attention. Such an introduction invites and persuades the listeners to give heed to the message because it has something useful for them. Robinson rightly states that in preaching, "Ultimately, we are using the Bible to talk to people about themselves. We're not talking to them about the Bible."[24] This is a matter of rele-

---

22. Jay Edward Adams, *Truth Applied: Application in Preaching* (Grand Rapids, Michigan: Baker, 1990), 72. Andrae Crouch, an American gospel artist, sings, "Jesus is the answer for the world today. Above him there's no other; Jesus is the way." Such an introductory purpose should pull listeners to this only perfect source of solutions to life's challenging issues.

23. Vines and Shaddix quote Adrian Rodger's idea. They explain this thus: "Hey! is a catchy word used to declare the essence of the sermon and get attention. You! intends to convince the listener that the subject at hand applies directly to them personally; it is for him or her; because it certainly has something the listener needs to hear. Look! presents before an individual listener the graph, that is, the content of the sermon that concerns him or her. It supplies summary information about the subject he or she must hear. Do! points to the course of action on the sermon." See Vines and Shaddix, *Power in the Pulpit,* 220.

24. Robinson, *Expository Preaching,* 172.

vance. Otherwise, of what use is it to talk about the Bible without its impact on the listener who is the "object of the sermon"?[25]

Sixthly, an effective sermon introduction is also intended to orient the listener about his or her contemporary environment, temptations and practical life experiences. Each person is different with unique individual needs and experiences in life. Even though some areas of similarities exist, yet, their disparities are also evident. This also presupposes that there are distinctive and peculiar challenges in life that each individual has to contend with. When a sermon's introduction touches on what the listener is experiencing in life, it becomes personal. As such, a listener will readily identify with the sermon and will want to listen to it anxiously and expectantly. Robinson agrees no less as he correctly points out, "The strongest introductions will usually be personal. . . . Men and women will listen if they feel you are talking about the strains and temptations they feel as they try to keep their marriage vows."[26]

Additionally, people face various temptations wherever they may be found. While human nature and human conditions remain the same, the temptations that people face daily are primarily shaped by their environments. For us in Africa, our context of abject poverty forces many people to tell some "white lies" or dabble into some falsification in business deals. Some others struggle so hard to keep their moral ethics and purity as they are confronted daily with sexual temptations from ever-lowering morality standards. Some are forced by their parents or relations, friends or employers, or some other persons, to unintentionally do what is morally wrong, while some others feel compelled by circumstances to yield to various temptations.

____

25. Robinson, *Expository Preaching*, 172.
26. Robinson, *Expository Preaching*, 173.

Still others are intentionally becoming morally bankrupt in their quest to satisfy insatiable desires aroused by the shallow level of morality and society's diminishing respect for personal integrity. People who do such things, whose consciences are still responsive, feel a sense of emptiness and guilt inside them. As such, they will always wish to find some help in achieving lasting peace and find what truly satisfies in life. When an introduction to the sermon orients such listeners to finding the answer to their struggles and challenges in life in the Bible – an answer which the sermon of the day proposes to give - they will want to listen to the solution.

TYPES OF SERMON INTRODUCTION

Variety is said to be the spice of life. This suggests that a sermon can be introduced in many ways. Preachers should be conversant with and use them. Some of the types are discussed below:

Using Biblical examples.

This type of sermon introduction uses the Bible to kick-start the sermon. It can either refer to or direct attention to an appropriate incident in the Scriptures as its hook. A biblical passage, a parable or Bible story, a key event in the Scriptures, a statement, or a character could be used in this respect. For example, if one were preaching on the subject which suggests that ordinarily, people struggle in order to achieve something tangible in life, one would use something like this statement for an introduction, 'Everyone struggles in some way to get something in life, like Zacchaeus who had to climb a sycamore tree in order to see Jesus.' Here, a Bible character is used to introduce the sermon.

Zacchaeus was considered a rich man but a sinner in the eyes of the religious leaders of the day and most Jewish people. His bad public image as a Roman tax collector and his physical stature as a short person appeared to militate against his coming in contact with Jesus. Aware of these obstacles, he struggled to see Jesus of whom he must have heard so much about. If Zacchaeus had not struggled hard the way he did, it is unlikely that he would have been able to see Jesus, let alone to have had the rare honour of hosting him in his house (Luke 19:1-10). Nigerians would describe Zacchaeus as a "hustler", a person who struggles hard to achieve something.

Story-telling or Human-interest Introductions.

This type of sermon introduction tells a short story of a human condition or narrates an experience. Such a story could be about a good or bad experience that someone had or it could be about a particular incident in society. Stories such as these, when appropriately chosen and used, easily capture attention. The preacher may even use his or her personal life experience in this regard provided that the ultimate goal for doing so is not to draw attention to himself or herself rather than to the message. A story should be brief and masterfully told.

Startling Statement Introductions.

A startling statement is a type of statement that is surprising and alarming because it is couched in a seemingly contradictory fashion. The primary aim is to get attention and arouse interest in the subject of the sermon.

Some examples of such type of introduction are: Firstly, "I died last night; even now, I am still dead." A human corpse is lifeless; therefore, it does not speak. How come that the one who died last night and is still dead could be speaking? The surprise element and seeming contradiction lie in this question. Secondly, Chapell reports Jay E. Adams' use of this startling statement to introduce a sermon:

> There is a murderer sitting in this congregation today. . . .
> Yes, I mean it. Just yesterday he murdered someone. He
> didn't think that anyone saw him, but he was wrong. I have
> a written statement from an eyewitness that I am going to
> read. Here is what it says, 'Everybody who hates his brother
> is a murderer.'[27]

This type of introduction sends surprise and curiosity in the listener to make him, or her want to listen to the subject.

Thought-provoking Questions.

This type of sermon introduction could either be a rhetorical question or one where a response is called for by the preacher. Such a question should both be provocative and engaging to blow the mind of listeners at the start to a sermon.

When using this introductory method, either a question or series of questions are asked simultaneously. For instance, "Does it matter if I sin, provided I confess my sin; after all God is a compassionate, merciful and forgiving God?" Alternatively, "Suppose you find your most trusted friend in bed with your spouse, or fiancé or fiancée, what will you do?" Each one of these examples provokes the listener into deep thinking regarding the implications of the question and their reaction. Such introduction hooks the listener's attention to the sermon subject ready to book them in the message.

Quotations.

A useful and relevant quotation can introduce a sermon. Here, the preacher uses his or her sanctified mind to use appropriate quotes

---

27. Chapell, *Christ-Centered Preaching*, 247. The Bible passage used as the text for the sermon from which Adams expertly used this startling statement is 1 John 3:15.

from numerous sources such as printed materials, documentaries and movies, and from hymns and songs or any other relevant source to introduce the sermon. Such quotes should be very related to the theme of the sermon. It must also be graphic so that it gets proper attention. Appropriate proverbs that relate to the subject of the sermon can also be quoted in this respect.

Historical or Situational References.

Each society experiences change because human life itself is dynamic. Good and bad events occur on an almost daily basis in human society, and individuals benefit or suffer as a result of such happenings. A skilled preacher could use a recent incident in society as the starting point of a sermon. This can quickly get the attention of the audience who would have been aware of the incident and readily identify with it.

Some examples of such references are the Al Qaida terrorist attack of the International Trade Centre on September 2011, and the bomb blast at Eagles' Square in Abuja, Nigeria, on October 1, 2010 during the celebration of the country's fiftieth independence. The successful rescue on October 15, 2010 of 33 Chilean miners who were trapped underground for 69 days, or the inhumane mayhem in Dogon Nahawa village of Plateau State, Nigeria, in March 2010 where over 500 children, men and women, and the aged, where reportedly murdered, are good examples. Particularly, if one were addressing a Nigerian audience, the incessant harassment and inhumane brutality of Boko Haram terrorists and Fulani militia in recent time, can be a very moving historical reference type of sermon introduction.

Recapitulation or Summary Introductions.

When a resident pastor or preacher is preaching systematically through a book of the Bible, or a series of sermons on a particular topic, the immediate previous sermon is recapped at the start of every new sermon in the series. Only the main thoughts are restated as it is not a repetition of the whole sermon. The purpose for such type of introduction is to refresh the memory of the audience and achieve continuity. It is also helpful for those members who missed the previous sermon and visitors so they will connect the day's message with the previous ones in the series.

Assertive Statements.

In this type of introduction, the preacher makes a simple assertion of intent for the sermon before or immediately after reading the text of the sermon. An assertive type of introduction should be particular and direct, and it must be addressed to a real existing situation within the particular congregation. Chapell gives one example, "'Today, I want to talk about how gossip is hurting our church and what we should do about it.'" He states that such an assertion can arrest an opening that will perk interest.[28] If I were to preach to an African audience, say to Nigerians, Ghanaians, or Cameroonians, I would say, for instance, "Church politics and the attitude of tribalism has affected the spiritual growth of our local church. I know some of you are not happy about it. I want to speak about these effects and what we can do to change it."

---

28. Chapell, *Christ-Centered Preaching*, 246.

Drama

A preacher may choose to introduce a sermon with a very short play-
let appropriate to the sermon subject. Preachers rarely use this method, though it is very useful. It quickly captures attention and creates
curiosity, thereby hooking the listener to the subject of the sermon.

Catalogues or Statistics.

What this type of introduction does is to stockpile related issues in
their particular category with the purpose of pointing to the particular theme of the sermon. Chapell says this method is the grouping
or listing of items, ideas, disasters, persons, et cetera in such a way
that they reveal the central concept of a sermon.[29] Such listing could
also include certain critical events in society as long as it does not
collide with the historical or situational reference type. The catalogue or statistical data type of sermon introduction tries to establish a particular fact of life such as acts of disobedience, failures to
learn from history, and so on.

Biography

This can be taken either from a biblical character or someone else, to
introduce a sermon. Care is needed to focus on a particular aspect of
the biography. If, for example, I were to use Paul, I could speak about
his pre-conversion and post-conversion religious zeal. I could also
speak about the role of his much learning or the persecutions that
he suffered.

---

29. Chapell, *Christ-Centered Preaching*, 247.

QUALITIES OF A GOOD SERMON INTRODUCTION

In both ancient and contemporary African societies, men do not choose wives indiscriminately. In ancient Africa especially, it was the father who searched for a wife and negotiated a marriage for his son. Like it was the case in ancient Israelite society, parents served as matchmakers when seeking spouses for their children. Careful observations, as well as careful research, were first made to be sure what kind of a wife was brought into one's family. In both ancient and contemporary experiences, Africans do not take wives for their male children from families that are known for laziness or deceit and lies, or theft. They won't also consider a woman from a family that has a history of bad health and constant death or barrenness for a wife.

No father would negotiate a marriage between his son and a lady from a family where the wife or her mother has any record of bad character, such as stinginess, lack of submission, rudeness, insubordination, bad behaviour or being sarcastic. For example, among the *Miship* people of Nigeria, the exhibition of such bad character and bad behaviour by a wife is described as *mat kah ting kih dilang*. It literally means that a wife has climbed a tree with a clay water jar on her head. It is a proverbial expression that captures her attitude of disobedience and rebellion, stubbornness and insubordination, or disrespect to elders in her community. For this reason, care was taken in the choice of a future wife because each African family and clan look out for good qualities in the woman that is to be brought into the family and clan as a wife. A wife of outstanding character is highly valued but the one that has a bad character, attitude and behaviour is a disgrace to the entire family and clan.

Like the search for a good wife, every good sermon introduction should have attractive qualities, not bad ones. Listeners will always love to listen to preachers who are mindful to incorporate such enriching qualities in their sermons. Some of these qualities are discussed below.

Brief and Sharp.

The introduction serves as the gateway to the sermon and not the sermon itself; therefore, intrusive words should be avoided. A brief and sharp introduction helps in keeping the interest of the listeners, and it maintains their focus in the sermon as well. Olford and Olford explain,

> A lengthy introduction can lack focus and can contain a lot of material that could have been expressed within the flow of the [sermon body] ... A lengthy introduction can take time away from the [sermon] itself, resulting in a sense of rushing through the [sermon] instead of a more deliberate pace needed to facilitate the understanding of the textual insights ... a lengthy introduction [results in] a thin piece of exposition that barely scratches the surface of the text.[30]

This thought cautions against the hazards and demerits of a lengthy sermon introduction which may likely make listeners disinterested in the preacher and the sermon from the start. Because a sermon's introduction is crucial, Larsen says, "Blessed is the preacher who can get the sermon airborne without too long a runway."[31]

Those who drive know the traffic road sign that reads, "No parking, No waiting, Keep moving." Drivers who disrespect such traffic signs put themselves at the risk of the law and constitute a great nui-

---

30. Olford and Olford, *Anointed Expository Preaching*, 193.
31. Larsen, *The Anatomy of Preaching*, 74.

sance to other road users. Preachers should obey the "No parking, No waiting, Keep moving" sermon instruction so they get quickly to the heart of the sermon and free it of any obstacle on its way.

Direct and Forceful

A good sermon introduction must be direct and forceful to make the subject of the message personal. It must not be generalised but personally directed to the listeners. When the listeners know without any ambiguity that the preacher is speaking directly to them, and by the force of the introduction, they detect that the message is for them, they will listen to it.

Real and Honest

An introduction should neither be illusive nor should it promise more than it can achieve in one sermon. It should be realistic and honest regarding being measurable and achievable. For instance, a preacher who promises in the introduction to present the biblical principles that will solve the challenge of poverty or bad governance in Africa cannot be taken seriously. Neither is the one who claims that the sermon will resolve all ethno-tribal wars in Africa be considered as being serious enough to be listened to.

The adverse effect of such a bad introduction is as Robinson explains, "When you fail to meet the need you have raised, the congregation feels cheated"[32] because the promises made and the high expectations raised are not met but rather dashed at the end. So, like the wise and experienced African farmer, preachers must always cultivate only the portion of land they know can be properly managed within a farming season to achieve good yields.

---

32. Robinson, *Expository Preaching*, 173.

Relevant and Varied

The introduction should both be relevant to the needs of the listeners and the main thrust of the sermon. Relevance functions as a centre of attraction that forces the audience to listen. No one cares to listen to stuff that does not concern them. On the other hand, preachers should also vary the introductions to the sermons they preach. This is important in order to sustain interest and keep attention in an audience that sits to listen to the same preacher Sunday-in Sunday-out.[33]

If "Variety is the spice of life", it also presupposes that monotony dulls the excitement of life. Most Africans already live in a hostile environment, though of various degrees, and life is unfair and quite stressful for them. The African preacher should help to relieve the listener of such burdens of life rather than add to it by a dulling-sleepy sermon introduction.

Appropriate and Accurate

Every sermon should carry the mood and tone that appropriately and accurately reflect the subject, occasion, and audience. In the same vein, it should also accurately reflect the mood of the text under consideration. Depending on the type of genre of literature and the expressions used by the author, the various contents of the biblical text reflect varying moods. Therefore, since an aspect of the introduction is also to set the mood and tone for the sermon, the mood of the text, subject, and that of the audience should be matched appropriately. For example, as the preacher, "You do not want to begin in a frivolous

---

33. Vines and Shaddix point out that, "Because texts, audiences, and occasions vary, the sermon introductions that serve each one should vary as well." See Vines and Shaddix, *Power in the Pulpit*, 222.

manner when you will be discussing something serious."[34] Neither should you introduce a sermon that is all about the message of consolation to a hurting congregation with a fierce tone that creates a much-tensed atmosphere.

Serious and Convincing

A good sermon introduction must capture the seriousness and conviction of the message. An introduction that is floppy and casual is a bad one. Its tone should reveal the sermon's seriousness and conviction, thus deserving due attention from the listener. Such a tone is set by the seriousness and conviction with which the preacher approaches the sermon itself.

Relationship and Care

The tone and body language with which a preacher exhibits during the introduction opens the preacher up to the listeners' judgement. The attitude could either be judged as that of respect for the audience and care for them or that of arrogance and a flamboyant one. Public communication requires a good relationship between the speaker and the audience for receptivity. A positive attitude demonstrated by the preacher develops a relationship with the audience. Really, "'People don't care how much you know unless they know how much you care!'" This is a clear indication that "The preacher who is interested in communicating God's Word to people will be most interested in securing their attention"[35] by exhibiting an inherent and outwardly expressed attitude of care, compassion, love, friendliness and sensitivity towards their needs.

---

34. Vines and Shaddix, *Power in the Pulpit*, 222.
35. Vines and Shaddix, *Power in the Pulpit*, 223.

We have stressed in this chapter the need not only to introduce a sermon, but to do so adequately and appropriately. A sermon properly introduced helps the preacher to preach it and prepares the listeners to listen to it. This is why the next chapter addresses how to preach the expository sermon just introduced.

CHAPTER 12

DRIVING THE EXPOSITORY SERMON

The principal purpose for igniting a car is to drive it; unless the driver only intends to warm the car to keep the battery from running down. Similarly, the preacher drives a sermon so the audience or listeners can enjoy the ride. This driving imagery is the act of preaching the expository sermon.

Oral tradition in Africa is powerful. Stories about family, clan, tribal and ethnic heroes and heroines are transmitted orally from generation to generation. Some of them attained their heroism in such areas as war or farming, hunting or musicology and dance; and others through skills such as wrestling, craftsmanship and medicine. More attain heroism in cultural rhetoric and wisdom speech as sages. While their story is told and retold down the generations, the main content of the script hardly gets corrupted because it has been preserved in its oral form.

Like the African oral tradition, the biblical text tells an old story with timeless meaning for people of all generations and ages. This old story, to be effectual, then, must be told in a masterly contemporary manner, yet without distorting its content. Ramesh Richard captures this point aptly when he says contemporisation is the primary task of the expository preacher. Accordingly, the preacher takes what was written centuries ago and contemporises it for present-day audiences.[1] This means the message of the ancient sacred text of the Jews and Christians is carefully and adequately translated to the contemporary context without any distortion.

Today, we live in the age of Information and Communication Technology (ICT). Communication itself, as a medium of the exchange of useful information, attempts to build a bridge across borders by linking people and organisations via the transfer and sharing of information. If the process is fraudulent or the medium through which information is processed is fraudulent, the intended message stands the risk of being corrupted and misunderstood. When such corruption occurs in the communication process, it becomes detrimental to the information source, or the target audience, or both.

Similarly, expository preaching endeavours to pass the message of the inspired, infallible, and inerrant Word of God to the world of human beings. In our case, it is to translate God's written Word through oral communication to an African audience that is far removed from the time of its original hearers or readers. Since a massive gulf stands between the world of the ancient sacred biblical text and that of its contemporary African readers, care should be taken to properly transfer its message to the contemporary listeners in such a mode that best communicates meaning, and in a manner that its originally intended message is neither corrupted nor lost.

To this extent, the manner in which the developed expository sermon is delivered is very crucial. If it is not properly communicated, the meaning is lost in the process. The role of language in communication, Murthy says, is communicating correctly with our fellow people to be successful in society.[2] An expository sermon is

---

1. Ramesh Richard, *Scripture Sculpture: A Do-It-Yourself Manual for Biblical Preaching* (1995; repr., Grand Rapids, Michigan: Baker Books, 1997), 18.
2. J. D. Murthy, *Contemporary English Grammar: West African Edition* (ed., Ben Lawrence, Lagos, Nigeria: Book Master, 2007), 4.

successful only to the extent that it is clearly and adequately delivered, and the intended message by the preacher is correctly decoded and understood by the listeners.

The attempt to get the prepared expository sermon across to the audience is the act of sermon delivery. The preacher, like a driver, needs careful attention, focus, alertness, and good judgement to get its content across to a congregation. Sermon preparation and development, as well as its presentation or delivery, are equally essential. Otherwise, of what use is it to spend long, laborious hours, expending much energy preparing a sermon only to throw it into the garbage bin through poor delivery? Would it not be a wasteful venture and a regrettable effort? As Vines states,

> Sermon delivery is an essential aspect of the preacher's
> work. At this point, many preachers fail. They may gather
> excellent material for their sermons. The sermon itself may
> be well organised and skilfully done. Yet when the preach-
> er opens his[her] mouth in the pulpit, the sermon dies. . . .
> The preacher must not only prepare his[her] sermons well,
> he[she] must also deliver them well.[3]

---

3. Jerry Vines contrasts the sermon development and delivery with a production enterprise that has to manufacture and market its product. He sees sermon development as the manufacturing aspect of the preaching enterprise while its delivery as the marketing aspect. Just as the customer will not buy a company's product, no matter how good, if it is poorly packaged and marketed, so is a sermon poorly delivered. Vines, therefore, encourages preachers to know how to effectively and attractively deliver the content of the developed message to the audience. See Jerry Vines, *A Guide to Effective Sermon Delivery* (Chicago, Illinois: Moody Press, 1986), xiv. Readers should note that the term sermon construction, development, and preparation all mean the same thing while sermon communication, delivery, and presentation also all mean the same thing. They are a paired triplet: Sermon construction and communication; sermon development and delivery; and sermon preparation and presentation.

The only aim of sermon development is its final delivery for the benefit of the listeners. Sermons are prepared to be presented or constructed to be communicated to an intended target audience.

Let me illustrate this point. In ancient Africa, children got excited when the mother was cooking food either in the kitchen or in an open space within the family compound. This is particularly significant in many homes when it was rice that was being prepared because rice was a rare meal in most societies. It was served, perhaps, only once a year on Christmas Day in most homes. So, children always looked forward to the Christmas season so they could eat rice, and of course, wear new clothes. When some children were sent on an errand to the neighbourhood while the rice was not yet done, they would run their hearts out so as not to be late returning when the food would have been done. However, it would be a terrible disaster for these excited and anxious African children if the long-awaited prepared rice was accidentally poured out on the ground, and could no longer be eaten by humans except the dogs. Similarly, a well-prepared sermon poorly delivered compares with this analogy. The expository preacher should circumvent those factors responsible for the death of a well-prepared sermon in the pulpit.

OBSTACLES TO SERMON DELIVERY

Speed bumps are put at some points on the road for specific reasons. While such bumps are helpful for safety, they slow down the traffic flow and the journey, thus, constituting an obstacle. The ability to manage correctly certain elements that make for a smooth presentation can become an uphill task for the preacher. When a preacher appears unsure in the pulpit, looks frigid and stumbling at the sermon presentation, and becomes disorganised at some point during the presentation, this is a sign that certain militating factors are responsible. We consider below both some enemies of the preacher that attempt to kill the sermon in the pulpit and some antidotes to such enemies.

Five Obstacles

A preacher may ask, "How do I deliver the prepared sermon effectively?" Careful adherence to homiletical principles and sensitivity to certain intruders during the delivery is the answer. Certain imbalances in the preacher's body instruments such as his or her body, eyes and voice, or his or her mind and emotions, all act as obstacles to effective sermon delivery. A crucial part of the sermon delivery is being sensitive to and ensuring a good synergy among these body instruments, and their appropriate co-ordination as well by the preacher when in the pulpit. For the slightest alteration in any one of them distorts the flow of the sermon, no matter how well-prepared. Sometimes, certain intrusive "pop-ups" to sermon delivery become unavoidable.

First, tension is one of the obstacles to the effective delivery of a well-prepared sermon. It can alter the mind and emotions of a preacher when he or she is in the pulpit. Stage fright or nervousness can cause tension for a preacher. However, the experience of these emotional feelings is a very natural part of human beings.

Being tense, frightened or nervous can be caused by a number of factors. For instance, the looks on the faces of the listeners can be intimidating and quite frightening. A church wedding was being conducted in one village. Before the solemnisation of the marriage, the usual statement of inquiry came on, "If anyone has a just cause why this wedding will not hold, let such person now speak, or else, forever, they should hold their peace." A hand went up soon after the statement. The officiating clergy invited the person to come forward.

The paternal uncle (father) to the bride had raised his hand to lay a complaint. (In Africa, even very distant relations within a clan and tribe are either one's brothers and sisters or fathers and mothers, because one is related only either as a parent, brother or sister. The Western concept of uncles, aunts, cousins, nephews and nieces is foreign to the African understanding).

However, when the uncle (father) stood before the audience and looked at their watching eyes, he became speechless. Instead of speaking, tears began to run down his cheeks. When, after they had entered the vestry, the solemnising minister inquired why he came forward but could not speak but wept instead, the man said all he had wanted to say was that the bride was his daughter (niece), but she did not come to inform him about her wedding. However, when he stood and saw the curiously watching eyes of the audience, he was terrified and began to weep instead of speaking. Just as with the experience of this man, the many glittering eyes of an audience can be very intimidating to a preacher; worst, to a beginner preacher.

Second, the feelings of intimidation can stand in the way of good sermon delivery. If a preacher is addressing an intellectual audience, for example, the thought of their much learning and how they might critique the sermon can be quite daunting for the preacher. Alternatively, when one is standing before a congregation that has rich and or highly placed people in society, this can be intimidating. The presence of one's professional colleagues or, in particular, one's teacher in the congregation, can even make one more intimidated. I have always told my students in the class of homiletics and expository preaching not to be deterred by my presence or that of any other of their teachers in the congregation. I have equally counselled them to always focus on the audience and the message from God for them, not on personalities.

Third, the physiology of a person can also either make people like or reject the person. The analytical ability of the members of the audience to critique the preacher and decide to accept or reject the sermon can as well cause some stomach upsets. Aware of this, as the preacher walks into the pulpit apprehensive questions will naturally "pop-up": "Will this audience accept or detest and reject me?" "How does the audience perceive me – as someone friendly or hostile?" "How do I present the sermon within the context of the audience in such a manner that they understand it?" "Will I be able to keep the interest and attention of the audience to the end so they could respond positively to the message of the sermon?" "Will the audience be appreciative and complimenting of the sermon or be offensive and vengeful?" "Will some even walk out on me?" The thought of these questions can affect the psychological and emotional balance of the preacher.

In the case where the preacher is an invited speaker, other pertinent questions usually would be, "Will I ever be invited again by this congregation given the way and manner in which I will preach?" "Will anyone care at all to give me some words of greetings and a handshake after the sermon?" These "pop-ups" can cause great discomfort to the preacher and make him, or her feel uneasy and inadequate before the sermon delivery. Larsen describes such "pop-ups" as "butterflies" in the stomach that conspire against proper breathing and cause dry mouth.[4] They can also cause a choking throat creating some difficulty in the preacher's diction and articulation in the sermon delivery.

---

4. David L. Larsen, *The Anatomy of Preaching: Identifying the Issues in Preaching Today* (Grand Rapids, Michigan: Baker Book House, 1989; Grand Rapids, Michigan: Kregel Publications, 1999; & Ibadan, Nigeria: CHRIST & WE PUBLICATIONS, 2000), 184.

Fourth, the feeling of arrogance and or timidity stands in the way of sermon delivery. The disposition of arrogance and timidity are opposite extremes in the pulpit. Paul recognised these hiccups and said, firstly, of the arrogant, "They want to be teachers of the law, but they do not know what they are talking about or what they so confidently affirm" (1 Tim 1:7 NIV). Secondly, he said of Timothy's timid spirit, "For God did not give us a spirit of timidity, but a spirit of power, of love and of self-discipline. So do not be ashamed to testify about our Lord, or ashamed of me his prisoner" (2 Tim 1:7, 8a NIV). A nervous feeling not only impairs good preaching but also deprives Christians of being at their best in the exercise of their spiritual gifts in Christian service.

Fifth, the feeling of inadequacy and lack of confidence can stand in the way of a preacher in the pulpit. To be clear, self-confidence is different from self-arrogance. While arrogance says "I know it all and am superb at it", confidence says "By God's gifted ability and his guiding grace, I am able to do it". When a preacher thinks he or she would not be able or is not adequately prepared for a sermon, such feeling of inadequacy can sure stand in the way of the flow of a sermon.

Overcoming Obstacles

African domestic rats can be very destructive, especially the tiny black ones. Because rats can be a nuisance in the home, housewives devise several means of keeping them off the house. Some use traps, others use poison, and still others keep cats in the house. Hence, it is said, "There are many ways of killing a rat." Similarly, there are equally several things a preacher can do to serve as an antidote to these intrusive "pop-ups" to effective sermon delivery.

First, complete dependence on the Holy Spirit is critical in sermon delivery. A preacher's success in the pulpit ministry is not consequent upon human ingenuity but God's power. Expositors of God's Word should always depend on the power of divine grace and the inward enabling strength of the Holy Spirit. Preaching is declaring the whole counsel of God. Therefore, it should be done entirely on the merit of the empowering ministry of the Holy Spirit; for the task is done "Not by might nor by power, but by my Spirit, says the Lord Almighty" (Zech 4:6 NIV). Preaching by the inspiring power of the Holy Spirit is what builds confidence in the preacher. Paul says, "I can do everything through him who gives me strength" (Phil 4:13 NIV). This resonates well with what Christ says, "'. . . Remain in me, and I will remain in you. No branch can bear fruit by itself; it must remain in the vine. Neither can you bear fruit unless you remain in me'" (John 15:1, 5 NIV).

Second, a quiet attitude is also important to sermon delivery. This attitude helps in boosting the self-confidence of the preacher. Every preacher should learn to be relaxed in mind, always to be himself or herself, and to be natural whenever they get into the pulpit to preach. As well as helping to overcome nervousness this helps to bring out the full potential of the preacher. This way, a preacher can build self-confidence to overcome feelings of inadequacy, fright and timidity.

Third, pre-preaching a sermon is helpful in fighting against intrusive "pop-ups." Let me illustrate; singing groups within a congregation rehearse their songs before they present them. In the same way, some self-drill in the area of an imaginative and actual methodology of speech, posture, pace, and gestures, way ahead of the preaching time, is a helpful exercise. One can go into the bush or lock oneself inside the room to pre-preach the prepared sermon. This homiletical self-drilling exercise is helpful to develop self-confidence in the preacher. It also assists the preacher to have a good idea of the length of a sermon before its actual delivery.

Fourth, tension and nervousness affect the free flow of air in the lungs as well as the quality of the preacher's voice. These should be defused before the time of the delivery of the sermon. The preacher should sip water before going into the pulpit because it helps to soften the dry throat. Some homiletical authorities suggest breathing exercises before getting into the pulpit. For instance, Robinson says, "When you are nervous, tension can make your voice high and squeaky. Therefore[,] you need control in order to speak your opening words in a composed, relaxed manner. Take a deep breath before you start."[5]

Also, to further help in defusing tension and nervousness, a preacher should start speaking slowly and go gradually. Even before starting the main introduction to the sermon, a preacher should begin the sermon journey by first taking a gentle look at the audience, give them a beautiful natural smile, and greet them nicely and warmly. Like a competent and capable driver, first, ignite the engine and let it warm up, engage the car to gear one, and then accelerate gradually before engaging the other fast gears as you increase the acceleration.

Fifth, another longstanding obstacle to the sermon delivery is insufficient time. In Africa where an event is what matters, time-consciousness will appear immaterial. However, in reality, insufficient time has proved, over and over, to be an enemy to the preacher during sermon delivery. When much time is used up for other activities during the service and less is given for the preaching of the Word, this can be a very frustrating moment for the preacher, no matter how experienced.

____

5. Robinson, *Expository Preaching*, 175.

On the other hand, some preachers do not just utilise time well even when sufficient time is given for the sermon; they waste it with irrelevant stuff. Such failure causes in the audience the feeling of uneasiness, unhappiness, dissatisfaction, dislike, and can even kill interest. The audience may not wish to listen to this type of preacher ever again. The necessary warrant for the preacher's presence in the pulpit is to do just one thing – to preach God's Word, nothing more. Therefore, preachers should avoid time wasting while in the pulpit. Like a soldier in the battlefield, position yourself, aim at your target, pull the trigger, and then release it and hit the target. So, while preaching, always be very observant to read the psychology of the audience. By their looks, moods, and movements, they could be saying to you, "We do not understand what you are saying preacher," or "When will you be done, preacher? We are tired and want to leave."

As an antidote to poor use of time, preachers should apply the *TA-SALE* principle during sermon delivery. This principle means *Take, Say,* and *Leave.* When it is time for the presentation of the sermon, please, preacher, *take* the pulpit and waste no time. Once you are already in the pulpit, use it productively by *saying* what you have to say in the pulpit. Your warrant for being in the pulpit is to represent God by preaching his Word, the truth of it, and the whole of it; therefore, do just that. Lastly, when you have finished preaching, *leave* the pulpit, and say no other word. Even when you think you omitted something very crucial that should have been said, please, leave. Resist the temptation of wanting to go back on the sermon to say what was skipped or forgotten. Doing so distorts and waters down the effects of the message. After all, the listeners do not know your "skips" in the sermon. So, never feel guilty.

EFFECTIVE SERMON DELIVERY

Just as certain factors combine to make for effective public communication, the same holds for expository preaching; for poor use of them can mar the effectiveness of a sermon presentation. Therefore, the expository preacher should, of necessity, give careful attention to them. These crucially indispensable components are the preacher's body instruments, such as the voice, eyes, gestures, moods and possibly style. Chapell says, "Our bodies combine with our voices in the communication process. Our eyes, faces, hands, and movements participate in what we say or may carry a message all their own that we never intended to communicate."[6]

Good use of these components will accentuate the interest of the listeners in the sermon, but a bad use impedes it. Appropriate use of them improves the quality of the sermon. According to Robinson, "The effectiveness of our sermons depends on two factors: what we say and how we say it. Both are important."[7] Appropriating these necessary components helps a preacher to ". . . preach in an appealing, attractive, and compelling manner."[8]

Use Your Voice

Verbal communication depends on the voice to convey an intended message, but wrong use of it "can get in the way."[9] The voice serves as the medium through which a preacher passes God's message to the audience, yet, it can also serve as a significant obstacle by distorting the same message. Vines and Shaddix stress the role of the voice,

---

6. Bryan Chapell, *Christ-Centered Preaching: Redeeming the Expository Sermon* (2nd ed., 2005; repr., Grand Rapids, Michigan: Baker Academic, 2007), 334.

7. Robinson, *Expository Preaching*, 201.

8. Jerry Vines and Jim Shaddix, *Power in the Pulpit: How to Prepare and Deliver Expository Sermons* (Chicago, Illinois: Moody Press, 1999), 313.

9. Larsen, *The Anatomy of Preaching*, 190.

> The preacher speaks the [W]ord of God in the words of
> men. Thus, preaching is the most important kind of public
> speaking known to humanity. The expression of the sermon
> ultimately will be manifested via oral communication
> during the delivery of the message. Although various ele-
> ments of nonverbal communication are important matters,
> the preacher's first attention should be given to the quality
> of his verbal expression.[10]

It is clear, so far, that the voice is the most important tool for the expository preacher. In as much as the other instruments are crucial to communicating the divine message, they only play a supporting role to the voice. Knecht equates the voice and tongue as the propelling force for preaching with the fire of Pentecost. He says, "The revived preacher possesses but one instrument, but having that he needs no other. He has a tongue of fire, the very weapon given to the church on Pentecost. His tongue, energized by the Holy Spirit, is the means of articulating to the world the truth of God in such a way that hearts are changed and heaven comes to earth."[11] This is critical for us in Africa. Proverbs play a vital role in African speeches, particularly among the elderly. The use of proverbs usually punctuates oral communication because they heavily embed the speech patterns of the African peoples. This makes the care and use of the vocal instrument very essential for the African expository preacher.

The voice is described as a royal instrument that ". . . is unsurpassed in its ability to express with depth and meaning the intended message of its user."[12] The quality of its sound and tone need appropriate regulation. Charles Spurgeon once lamented the effects of

---

10. Vines and Shaddix, *Power in the Pulpit*, 229.

11. Glen C. Knecht, "Sermon Structure and Flow," in *The Preacher and Preaching: Reviving the Art* (ed., Samuel T. Logan Jr., Phillipsburg, New Jersey: Presbyterian and Reformed Publishing, 1986), 275.

12. Vines and Shaddix, *Power in the Pulpit*, 263.

poor voicing in preaching, "There are brethren in the ministry whose speech is intolerable; either they rouse you to wrath, or else they send you to sleep.... no human being, unless gifted with infinite patience, could long endure to listen to them, and nature does well to give the victim deliverance through sleep."[13] A bad voice not only distorts the divine message in the sermon but causes discomfort to the listeners as well. As the "royal" instrument in the hands of the expositor, the appropriate regulation of the rate or pace, volume, and tone or pitching of the voice in sermon delivery cannot be overemphasised.

Voice rate or pace has to do with the speed with which the preacher speaks, whether the speaker is fast or slow. Baumann says a proper rate is one that is both varied and sufficiently rapid to ensure interest in the sermon movement.[14] The volume of the voice also has to do with how loud or low it sounds. Still, the pitching of the voice refers to the filtering light or deep sound, that is, the high or low tone of the voice when one is speaking. As both a "royal" instrument and "God's given tool," a great deal of the effectiveness of the preacher's message depends upon the manner in which the vocal mechanism is handled.[15]

---

13. This is taken from *Spurgeon's Lectures to His Students* on page 199 as quoted by Daniel Baumann. See J. Daniel Baumann, *An Introduction to Contemporary Preaching* (1972; paperback ed., 1988; repr., Grand Rapids, Michigan: Baker Book House, 1990), 191. Jerry Vines cites Hoffman as saying, "If the preacher cannot be heard, then nothing else matters." See Vines, *A Guide to Effective Sermon Delivery*, 34. To speak either so soft and low that you cannot be heard, or so loud that the ears of the people are overwhelmed with a roaring sound are two dangerous extremes when using the voice in sermon delivery.

14. Baumann, *An Introduction to Contemporary Preaching*, 191. Baumann says an acceptable average range of voice rate is given as between 125 – 190 words per minute. Though every speaker has his or her speech rate, communication can be hindered when one speaks too fast or too slow. The same also holds when one speaks either too loud or too low.

15. Vines and Jim Shaddix, *Power in the Pulpit*, 265.

Mastery of the voice when preaching is of immense benefit both to the preacher and the audience. It improves the listening pleasure of the audience as the preacher's voice becomes as good music to their ears,[16] and it also improves the quality of the preacher's professional skills and expertise. Raising or dropping the voice is helpful when emphasis or attention is desired. Chapell says, by the appropriate regulation of the voice, whether to express joy, humour, seriousness, or contemplation, the tone, pace, and volume should indicate what the words mean.[17]

Many African preachers need training in regulating the voice in the pulpit. Some of them shout almost throughout the sermon. An underlying assumption behind this practice is that such action is a sign of an 'anointed' or 'powerful' preaching. On the contrary, it reveals a clear sign of ignorance of homiletical principles and a demonstration of professional immaturity or amateurship and incompetence instead. No matter how well-prepared a sermon is, the message and its essence are lost through poor voice regulation during its delivery. A poorly moderated voice kills interest, distracts attention, causes discomfort for the audience, and upsets and creates boredom in them.

Loudspeakers Assist

Professional public speakers or people directly involved in public relations are generally trained to speak in such a manner that they can be heard, understood, and followed through. When one is speaking to a large congregation, being heard by everyone can be a challenge. Communication support or voice aids are designed to make up for or assist the public speaker in overcoming this area of challenge. The

---

16. Vines and Shaddix, *Power in the Pulpit*, 268.
17. Chapell, *Christ-Centered Preaching*, 333.

most common of these is the use of the loudspeaker. However, the way and manner in which some preachers use the loudspeaker turns this needed supporting companion for the speaker into a dreaded enemy for the listening audience.

The use of the loudspeaker should be maximised to achieve the listening pleasure of the audience. In order to avoid a blasting sound and echo, a preacher should ensure first that the loudspeaker's volume is appropriate for the size of the room and number of people attending, and second that there is a reasonable distance between his mouth and the microphone. [18]Also, a preacher should be conscious to regulate the volume of their voice, particularly where there is no qualified sound engineer to do so. Chapell states, "Pulpit microphones work best (carrying the full dynamics of your voice) if you project over them rather than speak into them."[19]

When a speaker comes blasting through the loudspeaker and worst, when it also echoes, the effect is a distortion of the voice and an aching of the listeners' ears. A disconnect in communication becomes the result. Some African preachers take this as fashionable. This is offensive rather than fanciful. We cautioned preachers previously not to shout when preaching but rather to raise the voice only when it is necessary. When the loudspeaker is used appropriately by a preacher, it becomes a friend to the listeners; but when it is used poorly, it unavoidably becomes a foe to them.

---

18. Because bodies absorb sound a room full of people will require a higher loudspeaker setting than an empty room. Loudspeakers should be set so that the speaker (or singer) can be heard comfortably, without distortion or pain to the listener.

19. Chapell, *Christ-Centered Preaching*, 332.

Use Gestures

In African parenting, the rod is not spared as an aspect of child training and discipline. In ancient African societies, children were taught good morals and ethical behaviour by both parents and the immediate community they are a part of. They were also taught the value of respect for the elderly. Whenever the child misbehaved in public where either or both parents were present, the look on the face of the parent spoke volumes to the child. This is an aspect of gesture in child training. Similarly, in preaching, the body of the preacher is also actively involved in the communication process.

Gesture is the language of the body in preaching. It is the non-verbal aspect of the preacher's body parts that also communicates during the delivery of a sermon. This plays out by the movements made by a particular part of the preacher's body, each appropriately used in turn, in order to express meaning or emotion or to communicate an instruction. Put another way, the gesture is the way and manner in which the preacher consciously involves the movements of the body or limbs as a means of expression and to emphasise an idea.

A sermon will become dull without the effective use of these non-verbal communicative instruments of the human body. Gestures are significant because "Some thoughts are better expressed by gestures rather than words or facial expressions."[20] As Larsen also notes, one's posture ". . . makes a statement before one even begins to speak."[21] This suggests that the nonverbal aspect of the communication process can strike louder notes and tones than the actual verbal notes. This way, a preacher is at the risk of passing on to the listener unintentional messages by the use of inappropriate gestures.

---

20. Vines and Shaddix, *Power in the Pulpit*, 325.
21. Larsen, *The Anatomy of Preaching*, 191.

Gestures are expressed both by the use of body postures and movements. Our body fillers, replete in inflexions and actions, send quick signals to listeners. According to Robinson, a preacher's body inflexions ". . . transmit your feelings and attitudes more accurately than your words. . . . how we broadcast messages by the way we sit or stand, by our facial expressions, by our gestures, and even by how much space we allow between ourselves and those we meet."[22] For instance, a preacher who stands in a slightly bent position, leans on the pulpit with or without the palm on the chin, and kneels or sits down in a demonstration of a specific point, is exhibiting an aspect of postural gestures. The one that throws the hand in the air, pounds the pulpit or podium, shakes the head, grasps the pulpit with the hands and the like, exhibits parts of body movements. This goes to show that, "The eyes, hands, face, and feet say much to a congregation as the words we utter",[23] and even more. Accordingly, preachers should be aware that the use of gestures should be definite, appropriate, varied, timely and purposeful when and where they are used.

Movement or pacing in the pulpit is also a critical aspect of the expression of gestures. This should neither be aimless nor random, but specific and sparse. While it is good to move out of the pulpit, it should be done rarely with the aim of achieving specific goals at particular points in the sermon.

---

22. Robinson, *Expository Preaching*, 202.

23. Robinson, *Expository Preaching*, 203. Robinson directs that the preacher is to ". . . suit the actions and the words to the audience", because the purpose of gestures is "to help to explain and describe; to emphasise the speech; to maintain interest and hold attention; to put the preacher at ease to feel more confident and alert; and to help the listeners experience what we feel as they identify with us." This draws attention to the timely, appropriate and right use of gestures in such a manner that the particular point of the message does not slip away from the grips of the listeners. See pages 208-210.

In a cross-cultural context, the use of certain particular gestures can be offensive to specific audiences. In such cases, the preacher should be mindful what types of gestures are generally accepted and which may likely offend each type of audience. Preachers should always be on the lookout for particular circles where certain gestures are culturally and ethically inappropriate. Using such gestures can distort or even block the reception of the divine message in the sermon.

Use Your Moods

Moods refer primarily to facial expressions. These convey feelings and put life into the message. Moods convey the feelings of joy or sadness, of happiness or numbness/depression, satisfaction or dissatisfaction, acceptance or disapproval, and much more. Robinson states, "Because facial expression is very important, your people need to see your face"[24] so they can decode the message being expressed by your moods. At some point, a smiling face is appropriate while at some other point, a frowning face is also appropriate.

The appropriate and timely use of moods in sermon delivery is as critical as the content of the sermon itself. The human face, whether appearing in round, long, or spherical shape, is the only instrument that expresses various moods. The expository preacher's face is the first road sign or the first news caption where the listeners decode what to expect in the sermon. A Hausa proverb from Nigeria captures this idea quite vividly. It says, *labarin zuciya, sai a tambayi fuska*, meaning, the condition of a person's heart or state of mind is revealed by facial expression. When a person is happy, the face is the first place of expression. Also, when a person is sad, the face expresses it as well, even before a word comes on the person's tongue. The

---

24. Robinson, *Expository Preaching*, 212.

face expresses anger when it frowns and wrinkles, but it expresses happiness and approval by a smile and smoothened contours of its epidermis. The face serves more or less like a screen that is used to project steel photos. Being such a significant part of the sermon delivery, it should be strategically positioned to the proper view of all in the audience.

Use Your Eyes

The culture in the West requires that one looks straight into the eyes of the person that he or she is talking to. Failure here is considered as being dishonest or as hiding something. For us in Africa, however, the reverse is the case, at least for those who are born and nurtured in the African villages. Younger people do not look the elderly in the face when they are talking, let alone look straight in the eyes. When this happens, it is considered a gross act of disrespect that attracts some form of discipline. However, agemates or peers and friends can look each other in the eyes when talking with one another.

As a result of this cultural upbringing, some African preachers find difficulty in looking people straight in the eye even when they stand in the pulpit. There should be an exception to this good African cultural norm when it comes to the matter of the pulpit ministry. The preacher of the divine Word comes and stands before an African congregation, not before an African elder, with a serious and urgent message from God. Eye contact at this point is essential to reveal the weight of the message and the conviction with which the preacher delivers the divine Word.

Keeping eye contact with the audience is critical because they both listen to and look at the preacher. According to Robinson, "Eye contact probably ranks as the single most effective means of nonverbal communication at [the preacher's] disposal. Eyes communicate."[25] In contributing to this significant point, Larsen adds, "The eye is really an organ of speech. . . . [As such], Every break in eye contact is risky",[26] particularly so when it is at a crucial point where emphasis, application, caution/warning, or some serious point is being made. Consequently, when a preacher evades eye contact in the pulpit, it shows a sign of the lack of seriousness. In judging the preacher at this point, the audience will reason that, if what the speaker is saying were important, and if the preacher were serious about it, then he or she should have looked us in the eye.

Chapell explains the implications of evading eye contact further,

> A speaker who will not look people in the eyes is deemed aloof, afraid, and incompetent. One who looks at the ceiling while explaining how Jesus held little children appears distracted. One who looks at the floor while exhorting others to repent seems intimidated. One who looks overheads (or even at foreheads) instead of in the eyes of listeners seems untrustworthy. . . . You must look at people! . . . When you deny people your eyes, you really deny them yourself.[27]

A preacher who is afraid, timid, and lacks self-confidence can easily evade eye contact. However, eye contact in the pulpit is essential both for the benefits of the audience and the speaker. While listeners follow the preacher to decode what is being said by the preacher's moods, a good eye contact also enables the speaker to have feedback from their facial expressions. As such, the preacher should span the eyes from right to left and from left to the right side of the audience. This way, no part of the audience is robbed of the preacher's face and eyes. The preacher's eyes serve as a viewing screen, hence, should be well positioned for all to have a good view. Equally, the audience's

---

25. Robinson, *Expository Preaching*, 211.
26. Larsen, *The Anatomy of Preaching*, 188-9.
27. Chapell, *Christ-centered Preaching*, 334-5.

eyes function as a video camera that follows the action to capture it. Keeping the eyes in the centre is crucial. Is this not among the reasons why the pulpit is placed at the centre?

Some modern African preachers like to move back and forth in the midst of the congregation thinking such to be fashionable. However, standing in the pulpit to respectfully and reverently preach the Word of God is our evangelical heritage. The pulpit represents the altar of sacrifice in the Old Testament where a sacrifice was either accepted or rejected by God. Such rejection followed wrong attitudes and approaches either by the offeree or the offering priest. When a preacher stands in the pulpit, he or she stands on the platform of authority; and when the preacher calls attention to the Bible from which he or she is preaching, the preacher is appealing to higher authority deserving of absolute reverence and obedience. Standing in the pulpit to preach should not be taken lightly by African expository preachers. The pulpit signifies the Ark of the covenant that was placed in the holy of holies in the Temple in Jerusalem. Much more, frequent movement out of the pulpit into the midst of the audience distracts and likely distorts the message. It also robs the listeners of the preacher's face and eyes.

Over ninety per cent of any pacing should be in the pulpit where movement is needed at some appropriate stage in the sermon. When moving out of the pulpit, the preacher should balance the variation from both the left and right sides of the audience, so one side is not deprived of the preacher's face and eyes. Also, the preacher should not stay too long on one side before returning to the other side, or back to the centre and into the pulpit.

Using Your Style

Africans love to express themselves and their emotions through music and dance. Walter Rodney points out, regarding the apparent resemblances of ancient African communities, ". . . music and dance had key roles in 'uncontaminated' African society. They were ever present at birth, initiation, marriage, death, etc., as well as appearing at times of recreation. Africa is the continent of drums and percussion. African peoples reached the pinnacle of achievement in that sphere."[28] Similarly, Kato adds,

> The mere mention of culture brings traditional dancing to the minds of many people. In many countries of Africa, an official tour by a head of state or other government officials is incomplete without traditional dancing. In some countries, professional dancers are paid by the government to provide 'cultural dancing' on special occasions.[29]

Every type of dance has a unique style that accompanies its rhythm. Like it, individual preachers are inclined to have and express different preaching styles unique to the personality of every one of them. A style is understood essentially as the preacher's characteristic manner of expressing his thoughts.[30] It is the way a preacher preaches, described as the preacher's signature.[31] Style is a preacher's imaginative creativity, that is, an ability of "doing what other people

---

28. Walter Rodney, *How Europe Underdeveloped Africa* (2nd impression, London: Bogle-L'Ouverture Publications/Dar-es-Salaam, Tanzania: Tanzania Publishing House, 1973), 41

29. Byang Henry Kato, *African Cultural Revolution and the Christian Faith* (Jos, Nigeria: Challenge Publications, 1976), 7.

30. Vines and Shaddix, *Power in the Pulpit*, 230. This is a citation of John A. Broadus in the fourth edition of his *On the Preparation and Delivery of Sermon* on the issue of style.

31. Larsen, *The Anatomy of Preaching*, 170-71.

don't."[32] Our style in preaching is uniquely our individual identifying trademark evidenced in every message we preach,[33] described as being "the man himself."[34] As a preacher's pulpit trademark uniquely characteristic only of the personality of such preacher, style is not learned but rather an involuntary act and an unintentional expression of the specific characteristic nature of the preacher. Every preacher intuitively expresses some form of style in the pulpit.

We have given space to style to stress the point that African preachers should not mimic another preacher. The practice of being a copycat thwarts professional productivity. Paul says the gifts given to individual Christians are for the edification of the entire church (Eph 4:11-12). Instead of imitating someone else's preaching style, every preacher should instead channel such energy to developing and perfecting his or her unique preaching style.

In short, this chapter has addressed the methodology of preaching – what to do and what not to do when preaching. Preaching a sermon has a trilogy – introduction, delivery of content, and conclusion. So far, we have discussed the first two; what lies ahead is how to conclude a sermon.

---

32. Larsen, *The Anatomy of Preaching*, 108.

33. Larsen, *The Anatomy of Preaching*, 170.

34. Larsen is citing of George Louis Leclerc de Buffon in David L. Larsen, *The Anatomy of Preaching*, 170.

CHAPTER 13

BRAKING THE EXPOSITORY SERMON

When an automobile or a car is in motion, the journey is always smooth. However, when it heads towards a pothole, a bend, a turn, or any obstacle, the driver usually applies the brake to slow down or stop the car from moving. Particularly, when the driver gets to the destination of the journey, he or she applies the brake to halt the car. Braking to a stop signals to the passengers that they have arrived their destination. The end or conclusion of the expository sermon acts just like the brake to an automobile. It halts the sermon from moving.

Why is it necessary to conclude a sermon? What is lost or at risk if an expository preacher fails to conclude a sermon? Vines and Shaddix supply the answer: "Because the Word of God always demands a response . . . [and because] In reality, the sermon is not concluded until it is lived out in the lives of the people who hear it [,] all biblical sermons should culminate in a call for such action."[1] The need for a positive response demands that every sermon should always end with some concluding statements. Additionally, the sermon ". . . conclusion crystallizes, personalizes, and helps actualize the response

---

1. Jerry Vines and Jim Shaddix, *Power in the Pulpit: How to Prepare and Deliver Expository Sermons* (Chicago, Illinois: Moody Press, 1999), 207.

called for by the message . . . [being] intentionally the most confrontational aspect of the message."[2]

Let me illustrate why a conclusion is necessary. People who travel on African roads have several experiences. While some of the roads are smooth and good, some others are rough and bad. Both the tarred and untarred roads have potholes. Travelling on an untarred road, for instance, can be dusty; passengers would have to visit the laundry at the end of the journey to have their clothes washed as a result of the dust. Travelling on the roads with potholes too can be very discomforting. Also, some of the commercial cars and buses that ply the roads in Africa are bad; really bad – some have worn out engines, defective tyres, and torn seats. For example, in Nigeria, a traveller would usually come across broken cars and buses parked in the middle of the road instead of by the roadside. One would sometimes hear a driver of a broken-down automobile say to passers-by, "Abeg, mek una help me push." What the driver means is, "Please, give me a helping hand to push the vehicle." Do not assume that the driver is asking for help to push the vehicle off the road. It is actually to force it to start by pushing. When you travel on such bad roads or in such bad vehicles, it is very uncomfortable, and leaves you tired and frustrated. Time is wasted, and emotions are set on edge. Some of the drivers even lack manners and courtesy.

The expository sermon's conclusion is not like travelling on some horrible road or some lousy vehicle. It is not even marking the end of it like coming to the end of a short or long journey. Instead, the conclusion is like coming to the end of a very successful, enjoyable, satisfying, and meaningful journey. It is also like coming to the end of a self-fulfilling, adventurous and a rewarding journey. This is sig-

---

2. Stephen F. Olford and David Lindsay Olford, *Anointed Expository Preaching* (Nashville, Tennessee: Broadman & Holman Publishers, 1998), 194.

nificant because the conclusion of the sermon is not only the "sermon's destination,"[3] but most importantly, it is "the climax of the message."[4] Larsen says, "The conclusion of the sermon is where our intention or central idea should come into the clearest focus."[5]

All that preceded in the sermon has been "building toward a climax."[6] Accordingly, Robinson asserts that the sermon conclusion ". . . brings the central concept to a burning focus and drives home its truth to the minds and lives of the listeners."[7] Appropriately, then, the sermon conclusion is so crucial because this is where the sermon achieves its purpose statement – what it set out initially to achieve in the individual life of the listeners. The conclusion answers the "So what?" question of the listener. This is where the specific personal participation of the audience in the message of the exposed divine Word is demanded.

THE ROLE OF THE CONCLUSION

We cannot over-emphasise the fact that the sermon conclusion is critical. If we don't have a conclusion, a sermon would have loose ends, making it difficult for the listeners to respond, and for the preacher to evaluate as well. Olford and Olford explain that, ". . . it is in the conclusion that the preacher challenges the listeners to re-

---

3. Bryan Chapell, *Christ-Centered Preaching: Redeeming the Expository Sermon* (2nd ed., 2005; repr., Grand Rapids, Michigan: Baker Book House, 2007), 254.
4. Chapell, *Christ-Centered Preaching*, 253.
5. David L. Larsen, *The Anatomy of Preaching: Identifying the Issues in Preaching Today* (Grand Rapids, Michigan: Kregel Publications, 1999, and Ibadan, Nigeria: CHRIST AND WE PUBLICATIONS, 2000), 119.
6. Vines and Shaddix, *Power in the Pulpit*, 210.
7. Haddon W. Robinson, *Expository Preaching: Principles and Practice* (2nd ed., 2001; repr., Leicester, England: Inter-Varsity Press, 2004), 182.

spond to the main issue of the message."[8] The conclusion should lead to the question of action on the part of the listener like the gathered community at Pentecost in Jerusalem did ask when they heard Peter's simple exposition of current events (Acts 2:37; see also 16:30).

Expository preaching tells the listeners what God's demands and requirements are, what he has in stock for them, and what he expects them to do so they could benefit from it. Hence, "Now that you have exposed the listeners' minds to the truth of God's Word, the time has come for you to inspire them to act on it"[9] in the sermon's conclusion. The reason, as Chapell explains, is "Because listeners are more likely to remember a conclusion than any other portion of a message."[10] This is why "The last sixty seconds are typically the most dynamic moments in excellent sermons. With these final words, a preacher marshals the thought and emotion of an entire message into an exhortation that makes all that has preceded clear and compelling."[11] It is this compelling part of the sermon that leads the listener to the point of acting on the sermon without any delay. As such, the expository preacher needs extra care to neatly and finely tie all the important points in the sermon together in the conclusion so that the listener is left in no doubt as to what response is called for.

While preparing a sermon, expository preachers should always look out for what the appropriate response to the sermon should be. When a sermon conclusion fails to answer any or all of the questions of action by the listeners such as: "And so what?", or "What has it got to do with me?", or still, as Olford and Olford put it, "What do I need

---

8.   Olford and Olford, *Anointed Expository Preaching*, 194.

9.   Vines and Shaddix, *Power in the Pulpit*, 210.

10.   Chapell, *Christ-Centered Preaching*, 253.

11.   Chapell, *Christ-Centered Preaching*, 254.

to do about this message?",[12] then the preaching has failed to accomplish its purpose.

All expository preachers should ensure that the exposed divine Word ends with a good conclusion so it can have its desired effects on the listeners. Preachers should determine the definite purpose of the sermon from its beginning. This helps in arriving at a purposeful, realistic, tangible, achievable, and a measurable conclusion. A conclusion to a sermon is directed to a specific area of life. For example, a preacher must be clear in the mind which of these questions is the direction or aim of the sermon: "Are you hoping to effect a change of thinking or a change of behavio[u]r, or both? Are you trying to encourage, to motivate, to call for repentance, or to bring people to an encounter with the living God?"[13] This is where purpose matters. Purpose helps in giving ". . . an accurate, specific, clear, and personal answer for your listeners"[14] so they are not left wondering what to do about the message like a lost and helpless sheep in the bush.

The point of the conclusion is where the message now comes into its sharpest focus as it brings all things to a harmonious and moving culmination.[15] To raise the listener to this level, the conclusion must be relatively brief and well-shaped.[16] It should be clearly stated, straight to the point, and forcefully presented. Since the conclusion of a sermon is said to be the terminus of the sermon, "The wording of this terminus should . . . be striking enough to echo in the mind of listeners throughout the week. These expectations require a preach-

---

12. Olford and Olford, *Anointed Expository Preaching*, 195.

13. Gordon D. Fee, *New Testament Exegesis: A Handbook for Students and Pastors* (Philadelphia: The Westminster Press, 1983), 134, 135.

14. Olford and Olford, *Anointed Expository Preaching*, 195.

15. This is Baumann's citation of page 121 of Steps to the Sermon by Brown, Clinard & Northcutt. See Baumann, An *Introduction to Contemporary Preaching*, 142.

16. Larsen, *The Anatomy of Preaching*, 120.

er to plan for a definite, purposed, pointed end"[17] in the sermon. The point is simply this, that the expository preacher must expertly pull the material of the message "together and conclude strongly."[18]

The role of a good and accurate sermon conclusion is that crucial because it is the listener's take home. People who travel often return with a souvenir to remind them of such journeys. Similarly, sermon conclusions are like souvenirs and as such should be personally directed, emphasising a personal encounter with God – a compelling call to bend the knee and bow the head and heart before the Lord Almighty. The listener should be able to understand at the time of the conclusion that the moment of decision has come; that it is him or her, not everyone that the sermon invites to take personal action.

TYPES OF SERMON CONCLUSIONS

Africans are generally arable farmers. Most of the farmers regularly rotate their crops. Here, different crops are grown on the same land either at the same time or in succession. Similarly, just as sermon introductions are categorised into types, so are sermon conclusions. Sermons are not ended in the same manner, with the same material, and with the same tone. The shapes or forms that conclusions to sermons take depends on the nature of the sermon itself, the audience, and the personality of the expository preacher. A few examples follow below:

Recapitulation

This is a brief and concise summary of the main points and key thoughts of the sermon. It is the restating of the main points and a

---

17. Chapell, *Christ-Centered Preaching*, 256.

18. Larsen, *The Anatomy of Preaching*, 120.

tying up of the loose ends by reviewing the sermon's important as-
sertions.[19] Here, the highpoints, key thoughts and major emphases of
the sermon are very briefly restated without repetition and explanation and are succinctly re-echoed to remind the listeners about what
has preceded and what areas they need to act on. Care, however,
needs taken so that such summaries "sound like hammer strokes"[20]
to the ears and hearts of the listeners.

Exhortation

This is an articulated persuasive call to motivate, mobilise the wills,
and challenge the listener to action. The nature of an exhortative
type of conclusion can take the form of a plea, a citation of a particular hymn or Scripture that is relevant to the sermon, a relevant
saying common to knowledge or a proverbial statement, or some
wording that exhorts the heart.

The sermon context should ordinarily determine what aspect of
exhortation is used. For example, some sermon contexts that warrant different types of exhortation are the pain of bereavement that
is a general concern in the audience or the need for forgiveness for
some inhuman acts audience members have suffered such as terrorist murders. Alternatively, it could be the need for encouragement to
stand for the Master in the face of danger or persecution. Also, an
exhortative type of conclusion can as well be appropriate within a
particular sermon context where the spirit of commitment and dedication to the faith and Christian service is declining or lacking.

---

19. Robinson, *Expository Preaching*, 176.
20. Chapell, *Christ-Centered Preaching*, 255.

Altar calls

This is a call for listeners to commit themselves to act on the truth of the sermon, geared to either unbelievers or believers. This call to action encourages listeners to personally and specifically do something about the sermon, whether privately or publicly, by "Striking while the iron is hot."[21]

This type of conclusion may require people to stand in response or to come forward to the front. Note that the purpose of the sermon invitation goes beyond just inviting people to faith or salvation in Christ. It is also directed at Christians who may need to publicly stand or come forward and confess some sin in their lives. It calls on them to individually rededicate their life in personal commitment to the Lordship of Christ and make a definite commitment in service to him. It may even urge them to declare a public answer to a call to full-time ministry in the Lord's vineyard, and so on.

Prayer

The context of the sermon or the audience may require that a sermon end with a special prayer for the congregation. This is not a closing benediction to a church service. The context for such a conclusion could be special prayers for guidance and protection for the particular Christian community, or prayers for courage and confidence in the face of violence such as tribal strife and wars, or terrorist vandalism. Also, the need could be prayers for God's specific blessings upon the congregation, for comfort, strength of heart, and for maturity in faith. Still, the prayers may just be a concluding doxology at the end of the sermon such as, "The LORD bless you and keep you; the LORD make his face shine upon you, and be gracious to you; the LORD lift up his countenance upon you, and give you peace" (Num 6:24-26

---

21. Vines and Shaddix, *Power in the Pulpit*, 207.

NRSV). Or, "May the God of peace himself sanctify you entirely; and may your spirit and soul and body be kept sound and blameless at the coming of our Lord Jesus Christ" (1 Thess 5:23 NRSV).

Furthermore, the nature, mood, and force of a particular sermon may require that the preacher say a specific prayer to end the sermon without calling the congregation to prayer. Some examples of such relevant prayers are, "Strengthen our hands, O Lord, to move on . . . ," "O Lord, take the lead in our lives . . . ," "O God of all creation, please, comfort us . . . ," "O God, our Father, in your judgement, remember mercy. Please, forgive us . . . ." On the other hand, a sermon can end with an invitation to the congregation to join in a closing prayer to end the sermon with words such as "Let us pray" or "Shall we pray together?"

Questions

Questions are structured in different forms, and serve different functions depending on their purpose. A sermon can end with a specific, definite question. As Robinson says, "An appropriate question, or even a series of questions, can conclude a sermon effectively."[22] Skilled preachers sometimes end their sermons with powerful rhetorical question(s). The purpose of concluding a sermon with a rhetorical question is intended for personal reflection as it encourages listeners to consider more deeply the matters discussed in the sermon.[23]

Such questions should, of necessity, be provocative by their nature and tone. Here are some examples: "People die every day without hearing the gospel and go to hell. If we do not preach the gospel to save them, then, what shall we do?" Or, "If God did not spare the

---

22. Robinson, *Expository Preaching*, 178.

23. Chapell, *Christ-Centered Preaching*, 259.

city of Sodom and Gomorrah for their persistent sin; will he spare you when you persist in sin?" Every question or set of questions must relate to the subject and purpose statement of the sermon. Remember that the time of the sermon conclusion is similar to when a plane lands when the pilot needs to marshal all his professional expertise with utmost care to ensure a safe landing. The professional expertise of the expository preacher is quite crucial at this point so that such questions will sink deep into the hearts, bones and marrows of the listeners.

Thought-provoking

In this type of conclusion, the preacher ends the message with a statement, or even a question that challenges the listener to act, whether immediately or as they walk home. The specific purpose for the thought-provoking type of sermon conclusion is to force the listeners to ponder[24] the proposition and the main thrust of the sermon. An example of this type of conclusion could be something like, "God is looking for men and women today to stand in the gap in this corrupt and godless generation, and I want to be one of them." Or, "Esther saw the need to save her people from death (from total annihilation) by taking a great risk; hey, I want to be like her!" Also, another example could be: "Hey, the maxim states, 'When the going gets tough, the tough get going, because quitters never win a battle and winners never lose a battle.' Will you quit?" The anticipated response of such thought-provocation is to force deep reflection and inward questioning in the listener. It is a forceful challenge to the listener to decide to stand up for the Lord.

---

24. Vines and Shaddix, *Power in the Pulpit*, 208.

Song

In this type of conclusion, the preacher ends the sermon with a relevant chorus, song or an appropriate hymn. A stanza or even just part of a stanza of a hymn is most appropriate here. This type of conclusion is used to steer the listeners to action, to cheer the listeners to courage, and to light up hope in them. The expository preacher, depending on the purpose and goal of the sermon, could either quote the song, sing it, or involve the audience in singing it to conclude the sermon.

Specific Direction

As the name implies, this type of sermon conclusion gives specific and definite direction on the course of action that the listeners are to follow after the sermon. It answers specifically the listeners' "how?" question of the sermon. The preacher answers the question in the conclusion and tells and shows them how. This type of conclusion tells the listeners exactly how to apply lessons learned from the sermon to real-life situations during the week. It attempts to answer clearly how the biblical truth preached on can work in real life situations for different individuals – women, men, couples, students, workers, employers, business people, politicians, youths, and so on.

Abrupt Ending

The abrupt ending or the "surprise ending"[25] can also be masterfully used as the final action of the expository preacher in the pulpit. This type of conclusion can send graphic and shocking waves into the veins and nerves of the listeners. At this juncture, after the preacher has made a forceful statement or raised a critical question, he or she

---

25. Larsen, *The Anatomy of Preaching*, 128.

marshals critical points of the sermon appropriately and succinctly, and then ends with a statement like, for instance, "Think about it!" Alternatively, to put it another way, at this point in the sermon, the preacher raises the emotions, hammers home the point of the message, calls the hearers to urgent specific action,[26] moreover, while the listeners are still expecting the next statement, the preacher leaves the pulpit quietly without saying further any other word. The goal is to help the listener go into some serious reflection and deep personal soul searching at that moment.

Quotation

It is also entirely appropriate to end a sermon with an appropriate quote. The aim of using a quotation is to reinforce what listeners have heard.

Every sermon situation determines the type of conclusion that is most appropriate. However, one basic fact remains; every sermon must end, and it must end well. As we earlier stated, preachers must not compromise on a definite, purposeful, forceful and concrete ending of every sermon, because the aims of all genuine preaching are ". . . to quicken the conscience by the holiness of God, to feed the mind with the truth of God, to purge the imagination by the beauty of God, to open the heart to the love of God, to devote the will to the purpose of God."[27] The seriousness of this final moment is to be heard clearly from the tone of the preacher's voice, seen clearly from the looks on the preacher's eyes, and decoded from the clearly observed expressions of the preacher's moods.

---

26. Chapell, *Christ-Centered Preaching*, 258.

27. James Stewart, *Heralds of God* (Grand Rapids, Michigan: Baker, 1972), 73. John Piper says this quote comes from William Temple who formulated it to define worship, but that Stewart borrowed it as giving precisely the aims and ends of preaching.

CHAPTER 14

KNOWING THE TEXTUAL BACKGROUND

Having a good background knowledge about various life issues is an enormous help when decisions have to be made or your opinion is sought. When I was going into the fulltime pastoral ministry, my pastor advised me not to pull down any wall until I knew why it was built. This was a caution not to change anything I found until I knew the reason why it existed. Such a wise counsel about background knowledge on issues has stuck with me.

There are certain essential fundamental elements that preachers cannot ignore in the sermon making process. By *fundamental elements* one means those necessary and critical factors about the Bible that a preacher uses when constructing his or her expository sermon. The Bible was given to humans within a human context, and the human authors expressed the message of divine revelation in human words. The content was communicated both orally and in writing, following the standard conventions of the day. The Biblical authors also drew considerably on such factors as the cultures and customs of the ancient Middle East (Palestine then), and the Greco-Romans. They drew on their politics, economics and sociology; their agriculture and animal husbandry, ecology and geography; and on their hydrology and a host of other sources of their day as vehicles of transmitting the revealed Word.

Good knowledge of the background of the Biblical text enables its expositors to gain a good grasp of the content and message of it. This helps them to clearly interpret and properly relate the message of the ancient Biblical text in contemporary forms to the listeners. This is very important for us in Africa. We most times tend to assume the meaning of a particular passage because its context, especially that of the Old Testament, is closer to ours. However, what we see in the Bible may not turn out to be precisely what we think when we study the background of the passage. This is why a grounded knowledge of the textual background is essential for preachers.

The Bible is not only a religious text written primarily to a Jewish community, but it is also quite ancient and far remote from the modern readers in Africa and elsewhere. Consequently, the modern expository preacher needs to get acquainted with its general background, textual contexts, good working knowledge of its exegesis and hermeneutics, and its theology in his or her attempt to place its message in the hands and hearts of contemporary listeners. These unavoidable fundamental elements enrich the expository sermon, acting like a delicious meal prepared with all the required ingredients that make a good tasty meal.

UNDERSTANDING THE BIBLICAL BACKGROUND

In ancient Africa, even in some parts of Africa today, certain places found in every community were considered sacred. No one trespassed on them without facing the wrath of the gods of the land as well as that of the community. Also, in some parts of ancient Africa, a host who offered a drink to a visitor was required first to take a sip. The idea here suggests that if there was death in the drink, it would also kill the host. Leprosy was among the diseases used by some African communities to achieve a mischievous purpose to kill other people out of rivalry or hatred. It was usually added to local drinks or food through evil means. A person, therefore, who does not know the background to such practices might likely misjudge and misinterpret such communities.

The background of the ancient Biblical text refers to the "setting" of the entire Bible, that is, the context within which the original message was given. As in our illustration above, without a clear understanding of that "setting" of the Biblical text, communicating its meaning is difficult, if not impossible.[1] McQuilkin reasons that, since Scripture is rooted in history and claims to be a historical document, we must understand it in the context of its history – the history of the author's situation and that of his audience.[2] Understanding the background of the Bible presupposes that one seeks to know the peoples' way of life and certain practices such as their cultural milieu, customs and traditions, worldviews about public life and relationships, and the kinds of values that their lifestyles reflected. It also means seeking to understand certain functional systems and institutions of their day.

General background knowledge of the entire Bible and particularly that of individual books is essential. This facilitates understanding and explanation of a chosen text and its context by a preacher. For example, what the Prophets Hosea and Isaiah saw is not necessarily the same with what Jeremiah and Ezekiel did; neither is that which Nahum and Malachi saw. Also, what Matthew saw, heard, comprehended and reported in his gospel is not precisely what Paul espoused in his theological discourses. David Bosch, in his

---

1.   J. Robertson McQuilkin, *Understanding and Applying the Bible,* 2nd ed. (Chicago, Illinois: Moody Press, 1992), 91.
2.   McQuilkin, *Understanding and Applying the Bible,* 91.-104.

reflections on the New Testament, underscores the necessity of understanding the context of the text today,

> . . our task today is far more difficult than that of the New Testament authors. Matthew, Luke, Paul, and the others lived in cultures radically different from ours and faced problems of which we have no idea (just as we face problems of which they knew nothing). Moreover, they used notions their contemporaries immediately understood but we do not.[3]

It is true that Christians today are faced with the problem of meaning when they come to the Bible. Some African readers of the Biblical text today impose their experiences and cultures upon the text. Though they are all Africans, the way a Ghanaian, Kenyan, Nigerian, South African, and a Tunisian reads the Bible from their cultural contexts, will not give the same understanding. Our cultural and experiential imposition further compounds the problem of meaning. For example, the Bible calls upon children to obey their parents (Eph 6:1-3); women to submit to their husbands (Eph 5:22-23; Col 3:18; 1 Pet 3:1-6); and members of society to obey their leaders (Rom 13:1-8; Heb 13:7). However, is this a blind demand or one that is rational? Imposition of modern meaning on an ancient sacred text is a miscarriage of its original purpose and intention. Modern readers and interpreters of the Biblical text are not its primary and original recipients; neither do they have the same experiences of the people the text was addressed to. Instead, doing our best at background understanding is helpful; otherwise, we are found to be irrational and unfair to the text when we impose our assumption of meaning on it.

---

3. David Jacobus Bosch, *Transforming Mission: Paradigm Shifts in Theology of Mission* (1991; repr., Maryknoll, New York: Orbis Books, 2009), 21.

Consequently, a wide background knowledge of the culture of the Scriptures is essential for the African expository preacher so he or she can adequately preach the Scriptures according to the correct rhythm. As Ralph Gower points out, "God's Word came in particular places, at particular times, to particular people. It is when we stand in those people's shoes and understand what God was saying to them that the words can have full meaning for us."[4] So, an African expository preacher needs to understand, for example, what the royal culture of a king holding the golden sceptre to a person meant when preaching from Esther 4:11; 5:2; 8:4. Cultural and customary practices differ; some also change over time. Therefore, as Gower explains, readers of the Bible today can get a better feel of its background when we understand its language and terminology by placing ourselves back into the context of the Biblical era, seeking to understand the lifestyle of the people of the Book with all their variations. He notes,

> Life for the poor was not the same as life for the wealthy; life in the hot valley of the river Jordan was different from life on the cool mountains surrounding Jerusalem; life in summer was different from life in winter; life for the nomadic herdsman differed from life for an urban tradesman; and in a land that was subject to continual warfare, life was different under the occupation of the Assyrians from life under the occupation of Greeks and Romans[5]

Since the background understanding of the Biblical text is crucial to understanding its meaning and message, preaching without such adequate understanding not only risks proper communication of God's truth but also fundamentally and crucially risks planting the seed of heresy.

---

4. Ralph Gower, *The New Manners and Customs of Bible Times* (rev. and updated ed., Chicago, Illinois: Moody Bible Institute, 2005), 5.

5. Gower, *The New Manners and Customs of Bible Times*, 6.

UNDERSTANDING BIBLICAL THEOLOGY

In African Traditional Religious practices, libations and sacrifice are a critical part of its worship. For instance, when a group of elders from the Miship community in Nigeria sit to discuss either social or religious matters of concern to their community, or even at a place of relaxation, locally brewed beer is usually served to them. Before the senior elder takes the first sip to permit every other elder to drink, libation always precedes it. He pours a few drops of the drink to the ground, saying, "Our ancestors, taste this drink and bless it." There is an undergirding philosophy behind this practice. It is an act of respect for the gods of the land and the ancestors. Such practice of libation is also asking for their permission and guidance to proceed with the discussion.

Also, when an African religious priest or a medium is summoned to consult the gods about a particular matter, he would generally begin by calling on the heavens and the earth by looking up to the sky and down to the ground, pronouncing, *Naan ne, yil e,* (God and earth) before he would begin the consultation by making certain incantations. Such act also carries with it a clearly defined philosophy. A bystander who is foreign to such African religious systems stands the risk of wrong evaluation and misinterpretation of these practices. However, the quest to first understand their embedded meaning will lead to a purposeful discovery of it.

Christian theology finds its expression from the Biblical text as its source material. Our very first understanding of the theological necessity of expository preaching borders on what is better put in Bullock's words, by theology, ". . . we mean the theology of the book in which the passage under consideration is found, the theology of the literary genre to which that book belongs, and the theology of the Bible as a whole."[6] African expository preachers should seek to understand what the ancient Biblical text broadly teaches about God and his plans for humanity. Every aspect of the Bible, even things considered as mundane by some people, has an embedded theology. Preachers should always ask what God teaches as they seek to understand recorded historical events and what is described and prescribed in the books of the Old and New Testaments. George E. Ladd captures it well by pointing out that since Biblical theology sets forth the message of the books of the Bible in their historical setting, and has the task of explaining Biblical theology in its historical setting, it must be done from a starting point that is Biblical-historical in orientation.[7]

History and events are very significant in discovering the theology of Biblical books. As Ladd states, "The Bible is a compilation of ancient religious writings that preserves the history of an ancient Semitic people."[8] Such preserved ancient religious document has a unique emerging theology[9] that modern Biblical preachers in Afri-

---

6. C. Hassell Bullock, "Interpreting the Bible," in *The Literature and Meaning of Scripture* (ed., Morris A. Inch, Grand Rapids, Michigan: Baker, 1981), 17.

7. George Eldon Ladd, *A Theology of the New Testament*, rev. and edited by Donald A. Hagner (Grand Rapids, Michigan: William B. Eerdmans, 1993), 20-21.

8. Ladd, *A Theology of the New Testament*, 14.

9. The theological understanding that is needed in expository preaching is a comprehensive one. Theology asks, "What is God teaching here?" A theological quest of the Biblical text begins by seeking to understand the theology of the entire Bible, and then the theology of each of the Testaments (Old and New). This is followed by the theology of the various literary genres in the Testaments – narrative, prose, poetry, prophetic, apocalypse, Gospels, letters; then the theology of the individual books; and lastly, the theology of the book under study where the sermon text is located. Peter Adam submits to this effect that, "Every preacher knows that a text out of context is a pretext. Biblical theology reminds us to look not only at the immediate context, but also at the Old or New Testament, and finally at the Bible, as the theological context for every

ca ought to pay careful attention to in order to correctly unveil the theological content. God who is the Lord of all history has uniquely revealed himself to Israel in a series of historical events as he has done nowhere else. The preacher's task of correctly unveiling the undergirding theology of a text is so that the listener goes away with its correct understanding; for true Christian theology is what is to be applied to life. Theological correctness and accuracy are particularly crucial in preaching.

UNDERSTANDING THE TEXTUAL CONTEXT

Kamdang was laughing when he walked pass Yilbis who had been crying because of some misfortunes he had recently suffered. When from afar he saw Kamdang laughing, he rained insults on him because he assumed he was laughing at him. However, upon hearing what had happened to Yilbis, Kamdang came back to sympathise with him. Yilbis challenged him, demanding to know why he laughed at him. Kamdang, who had not even seen Yilbis, explained he was laughing at a drunken man who fell off his bicycle. Lack of proper contextual understanding leads to the wrong assumption. Context means a background motivating factor that informs/causes an action or a statement.

The term *context* is used here about the immediate as well as the distant surrounding environments of a particular Biblical passage. The context of a text refers to the surrounding source of information that throws light on the text. A textual context is mostly located within the book from where a text is taken and sometimes somewhere within the whole Bible. Textual context is essential for understanding the message of a Biblical passage. McQuilkin expresses the

---

text." See Peter Adam, *Speaking God's Words: A Practical Theology of Preaching* (Leicester, England: Inter-Varsity Press, 1996), 111.

importance of context when he says, ". . . it might even be said that 'context is king'! It is through the context of any passage, in the final analysis, that we determine meaning."[10] McQuilkin is correct in his assertion. The different parts of the entire Scriptures connect to the Bible as a whole. The whole Bible relates to the parts, be they the individual units of the Old and New Testaments (for example, the historical books in the OT and the Gospels in the NT). Finally, the different books in the Bible, including the chapters, paragraphs, or even the sentences all relate as a whole.

Bullock sheds light on this point of contextual relatedness of the parts of Scriptures when he notes that Matthew's citation of Isaiah's prophecy can be fully comprehended only against its *historical context* (Matt 1:23; see also Isa 7:14). For him, "To interpret that prophecy out of historical context is to risk misunderstanding its theological thrust."[11] In the Isaiah passage, King Ahaz of Judah was faced with the threat of an alliance between Aram and Israel. Hence, God gave the sign of Emmanuel as an assurance that salvation would come for the king and Judah only by trusting in the mercy and saving power of God, not by a political and military alliance with a foreign army (see 2 Kgs 16:5-11; Isa 7:1-17).

The second area of contextual understanding of a text, besides its historical context, is the *cultural context*. The Biblical writers were

---

10. McQuilkin, *Understanding and Applying the Bible,* 123. Gordon D. Fee says, before the investigation of any sentence, paragraph, or any other subsection of the document, one should always have a good overview of the entire document by raising specific critical questions that would help to determine meaning. Such questions reflect on who the author and the recipients are; what the relationship between the author and the recipients is; where the recipients live and what their present circumstances are; what historical situation occasioned this writing; and what the author's purpose is and the overall theme or concerns as well. See Fee, *New Testament Exegesis,* 28.

11. Bullock, "Interpreting the Bible," 15.

influenced by the cultural contexts of their day when they wrote. Cultural context seeks to understand the existing laws, social customs and norms, and the religious practices which were features of the particular society and historical timeframe at the time of their writing. For example, as Bullock submits, passages like Genesis 30:3 and Hebrews 1:2; 2:5b can only be fully understood against their cultural contexts. In this connection, Bernard Ramm presents four levels of contextual analysis for a fairer interpretation of the Biblical text. First, he notes that the context of any verse is the entire Scripture because "Scripture interprets Scripture." From this statement, he asserts, ". . . we can understand a particular passage only if we know what the whole Scripture teaches; but we can only know what the whole Scripture teaches by knowing the meaning of its parts," that is, a rotating or spiralling from part to whole and from whole to part.[12] Secondly, Ramm notes that the context of any passage is the Testament it is in – Old or New, because each Testament has unique features of its own such as theological, economic, political, and much more. He also follows with the third context which is the particular book in which the passage occurs. To illustrate the point, Ramm cites the example of the Galatian and Revelation contexts,

> The interpreter must know what the 'Galatian heresy' was all about properly to interpret passages in Galatians. The interpreter of the book of Revelation must understand the history of martyrdom and the theology of martyrdom of the early church, or else he turns the book of Revelation into a kind of Ouija board for prophetic speculation.[13]

---

12. Bernard Ramm, *Protestant Biblical Interpretation: A Textbook of Hermeneutics* (3rd ed., Grand Rapids, Michigan: Baker Book House, 1970), 138.

13. Ramm, *Protestant Biblical Interpretation*, 139.

He notes lastly, that the fourth context of any passage is the materials immediately before it, and immediately after it. If these are understood or tracked, then the interpreter will have set in place the framework in which the passage is to be understood. When an expositor disrespects context, the meaning is always at risk; and the audience is exposed to the danger of misunderstanding, misinterpretation, and misapplication which potentially leads to heresy.

Why does context matter for expository preaching in Africa? Many African preachers preach sermons that fail to emerge from the textual context, thereby, misrepresenting the message of the text. Some of them assume meaning and preach the Bible as though it was written in their culture and in their day. Some others perceive the Bible as if it was dropped from heaven. Such preachers need to understand that although the Bible is an inspired religious book, it is a literary text that is the product of divine and human contributions. It developed from a specific literary background that should be rightly understood by anyone who seeks to interpret or preach from it. Its interpretation must necessarily be rooted in the literary convention of its day, not ours. This reduces the risk of misinterpretation, misunderstanding, and misapplication of the Biblical message.

BIBLICAL EXEGESIS

Although exegesis, strictly speaking, is not an aspect of Biblical background, yet one's background understanding of the Biblical text influences one's exegesis. The Bible is accepted within evangelical circles as a religious book that is the inspired, infallible, and inerrant Word of God. Yet, it remains a literary material. The divine stamp on the body of Scriptures does not empty it of its literary content. Upon this, as we seek to preach the Bible in Africa, we must first seek to exegete it as a literary work.

However, what is exegesis? Douglas Stuart says, "An exegesis is a thorough, analytical study of a Biblical passage done so as to arrive at a useful interpretation of the passage."[14] Elliott E. Johnson also notes, "Biblical exegesis is the unfolding of the meaning of a passage or a book of the Bible." He explains that the Greek *exaggeo* from which the English *exegesis* is derived, literally means, 'a leading out,' with the purpose of setting forth by explaining an author's unfolding intended meaning and its full implications.[15] The primary task of exegesis is the discovery or the unveiling of textual meaning. We cannot understand what a Liberian means when someone is addressed as *Mame* or what a South African means by addressing someone as *Ma Bru* without exegesis.

However, in our attempt to exegete a Biblical passage, we may likely muddle things up if we fail to give careful attention to putting every part of the text in proper perspective. This is significant in our attempt to locate lexical meanings as lexical or grammatical meanings can take various meanings. Gordon D. Fee prescribes particular determining questions to ask in order to ascertain the right lexical and grammatical meaning of a word within the textual context. Such questions are: "Which of these lexical meanings is the author's intended meaning? Which of these grammatical meanings is the author's intended meaning? Does the author intend all the options listed, only some, or only one?"[16] These exegetical questions serve as an excellent guide to locate meaning.

---

14. Douglas Stuart, *Old Testament Exegesis* (rev. ed., Philadelphia, Kentucky: Westminster John Knox Press, 1980), 21.

15. Elliott E. Johnson, *Expository Hermeneutics: An Introduction* (Grand Rapids, Michigan: Zondervan, 1990), 142.

16. Gordon D. Fee, *New Testament Exegesis: A Handbook for Students and Pastors* (3rd ed., Louisville, Kentucky: Westminster John Knox Press, 2002), 71-82. Honest exegetical questions serve to lead to correct meaning. According to Johnson, "Every exegete desires to lead out the answers the author intended and not the

African expository preachers must give great attention to accurate exegesis and correct hermeneutics; for it is upon them that correct Biblical theology is arrived at. It is this understanding that leads to a meaningful, relevant, contextual application of the Biblical text. However, the imposition of one's cultural and personal meaning upon the Biblical text is not in doubt when a sound Biblical theology that reflects on proper hermeneutics and exegesis is not followed.[17] Dealing with God's thoughts obligates preachers to take the greatest

---

answers his personal, experiential, theological, cultural, or other bias might lead him to which are not in the text." See Johnson, *Expository Hermeneutics*, 142. Fee also says asking the right exegetical questions of the text, that is, the questions of content (what is said) and the questions of context (why it is said) is critical to leading out the author's intended meaning of the text. Historical and literary exegetical questions are helpful. The first deals with the general setting of a document (for example, the city, people, geography, religion, and economy), and with the specific occasion of the document; while the second deals with why a given thing was said at a given point in the argument or narrative. Also, four other questions of content are helpful.

(1) Textual criticism (determining the author's actual words and order, that is, the science that seeks to recover the original form of hand-produced documents);

(2-3) Lexical and grammatical data (lexical determines the meaning of words and grammatical determines the relationship of words to one another); and

(4) The historical-cultural background that is, determining the relationship of words and ideas to the background and culture of the author & his readers.

According to Fee, proper exegesis is the happy combination or careful integration of all these data into a readable presentation. See Fee, *New Testament Exegesis*, 25.

17. Kevin J. Vanhoozer, "Exegesis and Hermeneutics," in *New Dictionary of Biblical Theology*, (eds., T. D. Alexander and Brian S. Rosner, Leicester, England: Inter-Varsity Press 2000), 52-64.

pains to understand them adequately and honestly, and to faithfully explain them, and relevantly and clearly apply them.[18]

Africans are seeking the *truth* of God as solutions to their myriad challenges in the face of collapsing human systems. Many fall prey to African predatory impostors and fake prophets for this reason. As such, honest expository preachers who sense the obligation of such a task must help them to find this *truth* through true Biblical preaching. They need to hear this *truth* soundly expounded from the African pulpit by preachers who know and value the truth themselves. African expository preachers must sense the need, see the need, and rise to the challenge of this urgent need of leading out God's truth from the Bible through sound preaching in order to achieve quality spirituality for the Christian church in Africa. The task of quality expository preaching in Africa is not only an awesome responsibility that God has placed in the hands of those who preach and teach the Bible, but much more, because God's people look up to preachers and teachers of the Bible for insight and direction[19] in a disoriented, confused, and a growingly directionless world.

BIBLICAL HERMENEUTICS

Biblical exegesis and hermeneutics are two sides of the same coin. While exegesis deals with Biblical words, hermeneutics deals with the meaning of the written text of the Bible following specific particular rules. Ramm says the primary and fundamental need of Biblical hermeneutics is to ascertain what God has said in sacred Scriptures and to determine the meaning of his Word. Accordingly, he sees

---

18. Donald Anderson Carson, *Exegetical Fallacies* (2nd ed., Grand Rapids, Michigan: Baker Books, 1996), 15.

19. Robert B. Chisholm, Jr., *From Exegesis to Exposition: A Practical Guide to Using Biblical Hebrew* (Grand Rapids, Michigan: Baker Books, 1998), 10.

hermeneutics as the science and art of Biblical interpretation. He explains, "It is a science because it is guided by rules within a system, and it is an art because the application of the rules is by skill, and not by mechanical imitation."[20] It is said that hermeneutics is at the heart of the Christian faith.[21] Christians cannot adequately know God experientially and be able to obey and serve him until they have clearly heard his voice from the exposition of the Biblical text and have properly understood its meaning for them.

This need is quite critical. For example, we earlier stated that communication attempts to build a bridge across borders by linking people and organisations via the transfer of information. When the process is fraudulent or the medium through which information is processed is faulty, the intended message stands the risk of being corrupted and misunderstood. Similarly, Biblical hermeneutics endeavours to correctly interpret the inspired, infallible, and inerrant Word of God, and then appropriately pass its message to men and women. Expository preachers in Africa, in their attempt to achieve this task, should always remember that a vast gulf stands between the world of the ancient sacred Biblical text and that of Africa today. They should be careful to bridge the two worlds in their attempt to best communicate meaning to the audience.

While African preachers seek to bridge the gap by relating the message of the Bible to Africans today, they should not forget that the Bible is unique in its own right because it consists of sacred writings. It is unique also because it lays claims to particular inspiration in a way that no other religious literature has done and can do (see Gen 1:1; 2 Tim 3:16-17; 2 Pet 1:21). Therefore, the Bible should be preached out of genuine respect and reverence for its divine author, and its

---

20. Ramm, *Protestant Biblical Interpretation*, 1-2.
21. Bullock, "Interpreting the Bible," 11.

message should flow out of a heart with deep conviction in the God of the Scriptures. To do otherwise is not only to empty Christianity of its authentic claim but to negate divine supremacy and Biblical authority over human lives.

Undoubtedly, background is so critical to understanding a story or an event; so also with the message of the biblical text. Without a proper understanding of the background of the literature of the ancient sacred Biblical text, the actual meaning is lost; and the attempted application of the text also is a fraud. Yet, not only is adequate textual background necessary for expository preaching in Africa, but the background of the audience as well. A knowledge of these two backgrounds helps in making the appropriate connections between these poles.

CHAPTER 15

KNOWING THE AUDIENCE'S BACKGROUND

We all have, or have had parents. Some of the parents are good ones, but some others are not. Most good parents teach their children some security tips. One such instruction is not to talk to strangers. Some strangers can be dangerous, and good parents do not want their children harmed. However, even if a stranger is a good one, being a stranger in a place can sometimes be frustrating through lack of acceptance. I suffered this when I went to America last year on my sabbatical leave. A person is accepted by other people only when they know him or her reasonably well and can trust the person.

Preaching is an aspect of pastoral theology. In what Robert Dykstra describes as finding ourselves lost, preaching is to people, most of whom are overwhelmed by the challenges of life, while others are discouraged and hopeless because they have persistently been beaten down by such overwhelming challenges.[1] People matter; ministry is to people; and expository preaching should always have people at the centre because it is to them – to their hearts and in their hands

---

1. Robert C. Dykstra, *Finding Ourselves Lost: Ministry in the Age of Overwhelm* (Eugene, Oregon: Wipf and Stock Publishers, 2018), 2. Dykstra is the Chair, Faculty of Practical Theology at Princeton Theological Seminary, Princeton, New Jersey, USA. The main concern of his book is his personal struggle, as he explains, "to wrestle with and respond to the quandaries of finding ourselves lost in an age of overwhelm" as a person, Christian minister, and as a pastor-theologian.

– that the Word of God is proclaimed. An audience should not become strangers to any preacher who stands in the pulpit and enters into communication with them. Rather, preachers should seek to know the identity and situations of the people they are speaking to each time they stand up to preach. In an introduction to the book he edited, written by African-American preachers, LaRue explains that preachers are to be mindful of the happenings in their social, political, educational, and economic surroundings. Preaching, he says, should seriously engage "the whole of God's created order in its beauty and splendour, its disorder and unruliness."[2] The knowledge of the context of an audience is the art of audience psychology in the field of homiletics. Both the resident pastor/priest as well as an invited preacher must possess this knowledge.

Preaching is perhaps the most challenging ministry task to accomplish. In a sermon, a preacher speaks to tens, hundreds, and thousands of people in the audience. Each has issues that are most times, unique only to them. It is an even harder task when the audience members come from various disciplines, different cultural backgrounds, different statuses in society, and with different social and moral orientations. As a preacher preaches to such a diverse congregation, his sermon should address each listener's needs. This is quite a complicated job to undertake. Hence each preacher of the Scriptures needs to have a good working knowledge of the audience members' backgrounds.

This is what I do in order to help me understand my audience. Each time I am invited to preach to an unfamiliar audience I usually ask whom I am expected to meet. For preaching is speaking to people; it is speaking to souls that hang between heaven and hell; it is

---

2. Cleophus James LaRue, ed., *Power in the Pulpit: How America's Most Effective Black Preachers Prepare Their Sermons* (Louisville, Kentucky: Westminster John Knox, 2002), 7.

speaking to people torn between opinions whether to choose what is right in line with God's instructions for life or what is wrong; and it is addressing their different challenges and needs by providing answers to them from the Scriptures. This task of speaking to *people,* not just an audience, is not to be taken lightly by preachers. As a rule, then, every preacher must know or seek to know whom they are speaking to in an audience.

KNOW WHO IS IN YOUR AUDIENCE

Conrad Mbewe stresses the importance for a preacher to be aware of the identity and the situations affecting members of the audience. He explains that the people a preacher preaches to are not people from another planet; neither are they living in a utopian society. Instead, they are also people who are affected by the social, political and economic changes taking place all around them.[3] Preaching is to people, and it becomes effective only when it meets the needs of the listeners. The knowledge about who, what, and how are the audience members is critical for effective expository preaching. Who they are concerns the identity of the individuals; what they are concerns their status and vocations; and how they are concerns the social challenges and conditions the people face in society.

Knowing the people in the audience, helps in presenting the message of the Scriptures. It is particularly significant for the types of illustrations to be used and how the message of the sermon will be applied. For example, when an expository preacher is speaking to a group of students, or a group of professionals such as doctors or lawyers, or poultry farmers, illustrations drawn from their fields of profession will be more captivating and appealing to them.

---

3.   Conrad Mbewe, *Pastoral Preaching: Building a People for God* (Carlisle, Cumbria: Langham Preaching Resources, 2017), 117.

However, preaching to a mixed audience is more challenging. Let us suppose, for example, that a preacher is speaking to an audience that has couples. Some among them are happily married while others' marriages are in difficulties; some others are separated or divorced, and more are widows with a few widowers among them. What will the preacher do with this knowledge as he or she stands to preach to them? Alternatively, still, if the preacher is speaking to an audience that has market traders, farmers, students, vocational drivers, and the unemployed, how will he or she handle the issue of illustrations and the application of the message in the sermon?

Good working knowledge of an audience to the expository preacher is a valuable resource. This raw communication information helps the preacher in preparing the sermon. It guides him or her regarding what to emphasise, the tone of the speech, the types of gestures to use, the types of illustrations and areas of appeals to make. It also helps, particularly, in carefully crafting relevant and specific applications of the sermon to such a mixed audience.

LITERACY AND EDUCATIONAL LEVELS

Just as those that preach the Scriptures do not all have the same level of education and exposure in society, so are the people in the audience. They do not all have the same biblical literacy level neither do they have the same educational level. However, why does a preacher's knowledge of the audience members' literacy levels matter?

Good working knowledge of the literacy level of each in the audience is crucial. When a preacher stands in the pulpit to preach, the Bible MUST be central to the sermon, and it should be read before preaching. It is the Bible that is both the source material and the preacher's authority for preaching. However, some people in the audience may not know where to locate the books of the Bible or some particularly "notorious" smaller books of the Bible. Hence, they need careful guidance. As a preacher, you want the people to whom you are speaking to read the Scriptural passage(s) along with you. In the course of the sermon also, you may once in a while draw their attention to a particular verse, sentence, expressions, phrase, or a word in the passage. However, if the audience members are not able to follow you then they are likely to miss the point you are making.

In every society people attain different levels of education. Knowing your audience, therefore is helpful in the types of vocabularies and language expressions that the preacher can use. For example, a person that has at least a first degree will understand what a theory is, but a secondary/high school leaver may not, unless he or she has studied some sciences. Also, a person who has a second or even a third-degree will have no problem understanding the concepts of ideology or philosophy. So, the literacy level of the people in one's audience determines one's use or choice of vocabularies and the language level in communication. To further illustrate this need, every language has various ways of expression. For instance, the British or Americans talk about someone being *under the weather*, meaning, the person is in ill health or is sick. However, the Nigerian expression for the same subject is to say that the person *is down*. Equally, while someone at a lower level of education may not understand the proverbial expression *throwing in the towel*, the person who has a higher level of education may.

An expository preacher is always obliged to remember that standing in the pulpit is to *communicate* the divine Word. Moreover, the singular purpose of this *communication* is so that the people understand what God is saying to them, and so they know exactly how to respond to the message. Donald R. Sunukjian captures the point aptly: Preaching is presenting to the modern audience, not so much what God said then, but importantly, what he is saying to the audience now; "'This is what God is saying now, to you.'"[4] However, the preacher's inappropriate choice of vocabularies and language expressions can stand in the way of the audience's understanding and response to the divine Word. Hence, a fair knowledge of the literacy level of the audience is unavoidably necessary.

SOCIAL AND CULTURAL BACKGROUNDS

It is most appropriate to talk about "cultures" rather than "culture" in Africa because of Africa's tribal and ethnic diversity. Mbewe understands culture as ". . . the way in which people generally act or think in a given community or society. Some of it is very positive and commendable, but some of it is negative and unwholesome."[5] The African continent consists of different peoples with different socio-cultural understanding, estimated at 3,000 tribes or more. Every African country has a multiplicity of tribes and ethnic groups. For instance, there are the Zulu in South Africa, Kalenjin and Maasai in Kenya, San Bushmen in Botswana, Yoruba in Nigeria, Oromo in Ethiopia, Chaga in Tanzania, et cetera.

This multiplicity of nations also means that each has their language, cultural, social, and ethnic differences. For instance, while one thing may be accepted as normative in one culture, it may be a detestable thing in another. Also, while one word or language expression means one thing in one culture, it may mean an entirely different thing in yet another. Overall, some of these cultures go against those of the Bible that are expressed commands with timeless effects.

---

4. Donald R. Sunukjian, *Invitation to Biblical Preaching: Proclaiming Truth with Clarity and Relevance* (Grand Rapids, Michigan: Kregel Publications, 2007), 12.

5. Mbewe, *Pastoral Preaching*, 118.

Adequate knowledge of the socio-cultural backgrounds of the people in the audience is quite helpful in the area of the use of gestures and illustrations. Appropriate illustrations for a particular audience should be carefully chosen so that its use does not become offensive to some tribes or individuals in the audience. For example, concerning food in Africa, some tribes eat rats while some others do not. Some others eat snails while others do not. Still, some tribes eat pigs or donkeys while others abhor eating these animals. Dog meat, frogs, crabs, are a precious delicacy to some people in Nigeria; but some Nigerian tribes abhor and detest them. Just imagine how a preacher would offend those who eat a particular animal in the list above should he or she condemn eating them; it is worst if the preacher describes those who eat these animals as carnal at best or unbelievers at worst. On the other hand, some others will be offended when a preacher praises and approves of people who eat certain animals. In Africa, it is different strokes for different folks.

When the preacher is well-informed about the socio-cultural contexts of the different people in the audience, it makes communication of the divine Word easier. Drawing connections between the cultures of the Bible and those of the audience will become more meaningful. This is particularly important where a preacher is handling a passage that has some culturally and morally inclined issues. As Mbewe notes, "Understanding the cultural context in which the books of the Bible were written also helps . . . to know whether something that is taught in the passage is a principle that can be applied or a command that must be obeyed."[6]

---

6. Mbewe, *Pastoral Preaching*, 116.

ANSWERING SOCIAL AND MORAL ISSUES

Honestly, many people are hurting; they are asking critical questions without finding the right answers. Moreover, some of them sit in the pews with their eyes glued to the preacher. Is the preacher aware of this fact; and does the preacher know the factors that cause such discomfort? Whenever a preacher stands in the pulpit to preach, he or she will find it helpful to remember that he or she is standing before human beings; before real people with real human problems; and before people who are seeking solutions to their real arching life issues.

John Stott addresses in the fourth edition of his book, *Issues Facing Christians Today,* many challenging issues that people are grappling with today. These issues cover global, local contextual, social, and personal areas. He asserts, "At the outset of the twenty-first century, we are faced with a bewildering array of challenges which fifty years ago we could never have imagined."[7] The fast-changing events in the world are creating unavoidably more issues for humanity to contend with. The bewildered onlooker can only describe these changes as "Wonders shall never end!" because the things that were not, now are.

For us in Africa, there are more severe social and moral issues we have to contend with far beyond tribal and ethnic ones. Let us take Nigeria as a case study. The persistent cases of Boko Haram Islamic terrorist attacks that have killed many soldiers; the increasing cases of Fulani herdsmen's killing of people in the villages to achieve their agenda of gradual ethnic cleansing; and the kidnapping, assassination and armed robbery attacks; all go to suggest bad governance as government does not have the political will to end these menac-

---

7.   John Robert Walmsley Stott, *Issues Facing Christians Today* (4th ed., fully revised and updated by Roy McCloughry, with a new chapter by John Wyatt, Grand Rapids, Michigan: Zondervan, 2006), 23.

es. Also, the failed effort at eradicating corruption in every facet of the country; the failure of governments to provide quality healthcare and education for the citizenry in favour of overseas patronage by politicians and the rich; and the greed and selfishness that most politicians and people in government have exhibited clearly indicate that Nigeria is on her way to total collapse. Some of such people, instead of working for the good of society, choose rather to become heartless, without moral consciousness, and greedily scoop the wealth of their nation and leave the people in poverty. Additionally, Christian indigenes/citizens in Northern Nigeria have, for many years, suffered deprivation of their rights to religious expression and gainful employment. Severally, they have suffered deprivation of justice, forceful denial of and intentional confiscation of lands, and the right to university admission to read the course of their choice. These unfortunate anomalies are becoming a normal daily theme song in modern Nigeria. One's security in society is no longer guaranteed. The people who are meant to address these challenges to develop a good society have failed to do so because they have no personal incentive to do so. Their needs are adequately catered for and they are heavily protected from public funds, so why should they care?

To say that people are grossly affected is an understatement. Let me illustrate such effects regarding the questions people are asking vis-a-vis these issues. In the early 80s in Nigeria, The Great Commission Movement of Nigeria came up with an evangelism strategy in the Northern part of the country. It was quite catchy but kept the public in suspense for a while. The fliers carried the notice, "I found It." The logical response from the public was, "What have you found?" After a couple of days of waiting the Great Commission Movement supplied the answer – "Jesus." In other words, I have found Jesus. So, if Jesus is the answer, then what are the questions?

Hurting people today in Africa and the world are asking – "Where is Jesus with the answers to our questions and the solutions to our challenging issues of life?" The answers to such crucial question are in the Scriptures, and it is the preacher who helps people to see them in the Scriptures. Preachers are not only to tell what the answers are but to practically show how they work. When a preacher knows the myriad social and moral issues that people are going through in life, the exposition of the Scriptures becomes more meaningful in the way applications of the message is made to the listeners in their life situations.

The contextual sampling of the audience above, especially the negative ones, obviously indicates that preaching to people with diverse backgrounds can be a bit of a challenge. This is one reason why understanding the context of one's audience members is crucial. More attendant challenges to expository preaching in Africa today are discussed in the next chapter.

CHALLENGES OF EXPOSITORY PREACHING

No doubt, quality expository preaching is one of the missing links in the church in Africa today. However, like the African proverb says, "Water cannot have a sour taste without a cause." Expository preaching is being robbed of its beauty and presence as a missing link in the African pulpit for certain factors that pose as threatening challenges.

In my earlier book, *Preaching the Scriptures*,[1] I explained some of the challenges to biblical preaching in Africa. I pointed out that cultural barriers to communication, the lure of false preachers, the low level of biblical literacy, and the attack of the enemy are some of the areas of these challenges. The areas of challenges to biblical preaching, particularly expository preaching today in Africa, are so many. Several obstacles confront expository preaching in Africa, and the preachers who are genuinely called and prepared for the task of preaching the Scriptures will have to engage in a faceoff with them.

HERESY

The greatest onslaught on Christian spirituality in Africa today that also stands as a challenge to expository preaching is the increas-

---

1. Joel Kamsen Tihitshak Biwul, *Preaching the Scriptures* (Jos, Nigeria & Carlisle, UK: HippoBooks, 2018), 23-30.

ing presence of the heretical teachings being merchandised by fake preachers and false prophets. Many so-called churches and ministries are springing up in Africa. The way and manner in which most of the leaders of these churches and ministries handle the Scriptures is nothing but heretical. This is seen in the way such leaders explain the meaning and application of anointing oil and the use of handkerchiefs as a source of magical powers. Their theology of binding and claiming, and prayer for people/enemies to die by fire, is nothing but erroneous and heretical. Some of such people do absurd things by going as far as kissing or fondling the sexual parts of some female members to heal them from sickness and diseases. Some of them are nothing more than African traditionalists and spiritualists.

Heresy is going against the established fundamentals of the Christian faith by distorting its doctrinal paradigm and corrupting its truth. Bruce Shelly understands heresy as erring from the biblical truth, "When we err in our thinking we call it heresy or bad theology. . . . Heresy is not necessarily bad religion, but like all wrong thinking it may lead to bad religion."[2] Alister McGrath says, while earlier generations understood heresy as obscure and dangerous ideas, heresy is essentially not unbelief, ". . . but a form of that faith that is held ultimately to be subversive or destructive."[3] To summarise, heresy, then, is an intentional erring or a departure from sound biblical, doctrinal and theological truth with the goal of distorting, corrupting, and subverting biblical truths. Anyone, therefore, who preaches or teaches wrong doctrine, that which stands in negation to biblical truth, is a heretic.

---

2. Bruce Leon Shelley, *Church History in Plain Language* (2nd ed., Nashville, Tennessee: Thomas Nelson Publishers, 1995), 47.

3. Alister McGrath, *Heresy* (London: Society for Promoting Christian Knowledge, 2009), 1, 19, 33.

Paul used several adjectives to describe what heretics are. For example, in Titus 1:10, he used the Greek adjective translated as "insubordinate" (ESV, NKJ, NJB, RSV, YLT), "unruly" (ASV, KJV), "rebellious" (CJB, NAS, NET, NIV, NLT, NRS), "disobedient" (GNV), and "rebels" (NAB). This word depicts the attitude of one who refuses to be made subject to authority; one who asserts self-independence and one who resists being under control. The rebellious attitude of the heretics mentioned in Titus is classically their refusal to submit to the sound authoritative teaching of the Triune God and the apostolic authority of Paul.

However, Paul also used another Greek word in the same passage translated as "idle talkers" (NET, NKJ, NRS), "empty talkers" (ESV, NAS, RSV) or mere talkers, vain talkers and worthless talkers to describe heretics. Another Greek adjective that Paul also used is translated as "deceivers" (ASV, ESV, NET, NIV, NKJ, NLT, NRS, RSV). Indeed, the main aim of heresy is deceit. Heresy, by its nature and form, is cunning, manipulative and subtle. This is why many people readily believe it against biblical truth and ignorantly fall victims.

This rebellion against doctrinal truth and resistance to sound biblical teaching never goes away in the church. Right from the period of the false prophets in the Old Testament, people have always crafted ways to resist the truth (Jer 23:9-32; Ezek 13:2-9; see Exod 16:1-50). Paul cautioned Timothy in his parting words about the resistance that people would put up against the truth of God (2 Tim 4:3-4 NIV). He had suffered several bouts of opposition to the gospel he had preached (see Titus 1:5, 9; cf. Acts 14:23; 1 Tim 3:1-7).

The growing presence of heresy within the Christian community in Africa today is a significant obstacle to expository preaching. Like Paul forewarned Timothy in his day, many people today are no longer willing to take in the truth of God's Word; they abandon it for falsehood (2 Tim 3:1-5; 4:3-4). Many "supposed Christians" are turning into heretical preachers, teachers, prophets, and exorcists. By their preaching and teaching, attitudes and actions, they oppose the truth by manipulating it, so it appears right in the eyes and sounds correct in the ears of their undiscerning prey. I knew a woman in my denomination who had led the Women Fellowship of the local church for years. She later left for a New Generation church. When she took ill and on hospital admission, she sent to fetch a special garment "The Man of God" had given his members for healing. Covering oneself with such garment invokes healing. Sadly, she still died though even when she was covered by the spiritual garment. Such prey as this woman prefer falsehood to the truth of Scriptures, and quick solutions to their needs, so they seek spiritual help from these fraudsters.

UNPROFESSIONAL CONDUCT

Many years ago, in Israel, the *Qoheleth* (preacher, teacher, wise man) gave his counsel, "Whatever your hand finds to do, do it with all your might, for in the grave, where you are going, there is neither working nor planning nor knowledge nor wisdom" (Eccl 9:10 NIV). This wise counsel captures the need for the sincerity of purpose, excellence, devotion, dedication, and commitment to a task. Luke re-echoes this idea,

> Many have undertaken to draw up an account of the things that have been fulfilled among us, just as they were handed down to us by those who from the first were eyewitnesses and servants of the word. Therefore, since I myself have carefully investigated everything from the beginning, it seemed good also to me to write an orderly account for you, most excellent Theophilus, so that you may know the certainty of the things you have been taught (Luke 1:1-4 NIV).

The phrase, "do it with all your might" in the *Qoheleth* and "carefully investigated" and "an orderly account" in Luke are quite significant. This is the point of professionalism. A professional is a person who is specially trained to acquire necessary purposeful skills to perform a specific specialised task. Upon such acquisition, the person deploys skills, dedication, and commitment to the task.

The preaching arena in Africa today is being dominated by, and its climate also is beclouded by a majority of egocentric laypeople who are not called for the task. Such people are either untrained for the task or have received training only to achieve personal gains. Unfortunately, though, some who sense the true calling and have received quality theological training for the ministry are lazy at expository preaching. In both cases, expository preaching is suffocated in their hands.

However, there is a bigger problem. Some African pastors and preachers who occupy the pulpits are half-baked ministers and preachers, though trained in reasonably good theological institutions. Such people went to theological schools not primarily to train so they could contribute meaningfully to church and society. Instead, they aimed to obtain a certificate so they can achieve some personal desires such as promotion or election to an ecclesiastical office. I personally know of someone who came to train in the seminary where I teach for such sentiment. I also know of some tribes that are backward in theological education in my country who send their own people to the seminary for this purpose. People with such an agenda would not have bothered to learn the rudiments of expository preaching during their training. They can manipulate Scriptures and produce more dangerous heresies by disorienting the Christian spirituality of the church, thereby, becoming more dangerous than the untrained ones.

Closely connected to this also is the challenge of 'representation factor.' In Africa, every tribe or ethnic group and every geopolitical area wants to have a share of what may be described as the "national cake." Following this philosophy, some countries in Africa such as Nigeria apply the "quota system" to educational enrolment, employment into government jobs, political elections and the appointments of certain government functionaries to public office. This idea is gradually creeping into the church. It is not uncommon to find in some church denominations in Africa certain marginalised minority tribes or ethnic groups who purposefully send their representatives to theological institutions to train for the pastorate. For instance, elections to ecclesiastical offices in some District Church Councils in my church denomination are gradually being characterised by tribal and sectional sentiments. My discussion with pastors from other church denominations indicates that such practice affects more than a denomination. The presence of such pastors in the pulpit is to represent a particular human interest and not God. We should not expect professionalism from such people concerning expository preaching.

One other major challenge to quality expository preaching in Africa is the lack of the working knowledge of the original biblical languages. Some African preachers have never learned them. Even those who have some training in the Hebrew and Greek languages have not attained a reasonable level of proficiency that will aid their study of the original texts. Worse still, not many of those who do have some level of proficiency use the original languages when preparing sermons.

Although an African preacher may do a reasonably good job in communicating God's Word using available secondary materials, he or she would undoubtedly be better at expository preaching with a proper working knowledge and the use of the original languages of the Biblical texts. The original languages, no doubt, bring out the beauty of the Word far beyond what other translations can. Just the beauty of knowing the primary roots of the Hebrew grammar, the cases in the Greek and their uses, can be fascinating and enriching. Richard captures the point quite well, "When you can use the original languages in your study, your message will have greater precision, which will give you more confidence in your preaching." [4] Magary stresses such significance further, "The man or woman who has the responsibility to communicate to others what God has said needs to *know* exactly what God has said! A challenge far greater than learning Hebrew is keeping it vital and healthy for use in lifelong ministry. The whole point of studying Hebrew and Greek in seminary is to be able to have direct access to the biblical text – the very foundation for Christian faith and practice – in the languages in which God's Word was originally given."[5]

African preachers are obligated to preach Scriptures faithfully. Paul charged Timothy to prioritise his ministry in these words:

> In the presence of God and of Christ Jesus, who will judge
> the living and the dead, and in view of his appearing and
> his kingdom, I give you this charge: Preach the Word; be
> prepared in season and out of season; correct, rebuke and
> encourage – with great patience and careful instruction. For
> the time will come when men will not put up with sound
> doctrine. Instead, to suit their desires, they will gather
> around them a great number of teachers to say what their
> itching ears want to hear. They will turn their ears away
> from the truth and turn aside to myths. But you, keep your
> head in all situations, endure hardship, do the work of an

---

4. Ramesh Richard, *Scripture Sculpture: A Do-It-Yourself Manual for Biblical Preaching* (1995; repr., Grand Rapids, Michigan: Baker Books, 1997), 153.

5. Dennis R. Magary, "Keeping Your Hebrew Healthy," in *Preaching the Old Testament* (Scott M. Gibson, ed., Grand Rapids, Michigan: Baker Books, 2006), 30.

evangelist, discharge all the duties of your ministry (2 Tim 4:1-5 NIV).

Paul's emphasis is not only on commitment but professionalism as well. The person who is genuinely called for the task of shepherding and preaching is under a divine obligation to be faithful at it. Such a minister must stand their guard to resist the pressure to mimic what Pentecostal Televangelists do. The reason, according to Paul, is because of the day of final reckoning. Preachers and pastors who are conscious of this know that the task that demands their time and energy most is to be faithful in preaching the Word. It does not matter whether the people to whom they preach are ready to accept it or not. This obligation makes such preachers and under-shepherds to be focused, goal-oriented, and to set priorities in the discharge of the functions of their office.

CHURCH LEADERSHIP ABUSES

In Africa, a traditional ruler or king sits on the throne while the subjects sit on the floor or the ground thus indicating his superiority over his subjects. This philosophy is sometimes translated into the church and its leadership. It plays out mainly in the situation where the head of a particular congregation claims absolute superiority and total control over the members. Several Pentecostal pastors are faulted for such leadership posture. I also know of some intelligent pastors from mainline churches who have had to leave their church denominations because of the autocratic and dictatorial attitude of the leaders. In one situation I had to mediate between some aggrieved youths and an autocratic leader to ensure the stability of the church. This mindset serves as fertile soil to grow pride and arrogance, and as a prepared ground to nurture the spirit of power and control.

A church leader who claims superiority over the members usurps the greatness and authority of God. Such leaders can blatantly exhibit the attitude of greed and self-centredness; can easily become domineering, authoritative, coercive, and manipulative; and can also become insensitive to God and the feelings of those under their leadership. These so-called church leaders stand as a significant challenge to expository preaching in Africa. Pastors and preachers who are proud and arrogant are always full of themselves instead of being filled with the Holy Spirit and with awe for God (Gal 5:16-17; Eph 4:30; 5:18; 1 Thess 5:19). Those among them who lack the rudiments of homiletics and the principles of expository preaching will not subject themselves to learning from their other colleagues. They always claim that they already know how to preach.

The exhibition of such negative ungodly attitudes indicates a lack of the basic theological understanding of the identity, ownership and the essence of the church. John F. Balchin says the church is a group of people who find themselves in a new relationship with one another because of their new relationship with Christ.[6] This is why it is described as the *body* of Christ. The body imagery/metaphor for the church occupies space in the New Testament because all those who have been saved by Christ and who have pledged their loyalty to him have been united to him as he is their life (Acts 17:26-28). According to Charles C. Ryrie, the church stands unique in the purposes of God because it is that which God purchased with the blood of his own Son (Acts 20: 28). Besides, it is also unique because it is that which Christ loves, nourishes and cherishes (Eph 5:25, 29), and which he shall present to himself blameless in all her glory one day.[7] Addition-

---

6. John F. Balchin, "What the Bible Teaches about the Church" in *The Layman's Series* (ed., G. W. Kirby, Wheaton, Illinois: Tyndale House Publishers, 1979), 15.

7. Charles C. Ryrie, *Basic Theology* (1986; repr., Wheaton, Illinois: Scripture Press Publications, 1988), 397.

ally, the church is also described as the *Temple* of God. The image of Temple designates the idea of worship and residence as the gods in ancient times resided in and were worshipped in their temples. Peter O'Brien expresses the understanding that the church, being the community of the redeemed with the sanctifying activity of the Holy Spirit, stands as the *dwelling place* of God[8] (1 Cor 3:16-17; 2 Cor 6:16-18; Eph 2:20-22). God and his Holy Spirit dwell in and among the Christian congregation as well as inside its members.

Such a theological understanding of the church is very crucial because it affects expository preaching. Jotham Maza Kangdim states that the ultimate goal and desire for the church in Africa, ". . . is for leaders in Africa to be able to take the cue by seizing the opportunity to see and learn from both positive and negative aspects of the experiences of the leaders of ancient Israel."[9] This is quite significant because members will naturally model their lives after that of their leaders, a task which Christ has called church leaders to accomplish (John 13:1-17; see also 1 Tim 4:12). As Mbewe notes, ". . . preaching suffers when there are no mature believers in the church who are living out the principles being advocated from the Bible."[10] The need for spiritually qualified leadership as models for the church is so glaring for the present generation in Africa. The members of the local congregations are yearning for qualified spiritual leadership to give them spiritual nourishment and direction, and to teach them the biblical truth. However, such needed leaders are grossly lacking.

---

8. Peter T. O'Brien, "Church," in *Dictionary of Paul and His Letters* (eds., Gerald F. Hawthorne, Ralph P. Martin, and Daniel G. Reid, Downers Grove, Illinois: Inter-Varsity Press, 1993), 127.

9. Jotham Maza Kangdim, *Leadership Unveiled* (Kaduna, Nigeria: Baraka Press and Publishers Ltd., 2008), 9.

10. Mbewe, *Pastoral Preaching*, 43.

Consequently, many church members are straying into the den of ravaging wolves of our time.

Godless church leaders blur the image of God, and the lack of godly preachers robs Christians of the glory of God. Mbewe contends that the glory of God should be a primary focus of pastoral preaching; for preaching itself is done to glorify God, not human beings.[11] Consequently, the need for a spiritually qualified leadership to lead, nurture and direct the affairs of the local congregation is critically urgent for the church in Africa today. John Piper passionately argues for the dominance of the supremacy of God and Christ in Christian preaching. He contends that the *goal* of preaching is the *glory* of God and the *ground* for preaching is the *cross* of Christ.[12] Mbewe and Piper are right! The reason for Christian preaching is the presentation of Christ and the message of his Kingdom; the motivation for Christian preaching is the dissemination of the story of Christ and his Kingdom; the glory of Christian preaching is about Christ and his Kingdom; and the joy of Christian preaching is the self-exaltation of Christ and his Kingdom. In all, the purpose of Christian preaching is the declaration of the greatness and awesomeness of God. As Piper asserts, the "Preaching that does not have the aroma of God's greatness may entertain for a season, but it will not touch the hidden cry of the soul: 'Show me thy glory.'"[13]

---

11. Conrad Mbewe, *Pastoral Preaching: Building a People for God* (Carlisle, Cumbria: Langham Preaching Resources, 2017), 25-26.

12. See his revised work, John Piper, *The Supremacy of God in Preaching* (rev. ed., Grand Rapids, Baker Books, 2004). This little work is both a classic for Christian preaching and a masterpiece on the essence of preaching. Because of the worth of this little but powerful book for biblical preaching, I always make it required reading for the students in every homiletics class that I teach. Christian preaching today has to be properly grounded in the biblical text to achieve the glory of God and the goal of the cross.

13. Piper, *The Supremacy of God in Preaching*, 13.

ERRORS IN WORSHIP

Sociologists admit that because human beings are social animals, socialisation is a necessary aspect of them because it adds spice to life. In Africa, people love to congregate at the market square or at some place of public adventure to socialise. The primary goal for the existence of social fora where activities such as dance and celebration take place is for relaxation and socialisation.

That also seems to be the trend in much of African Christianity. Much of the singing and dancing and shouting "Hallelujah, praise the Lord" during Christian worship all point to this aspect of a socialised part of Christianity. I once pastored a church that had such tendencies and had to firmly correct it. In Jos where I live, I know of some Pentecostal churches, even few among the mainline churches, where members look forward to Sunday service to try out a new dance step. The preacher of one of them always excites his members with his charismatic preaching style, yet the excitement is not in the Word. Decorum in worship is almost outmoded in many Christian congregations in Africa today. The attitude of quiet reverence in solemn worship is gradually being replaced by emotional expression. This attitude and practice of a sober, reflective Christianity is fast giving way to a noisy type of Christianity. As a consequence, any Christian congregation that does not provide space for such contemporary prevailing phenomenon of socialisation stands the risk of losing its members to their neighbours next door.

When one observes closely the trend of events in most of the Christian congregations in Africa today, one would likely come away with the feeling that there is no clear-cut distinction between worship and social ceremonies. Some church members attend church worship service with the attitude of a social gathering where partying, ceremony and dancing dominate the atmosphere. Here, dancing and celebration, looking good and feeling nice is usually expected of the participants in ceremonies. So, when the attitude of ceremony instead of worship is carried over into church worship services, the characteristics of a ceremony will be exhibited. This way, the worshippers will always try out their newest dance steps. Some others would compete as they display their dance steps and styles of doing so. The younger generation of African Christians appears the most hit by this new phenomenon of Christian worship. This is one main reason why the Pentecostal churches are attracting more from the younger generation.

Despite the requirement for a serene atmosphere of reverence for God in Christian worship, the scenario above would not allow for it. With such a given, only a few congregants will feel drawn to the beauty of expository preaching. More and more Christians are becoming less interested in qualitative preaching in favour of an entertaining one. I have argued elsewhere that the effects of such a growing practice/attitude live on Africa a rootless and shallow type of Christianity.[14]

COMPETING RELIGIONS

Religious quest is an inherent part of human beings because they are created with an embedded religious consciousness. In Africa, there is the presence of a multiplicity of deities such as the gods of African Traditional Religions, the Allah of Islam, the Yahweh of Judaism, and the Christian God. All these variously conceptualised divinities compete for space in the lives of the African peoples, each demanding for equal allegiance on the part of the African worshippers. In the Middle East today, the religious contest is among the religions of

14. Joel K. T. Biwul, "Preaching Biblically in the Nigerian Prosperity Gospel Context," *Africa Journal of Evangelical Theology*, 32.2 (2013): 121-134.

the Abrahamic faiths – Judaism, Christianity, and Islam. In Africa, this contest is between African Traditional Religion, Christianity, and Islam. These religions persuasively propagate their gospels and clamour for adherents. Yet, the multiplicity of religions competing for space in Africa is only one out of many religious challenges to expository preaching.

A more recent and seemingly more significant challenge is that of escalating religious tension, strife, and war that is becoming a growing phenomenon in Africa. Take the case of Nigeria for example, where the issue of religious conflict and war has been a constant experience. Its characteristic pattern plays out in the burning of worship places and communities; the destruction of economic bases, the maiming and brutal killing of men, women and children; and in some cases, the issue is that of a clear case of genocide and systematic ethnic cleansing.[15] The, government seems politically incapacitated to deal decisively with the situation. The attackers are only described by the government as "unknown gunmen," while in fact, they are known. The situation is aggravated where some accused perpetra-

---

15. Since the religious faceup between Christian and Muslim students of College of Education in Kafanchan, Kaduna State, Nigeria, on March 6, 1987, such religious confrontation (Jihad) by Nigerian Muslims has escalated. For example, a senator of the Federal Republic of Nigeria (Senator Gyang Dantong) and a member of the State House of Assembly (Honourable Gyang Fulani) were both killed by Muslims in Kura Falls where they had attended the mass burial of the victims of Fulani herdsmen religious homicide. The Federal Government did nothing about such unfortunate incident. Instead, the remnants of Kura Falls have been sacked from their ancestral land to give space for Fulani occupation. Also, at least 15 people including two professors of Bayero University, Kano, were killed on April 29, 2012 during Sunday worship service when some gunmen detonated homemade bomb at them. At least no fewer than 17 other worshipers were killed on June 3, 2012 when Boko Haram bombed Living Faith Church in Yelwa, Bauchi State. The historical catalogue of such onslaught is unending.

tors are set free soon after their arrest by the security agents. Those victims who suffer the trauma of tragic losses struggle with the issue of true forgiveness and love for 'the enemy.' They wonder where a loving God was when such horrible assaults were launched at them. Such victims will find it quite difficult to reconcile the idea of God in the midst of their suffering. Such experience, then, would very likely become an obstacle to the preaching of the gospel of Jesus Christ.

SPIRITUAL WARFARE

Belief in the spirit world and spiritual warfare is a lived reality in Africa. This is why some theological training institutions in Africa teach a course in power encounter or spiritual warfare. This course builds on the already acquired knowledge on demonology treated in the course on doctrine/theology. The purpose is to orient students about the operations of Satan by providing some principles on how to withstand and counter satanic attacks in ministry. Paul speaks so much about the presence of satanic confrontation in ministry. In what Lisa Bowens describes as Paul's use of "martial imagery", she argues that he was unveiling an embattled reality. She asks the question, "In light of Paul's extensive use of martial language in these chapters [2 Cor 10-13], what might it mean for us as pastors, ministers, and laypeople to read Paul with a spiritual warfare lens?"[16]

The operations of Satan in opposition to divine purposes and programme are evident in the Old Testament. First, he used the principle of deceit, projecting God as one who deprives people of the right to equality. He did this in order to divert the affection and

---

16. Lisa Marie Bowens, "Painting Hope: Formational Hues of Paul's Spiritual Warfare Language in 2 Corinthians 10-13," in *Practicing with Paul: Reflections on Paul and the Practice of Ministry in Honor of Susan G. Eastman*, ed., Presian R. Burroughs (Eugene, Oregon: Wipf and Stock Publishers, 2018), 108-109.

loyalty of Adam and Eve from their Creator (Gen 3:1-20). Second, he infected the spirit of callousness in the hearts of people during the day of Noah, making them resistant and adamant to divine warning through Noah's proclamation (Gen 6:1-18). Also, when the Israelites were in transit from Egypt to Canaan, Satan attacked this travelling pilgrim community several times. For example, he instilled the spirit of ingratitude in some sectarians as well as individuals (Exod 15:23-24; 16:1-3; 17:1-3; Num 14:1-4); the spirit of rebellion (Num 16:1-50); the spirit of covetousness like in the case of Achan (Josh 6:26-7:21); the spirit of disbelief and idolatry as seen in the event of the golden calf (Exod 32:1-6); the spirit of sexual and religious immorality as demonstrated in the event of Shittim of the Midianites (Num 25:1-15); and several more instances.

Satanic confrontation is also evident in the New Testament. From the onset, Satan stirred in Herod's heart the spirit of jealousy when he pursued Jesus in his infancy to eliminate him. Such jealousy caused the death of many innocent male children in Bethlehem of Judea (Matt 1:1-23). When this evil plot could not succeed with Jesus, the enemy employed the strategy of temptation (Matt 4:1-1-11). However, when all his plots failed, particularly, when Jesus said in response to Peter's confession, ". . . on this rock, I will build my church, and the gates of Hades will not overcome it" (Matt 16:18 NIV), one would have thought that the presence of satanic oppression was over for Christians with the resurrection (see Matt 28:2-6; Phil 2:5-11).

On the contrary, Satan's onslaughts against God's agenda of human salvation is a continuous one. Hence the early church faced persecution from the Jews and the Romans. Paul, for example, was confronted severally by satanic opposition to his ministry. He was falsely accused, severally shipwrecked, beaten and left for dead, flogged, stoned, imprisoned, and always in danger (Acts 13:45, 50; 14:19; 16:19-22; 2 Cor 6:3-10; 11:23-33; 2 Tim 3-12). As such, he took careful notice of the havoc that the enemy of the cross can cause within the church when he said to the Corinthians, ". . . in order that Satan might not outwit us. For we are not unaware of his schemes" (2 Cor 2:11 NIV). Upon this truth, he counselled the saints in Ephesus when he said,

> Finally, be strong in the Lord and in his mighty power. Put on the full armour of God so that you can take your stand against the devil's schemes. For our struggle is not against flesh and blood, but against the rulers, against the authorities, against the powers of this dark world and against the spiritual forces of evil in the heavenly realms (Eph 6:10-12 NIV).

The subtle way in which the enemy is operating within the church in Africa today with the aim of destroying it is quite apparent. Satan is working so hard to steal the truth of God already planted in the hearts of people as a result of the preaching of the gospel. He is also making significant efforts to replace God's truth with falsehood in the church in Africa. The emergence of what may be described as spiritual crafting and spiritism in Africa today can attest to this reality. For instance, the mud from the Dead Sea and the water of River Jordan is believed to possess healing powers. African Christians, especially from Nigeria, who travel on pilgrimage to Israel, carry them along as souvenirs. Some within the church seek diabolical power to become prominent leaders while others seek such power for protection and to occupy positions to have control of local congregations. Some Christians in Nigeria and Ghana are reported to have consulted spiritualists for power to get elected into certain positions in the church.

A more alarming trend of satanic attack on African Christianity is when every preacher wants to become a miracle worker and an exorcist. As a result, some bury live animals, living human beings, or some spiritist's materials, mostly under the foundations of the auditorium or within the pulpit area of the worship auditorium. Here is an interesting live story. A pastor of an independent church in Nigeria was disgraced by a spiritualist he had consulted for power but refused to complete payment for the consultation fee. The spiritualist came to his church during a Sunday worship; performed certain incantation, and a live black goat the pastor had buried alive came out under the pulpit and ran outside. This was the end of his power and of that church because no worshipper went back to it. Some others use amulets, certain occult objects, or rub specific demonic prepared ointment to draw large crowds, thus becoming famous, and displaying extraordinary powers. For instance, a Pentecostal pastor from Nigeria invited his colleague as a guest speaker to a revival programme. Something extraordinary happened. The host pastor had entered the room of his guest in his absence and used his anointing oil. Such oil is believed to provide healing power and drive demons away. However, when the host pastor came during the evening programme, he shouted "Halleluiah" and waved his hand. To his surprise, people would fall whenever he waved. After the programme, the guest pastor enquired if he had used his anointing oil. He later explained to his host that sometimes, pastors need such power so members can believe and respect them.

The growth in the use of anointing oil in African Christianity today is unbelievable. It has almost literally become the object of worship rather than the God such people purport to worship. This religious behaviour, no doubt, is the enemy's subtle means of gradually dislodging Christ from the hearts of people who had hitherto believed in him. What aggravates this scenario is the quest for signs and wonders. People today, just as it was the case in the days of Jesus, are not looking for good sermons from the Bible but for tangible miraculous signs in order to believe (Matt 12:37-40). Many more African Christians today are being deceived into believing that any pastor or preacher who performs signs and wonders by casting out demons, raising the dead, breathing out money, or one who prays and automatic employment, admission for further studies, marriage partner, and quick wealth happen is a godly and powerful man or woman of God.

People with such kind of orientation are not patient or ready to listen to any sermon that does not promise them miracles. Even the Psalmist's claim that God says, "'Be still, and know that I am God; I will be exalted among the nations, I will be exalted in the earth'" (Ps 46:10 NIV) does sound absurd and as a mirage. These Satan engineered happenings pose a significant threat to expository preaching in Africa.

While we have argued that quality expository preaching of God's Word exposes God's truth to people, we have also acknowledged that there are certain obstacles to such a noble course. Growing erroneous teachings or heretical preaching and lack of professionalism are dangerous obstacles. They can divert attention of people from the truth into accepting falsehood. A wrong theological understanding of the nature of the church and its leadership, and the failure to clearly differentiate between worship service and an entertaining gathering serve to water down the force of Christianity and the gospel. Of course, the various strategies of satanic attacks on the church is a great hinderance to expository preaching in Africa. Matured Christians who are called by God for the task know the antidote – faith in the calling God, conscious dedication to studying the Scriptures, and unwavering commitment to preaching it.

CONCLUSION

We have made a case in this book for the necessity of expository preaching in Africa because of its key role in facilitating Christian spirituality for the church. Quality exposition of the biblical text will address some of the contemporary challenges being faced by church and society within the African context. We have endeavoured to argue that the expositor of the Scriptures will be more effective in the expository endeavour if the African contour is properly and carefully mapped. But this is not enough. We have also argued that the expositor must have a very clear understanding of the biblical warrants for preaching. Therefore, attention was drawn to certain biblical models upon which expository preaching in Africa should stand.

A quality preaching of the Scriptures by those whose lives are transformed and set aglow for reverencing the holiness and greatness of God is very much needed in Africa today. Africans are crying for the presence and help of God in their deplorable conditions. For instance, an infant will hardly cry unless it is hungry, wet, sick, or has some kind of discomfort. Otherwise, it spends most of the time sleeping on the mothers back, tied with the traditional African animal skin, to keep the child warm. Like a crying infant, expository preaching is inevitably necessary for the African context today to increase biblical literacy of Christians and offer hope to Africans vis-à-vis its many challenges. When God's will is explained through an effective exposition of his Word, it is expected that its transforming power will effect certain changes. This, to be effectual, requires the service of transformed and prepared men and women with the requisite knowledge in Bible and doctrine, hermeneutics and theology, and in expository expertise. This need is urgent; more and more Africans are starving for biblical truth.

Expository preaching will help to reshape and deepen the already existing knowledge of God that Africans have. It is only him as "Our Father" who can save and give life eternal to Africans, protect them from demonic harm, make them prosper, and give to them his peace and satisfaction in life. No one else and nothing else can. As such, true "Men" and "Women" of God who have truly been called, prepared, and tasked to "Preach the Word; be prepared in season and out of season; [to] correct, rebuke and encourage – with great patience and careful instruction" (2 Tim 4:2 NIV), are called upon to seriously take up this task. The church in Africa needs true preachers who will live and stand by their word; and whose lifestyle, well grounded in the Scriptures, would serve as a true reflection of Christ and his Kingdom.

The need for quality expository preaching for the African context is more urgent in view of the shift in the force of Christianity and the changing centre of gravity of the Christian gospel from the global North to the South.[1] Africa is better positioned to use such a paradigm shift to its advantage in view of the massive growth of Christianity in her. This historical change in church history creates a great opportunity for African Christianity and spirituality to blossom far beyond measure. A clear expository and appropriately relevant application of the biblical text to Africans will direct such a movement. African church leaders, therefore, are not only to encourage fruitful evangelisation but most importantly, also an effective exposition of the biblical text on the continent.

Africans today are longing to hear God speak to them in the various African tongues and languages. They are tired of hearing the

---

1. See Andrew Finlay Walls, *The Cross-cultural Process in Christian History* (2002; Fourth printing, Maryknoll, New York: Orbis Books 2007), 118. Also see Philip Jenkins, *The Next Christendom: The Coming of Global Christianity* (Oxford: Oxford University Press, 2002).

noise of false preachers, fake prophets, and the gymnastics of miracle workers and exorcists. They desire to resonate with the Scriptures within their different African contexts so it responds to their real needs and lived experiences. What then is the challenge? Truly transformed and reverential pastors and Christian scholars in Africa in the field of biblical, hermeneutical, theological and pastoral theology studies are to rise to the challenge to teach their people through their sermons and writings in ways that reflect both biblical content and contextual issues. Five critical things, then, African preachers must never neglect or gloss over – Preach the Word; Preach the Word; Preach the Word; Preach the Word; and Preach the Word!

BIBLIOGRAPHY

Achebe, Albert Chinualumogu. *Things Fall Apart.* Jordon Hill, Oxford: Heinemann, 1958.

Adam, Peter. *Speaking God's Words: A Practical Theology of Preaching.* Leicester, England: Inter-Varsity Press, 1996.

Adams, Jay Edward. *Truth Applied: Application in Preaching.* Grand Rapids, Michigan: Baker, 1990.

Adeleye, Femi. *Preachers of a Different Gospel.* Nairobi, Kenya: WordAlive/Bukuru: ACTS/Grand Rapids, Michigan: Zondervan Publishing House, 2011.

Agbogunrin, S. O., J. O. Akao, D. O. Akintunde, and G. M. Toryough, eds. *Christology in African Context*, Biblical Studies Series Number 2. Nigeria: Nigerian Association for Biblical Studies, 2003.

Baker, Kenneth et al. Editors. *The NIV Study Bible: 10th Anniversary Edition.* Grand Rapids, Michigan: Zondervan Publishing House, 1995.

Balchin, John F. "What the Bible Teaches about the Church" in *The Layman's Series.* Edited by G. W. Kirby. Wheaton, Illinois: Tyndale House Publishers, 1979.

Baumann, J. Daniel. *An Introduction to Contemporary Preaching*, 1972. Paperback edition, 1988. Reprint. Grand Rapids, Michigan: Baker Book House, 1990.

Bediako, Kwame. *Jesus in Africa: The Christian Gospel in African History and Experience.* Carlisle, Cumbria: Paternoster Publishing, 2000.

Biwul, Joel Kamsen Tihitshak. "The Challenge of Pastoral Hermeneutics in Africa: Suggestions for Effective Preaching by Nigerian Pastors." *TCNN Research Bulletin* Number 59 (September 2013): 28-42.

________ . "Preaching Biblically in the Nigerian Prosperity Gospel Context." *Africa Journal of Evangelical Theology* 32.2 (2013): 121-134.

________. "Reading the Virtuous Woman of Proverbs 31:10-31 as a Reflection of the Attributes of the Traditional Miship Woman of Nigeria." *OTE* 26/2 (2013): 275-297.

________. *Preaching the Scriptures.* Jos, Nigeria & Carlisle, UK: Hippo-Books, 2018.

Bosch, David Jacobus. *Transforming Mission: Paradigm Shifts in Theology of Mission,* 1991. Reprint. Maryknoll, New York: Orbis Books, 2009.

Bowens, Lisa Marie. "Painting Hope: Formational Hues of Paul's Spiritual Warfare Language in 2 Corinthians 10-13" in *Practicing with Paul: Reflections on Paul and the Practice of Ministry in Honor of Susan G. Eastman.* Edited by Presian R. Burroughs. Eugene, Oregon: Wipf and Stock Publishers, 2018.

Bullock, C. Hassell. "Introduction: Interpreting the Bible" in *The Literature and Meaning of Scripture.* Edited by Morris A. Inch and C. Hassell Bullock. Grand Rapids, Michigan: Baker Book House, 1981.

________ . *An Introduction to the Old Testament Prophetic Books.* Updated edition. Chicago, Illinois: Moody Publishers, 2007.

Carson, Donald Anderson. *Exegetical Fallacies.* 2nd edition. Grand Rapids, Michigan: Baker Books, 1996.

Chapell, Bryan. *Christ-Centered Preaching*. Grand Rapids, Michigan: Baker Books, 1994.

________. *Christ-Centered Preaching: Redeeming the Expository Sermon*. 2nd edition, 2005. Reprint. Grand Rapids, Michigan: Baker Academic, 2007.

Chisholm, Robert B. Jr. *From Exegesis to Exposition: A Practical Guide to Using Biblical Hebrew*. Grand Rapids, Michigan: Baker Books, 1998.

Collins, John J. Collins. "Introduction: Towards the Morphology of a Genre." *Semeia* 14 (1979).

Couch, Mal. General editor. "Introduction" in *A Biblical Theology of the Church*. Grand Rapids, Michigan: Kregel Publications, 1999.

Dykstra, Robert C. *Finding Ourselves Lost: Ministry in the Age of Overwhelm*. Eugene, Oregon: Wipf and Stock Publishers, 2018.

Fee, Gordon D. *New Testament Exegesis: A Handbook for Students and Pastors*. Philadelphia, Kentucky: The Westminster Press, 1983.

Gasque, W. Ward. "The Challenge to Faith" in *Introduction to the History of Christianity*. 2nd edition. Edited by Tim Dowley, 1990. Paperback edition, Minneapolis: Fortress Press, 2002.

Gibellini, Rosino. General editor. *Paths of African Theology*. Marknoll, New York: Orbis Books, 1994.

Giese, Ronald L. Jr. "Literary Forms of the Old Testament" in *Cracking Old Testament Codes*. Edited by D. Brent Sandy & Ronald L. Giese Jr. Nashville, Tennessee: Broadman & Holman Publishers, 1995.

Gower, Ralph. *The New Manners and Customs of Bible Times*. Revised and Updated edition. Chicago, Illinois: Moody Bible Institute, 2005.

Gula, Richard M. *Ethics in Pastoral Ministry*. Mahwah, New Jersey: Paulist Press, 1996.

Hogan, William L. "It is My Pleasure to Introduce . . . " *The Expositor* 1, 3 (August 1987).

Idowu, E. Bọlaji. *African Traditional Religion: A Definition*. London: SCM Press Ltd., 1973. Reprint. Nigeria: Fountain Publications, 1991.

Janvier, George Evans. *Biblical Preaching in Africa: A Textbook for Christian Preachers*. Bukuru, Nigeria: Africa Christian Textbooks, 2002.

Jenkins, Philip. *The Next Christendom: The Coming of Global Christianity*. Oxford: Oxford University Press, 2002.

Johnson, Elliott E. *Expository Hermeneutics: An Introduction*. Grand Rapids, Michigan: Zondervan, 1990.

Jusu, John. Supervising Editor. "Dedication" in *Africa Study Bible*. Carol Stream: Oasis International Limited, 2016.

Kaiser, Walter C. Jr. "'I Will Remember the Deeds of the Lord': The Meaning of Narrative" in *Introduction to Biblical Hermeneutics: The Search for Meaning* by Walter C. Kaiser Jr. and Moisés Silva. 2nd edition. Grand Rapids, Michigan: Zondervan, 2007.

Kangdim, Jotham Maza. *Leadership Unveiled*. Kaduna, Nigeria: Baraka Press and Publishers Ltd., 2008.

Kato, Byang Henry. *African Cultural Revolution and the Christian Faith*. Jos, Nigeria: Challenge Publications, 1976.

________ . *Biblical Christianity in Africa*, Theological Perspectives on Africa: No. 2. Achimota, Ghana: Africa Christian Press, 1985.

Knecht, Glen C. "Sermon Structure and Flow" in *The Preacher and Preaching: Reviving the Art*. Edited by Samuel T. Logan. Phillipsburg, New Jersey: Presbyterian and Reformed Publishing, 1986.

Kunhiyop, Samuel Waje. *African Christian Ethics*. Nairobi, Kenya: Hippo Books, 2008.

________ . *African Christian Theology*. Nairobi, Kenya: HippoBooks, 2012.

Kyomya, Michael. *A Guide to Interpreting Scripture*. Nairobi, Kenya: HippoBooks, 2010.

Ladd, George Eldon. *A Theology of the New Testament*. Revised and edited by Donald A. Hagner. Grand Rapids, Michigan: William B. Eerdmans, 1993.

Larsen, David L. *The Anatomy of Preaching: Identifying the Issues in Preaching Today*. Grand Rapids, Michigan: Kregel Publications, 1999; Ibadan, Nigeria: CHRIST AND WE PUBLICATIONS, 2000.

LaRue, Cleophus James. *I Believe I'll Testify: The Art of African American Preaching*. Louisville, Kentucky: Westminster John Knox Press, 2011.

________ . *Rethinking Celebration: From Rhetoric to Praise in African American Preaching*. Louisville, Kentucky: Westminster John Knox Press, 2016.

LaRue, Cleophus James LaRue. Editor. *Power in the Pulpit: How America's Most Effective Black Preachers Prepare Their Sermons*. Louisville, Kentucky: Westminster John Knox, 2002.

Leavell, Roland Q. *Prophetic Preaching, Then and Now*. Grand Rapids, Michigan: Baker, 1963.

Lingenfelter, Sherwood G. and Marvin Keene Mayers. *Ministering Cross-Culturally: An Incarnational Model for Personal Relationship.* Grand Rapids, Michigan: Baker, 1986.

Litfin, A. Duane. "Titus" in *The Bible Knowledge Commentary: New Testament,* 1983. Reprint. Edited by John F. Walvoord and Roy B. Zuck. America: SP Publications, 1988.

Logan, Samuel T. Jr. "The Phenomenology of Preaching" in *The Preacher and Preaching: Reviving the Art.* Edited by Samuel T. Logan Jr. Phillipsburg, New Jersey: Presbyterian and Reformed Publishing, 1986.

Magary, Dennis R. "Keeping Your Hebrew Healthy" in *Preaching the Old Testament.* Edited by Scott M. Gibson. Grand Rapids, Michigan: Baker Books, 2006.

Maigadi, Barje Sulmane. *Divisive Ethnicity in the Church in Africa.* Kaduna, Nigeria: Baraka Press and Publishers Limited, 2006.

Maxey, I. Parker. *Ministerial Ethics and Etiquette.* Owerri, Nigeria: World Parish Publications, 1990.

Mayhue, Richard L. "Rediscovering Expository Preaching" in *Rediscovering Expository Preaching: John McArthur, Jr. and the Master's Seminary Faculty.* Edited by Richard L. Mayhue and Robert L. Thomas. Dallas, Texas: WORD Books, 1993).

Mbewe, Conrad. *Pastoral Preaching: Building a People for God.* Carlisle, Cumbria: Langham Preaching Resources, 2017.

Mbiti, John Samuel. *African Religions and Philosophy.* 2nd edition, 1990. Reprint. England: Heinemann, 2008.

McArthur, John Jr. "Introduction" in *Rediscovering Expository Preaching: John MacArthur, Jr. and the Master's Seminary Faculty*. Edited by Richard L. Mayhue and Robertson L. Thomas. Dallas, Texas: WORD Publishing, 1993.

McCain, Danny. "THE CHURCH IN AFRICA in the Twenty-first Century: Characteristics, Challenges, and Opportunities." *Africa Journal of Evangelical Theology* 19.2 (2000).

McGrath, Alister. *Heresy*. London: Society for Promoting Christian Knowledge, 2009.

McQuilkin, J. Robertson. *Understanding and Applying the Bible*. 2nd edition. Chicago, Illinois: Moody Press, 1992.

Michael, Matthew. *Christian Theology & African Traditions*. Eugene, Oregon: Resource Publications, 2013.

Motty, Bauta Dauda. *Indigenous Christian Disciple-Making*. Jos, Nigeria: ECWA Productions Ltd., 2013.

Mugambi, Jesse Ndwiga Kanyua. *Christianity and African Culture*, 2002. Reprint. Nairobi, Kenya: Acton Publishers, 2009.

Murthy, J. D. *Contemporary English Grammar: West African Edition*. Edited by Ben Lawrence. Lagos, Nigeria: Book Master, 2007.

O'Brien, Peter T. "Church" in *Dictionary of Paul and His Letters*. Edited by Gerald F. Hawthorne, Ralph P. Martin, and Daniel G. Reid. Downers Grove, Illinois: Inter-Varsity Press, 1993.

O'Donovan, Wilbur. *Biblical Christianity in Modern Africa*. Cumbria, UK.: Paternoster Press, 2000.

Oladunjoye, The Rt. Rev. Dr. J. A. "Chairman's Keynote Address" in *Biblical Studies and Corruption in Africa: Biblical Studies Series Number*

6. Edited by Rev. Prof. Samuel Oyin Abogunrin. Ibadan, Nigeria: The Nigerian Association for Biblical Studies (NABIS), 2007).

Olford, Stephen F. with David Lindsay Olford. *Anointed Expository Preaching.* Nashville, Tennessee: Broadman & Holman Publishers, 1998.

Osborne, Grant R. *The Hermeneutical Spiral: A Comprehensive Introduction to Biblical Interpretation.* 2nd edition. Downers Grove, Illinois: Inter-Varsity Press, 2006.

Palmer, Timothy. *Christian Theology in an African Context.* Bukuru, Nigeria: Africa Christian Textbooks, 2015.

Parratt, John. "Introduction" in *A Reader in African Christian Theology,* SPCK International Study Guide. New edition, 1997. Reprint. Edited by John Parratt. Marylebone, London: SPCK, 2004.

Piper, John. *The Supremacy of God in Preaching.* Revised edition. Grand Rapids, Michigan: Baker Books, 2004.

Ramm, Bernard. *Protestant Biblical Interpretation: A Textbook of Hermeneutics.* 3rd edition. Grand Rapids, Michigan: Baker Book House, 1970.

Richard, Ramesh. *Scripture Sculpture: A Do-It-Yourself Manual for Biblical Preaching,* 1995. Reprint. Grand Rapids, Michigan: Baker Books, 1997.

Robinson, Haddon W. *Expository Preaching: Principles and Practice,* 2001. Reprint. Leicester, England: Inter-Varsity Press, 2004.

Rodney, Walter. *How Europe Underdeveloped Africa.* 2nd impression. London: Bogle-L'Ouverture Publications/Dar-es-Salaam, Tanzania: Tanzania Publishing House, 1973.

Ryken, Leland. *How to Read the Bible as Literature*. Grand Rapids, Michigan: Zondervan Publishing House, 1984.

________ . *Words of Delight: A Literary Introduction to the Bible*. 2nd edition, 1992. Reprint. Grand Rapids, Michigan: Baker Book House, 2001.

Ryrie, Charles C. *Basic Theology,* 1986. Reprint. Wheaton, Illinois: Scripture Press Publications, 1988.

Schnabel, Eckhard J. *Paul the Missionary: Realities, Strategies and Methods*. Downers Grove, Illinois: Inter-Varsity Press, 2008.

Schoville, Keith N. "Canaanites and Amorites" in *Peoples of the Old Testament World*. Edited by Alfred J. Hoerth, Gerald L. Mattingly, and Edwin M. Yamauchi. Grand Rapids, Michigan: Baker Books, 1994. Paperback ed., 1998.

Schreiter, Robert J. General editor. *Faces of Jesus in Africa*, Faith and Cultures Series, 1991. Reprint. Maryknoll, New York: Orbis Books, 2002.

________. "Introduction" in Diane B. Stinton. *Jesus of Africa: Voices of Contemporary African Christology*. Maryknoll, New York: Orbis Books, 2004. Reprint. Nairobi, Kenya: Paulines Publications Africa, 2007.

Shelley, Bruce Leon. *Church History in Plain Language*. 2nd edition. Nashville, Tennessee: Thomas Nelson Publishers, 1995.

Shorter, Aylward. *African Culture, An Overview: Social-Cultural Anthropology,* 1998. Reprint. Nairobi, Kenya: Paulines Publications Africa, 2001.

Sproul, R. C. Sproul. General editor. "Introduction" in *The Reformation Study Bible*. Orlando, Florida: Reformation Trust Publishing, 2015.

Stanley, Charles F. "Forward" in *A Guide to Effective Sermon Delivery* by Jerry Vines. Moody, Chicago: Moody Bible Institute, 1986.

Stewart, James. *Heralds of God*. Grand Rapids, Michigan: Baker, 1972.

Stinton, Diane B. *Jesus of Africa: Voices of Contemporary African Christology*. Maryknoll, New York: Orbis Books, 2004. Reprint. Nairobi, Kenya: Paulines Publications Africa, 2007.

Stott, John Robert Walmsley. *The Contemporary Christian*. Nottingham, England: Inter-Varsity Press, 1992.

_________ . *Issues Facing Christians Today*. 4th edition. Fully revised and Updated by Roy McCloughry with a new chapter by John Wyatt. Grand Rapids, Michigan: Zondervan, 2006.

Stott, John Robert Walmsley with Greg Scharf. *The Challenge of Preaching*. Carlisle, Cumbria: Langham Preaching Resources, 2011.

Stuart, Douglas. *Old Testament Exegesis*. Revised edition. Philadelphia, Kentucky: Westminster John Knox Press, 1980.

Sunukjian, Donald R. *Invitation to Biblical Preaching: Proclaiming Truth with Clarity and Relevance*. Grand Rapids, Michigan: Kregel Publication, 2007.

Tiénou, Tite. *The Theological Task of the Church in Africa,* Theological Perspectives in Africa: No. 1. 2nd edition. Achimota, Ghana: Africa Christian Press, 1990.

Turaki, Yusufu. *Foundations of African Traditional Religions and Worldview*. Nairobi, Kenya: International Bible Society Africa, 2001.

__________ . "Forward" in *Christian Theology and African Traditions* by Matthew Michael. Kaduna, Nigeria: Yuty Graphics, 2011.

Turnbull, Ralph G. Editor. *Baker's Dictionary of Practical Theology*, 1967. Reprint. Grand Rapids, Michigan: Baker Book House, 1982.

Unger, Merrill F. *Principles of Expository Preaching*. Grand Rapids, Michigan: Zondervan, 1955.

Vanhoozer, Kevin J. *Is There a Meaning in this Text? The Bible, the Reader and the Morality of Literary Knowledge*. Leicester, England: Apollos, 1998.

__________ . "Exegesis and Hermeneutics" in *New Dictionary of Biblical Theology*. Edited by T. Desmond Alexander and Brian S. Rosner. Leicester, England: Inter-Varsity Press 2000.

Vines, Jerry and Jim Shaddix, *Power in the Pulpit: How to Prepare and Deliver Expository Sermons*. Chicago, Illinois: Moody Press, 1999.

Vines, Jerry. *A Guide to Effective Sermon Delivery*. Chicago, Illinois: Moody Press, 1986.

Walls, Andrew Finlay. *The Cross-cultural Process in Christian History*, 2002. Fourth printing, Maryknoll, New York: Orbis Books 2007.

Wright, Christopher J. H. *Sweeter than Honey: Preaching the Old Testament*. Carlisle, Cumbria: Langham Preaching Resources, 2015.